D0923116

The aspiring mind of the Elizabethan
younger generation

Duke Historical Publications

The aspiring mind of the Elizabethan younger generation   Anthony Esler

Duke University Press
Durham, N. C.
1966

Library of Congress catalogue card
number 66-26025

Printed in the United States of
America by the Seeman Printery,
Inc., Durham, N. C.

Preface

This is a study of ideas and emotions which were originally felt and formulated in a world very different from our own. To remove some of the more artificial obstacles which four centuries have raised between these alien attitudes and modern readers, sixteenth-century spelling and punctuation have been modernized throughout. All passages in modern foreign languages have also been translated, by the author unless otherwise indicated.

I should like to thank Professor Arthur Ferguson for shrewd suggestions and frank criticisms. I should also like to express my gratitude to the staffs of the Duke University Library, the reading rooms of the British Museum, and the Folger Shakespeare Library for the use of their collections and for their unfailing helpfulness and courtesy.

A. J. E.

Contents

Introduction: a generational approach to Elizabethan England

One of the most difficult tasks of the historian has always been the analysis of human nature—as it existed in past ages. The cultural gap between humanity today and yesterday is much greater than we like to admit. How many modern men, for instance, are really capable of understanding the medieval fanaticism of the Inquisition, or of empathizing with knight errantry? How far beyond our grasp is even the most civilized man of the Renaissance, with his blood-feuds and superstitions, his passion for the garish and the beautiful, his strange combination of daring innovation and nostalgic traditionalism? No matter how much factual information the historian may accumulate about the past, the motivations and mental processes of past peoples still too frequently escape him.

Even as recently as the sixteenth century, and within the narrow compass of the England of Elizabeth, the picture seems strange and self-contradictory. What were the Elizabethans really like, after all? Were they the chivalrous gentlemen and poets of romantic tradition—or were they at heart the crassly materialistic bribers and takers of Neale's *Elizabethan Political Scene*?[1] Who was the true soul of the age—the cautious, conservative Queen, or her daring sea dogs? Even a single Elizabethan psyche may contain enough contradictions to undermine any generalization and baffle any attempt at synthesis. How is the honest biographer to reconcile Raleigh the heroic empire-builder, the truth-seeker, the patron of scientists and poets, with Raleigh the fawning courtier and the tricky businessman? And can the timeless genius that created *Hamlet* and *Lear* and *The Tempest* really have gloried in the construction of the second largest house in Stratford? Despite all that has been done to improve our understanding, the Elizabethan character remains to a surprising extent a baffling configuration of paradoxes.

The subject of this study is a single, crucial trait of this Eliza-

1. J. E. Neale, *The Elizabethan Political Scene* (London, 1948).

bethan character—or rather, of a particular group of Elizabethans. It is the quality of high aspiration, socially manifested as ambition, among the younger courtiers of late Elizabethan England. Succeeding chapters will seek to trace the origins and development, and to explain the nature and larger consequences of ambition among the young aristocrats of the 1580's and '90's, the last two decades of the reign of Elizabeth I.

This investigation thus seeks to comprehend, not only formal systems of ideas, but motives and attitudes, desires, fears, and passionately felt personal goals. It is an attempt to explore a portion of that no-man's-land where the life of the mind and the life of society meet and interact. In this hazy realm the historian must proceed with great caution, for the relationships between the inner and the outer lives of men are delicate and elusive. In this effort to penetrate the personalities of men long dead, the author has therefore turned for assistance to the concept of social generations. The historiographical theory of social generations, too seldom utilized by historians, may provide precisely the interpretative framework necessary for such a historical character study as this.

i. Social generations in Elizabethan England

The notion of social generations is an extremely simple one; yet it has intrigued a surprising number of first-rate minds, including such diverse talents as Goethe, Tolstoy, Sainte-Beuve, Dilthey, Ortega y Gasset, Karl Mannheim, Henri Peyre, and Ralph de Toledano.[2] In the twentieth century two streams of thought on the subject have emerged: a theoretical stream, largely the work of German, French, and Spanish scholars; and a more empirical tradition of generational literature, to which Anglo-Saxons have also contributed. Some of the fundamental emphases and discoveries of both these currents should be discussed here, for they have served as operating hypotheses for the study that follows.

2. The most readily available outline of the development of the theory of social generations is Yves Renouard, "La Notion de génération en histoire," *Revue historique*, CCIX (1953), 1-23. For more detailed surveys, see: François Mentré, *Les Générations sociales* (Paris, 1920); Detlev W. Schumann, "Cultural Age-Groups in German Thought," *PMLA*, LI (1936), 1180-1207; Julián Marías Aguilera, *El método historico de las géneraciones* (Madrid, 1949).

The scholars and thinkers—historians, sociologists, philosophers, critics of art and literature—who have examined the concept of social generations have frequently disagreed in their conclusions. There does, however, seem to be an area of basic agreement in the welter of conflicting theories from which a rough working definition of the concept may be derived. Basically, the theorists attempt to interpret history, especially cultural history, in terms of the development and interaction of succeeding generations of men. It is their view that the course of history is at least partially determined by this endless natural process operating within the context of a particular society. Men born about the same time, exposed in their plastic early years to a common educational experience, and passing through the same span of history at the same stages of personal growth, will develop enough common ideas and attitudes to justify studying them as a distinct social group. Such a social generation in fact comes to possess a group mind which, conflicting or co-operating with the group minds of older generations, helps to create trends and movements, to mold institutions, and to direct the course of history.

Henri Peyre has thus summarized the ties that bind a social generation in its youth:

They studied in the same handbooks, acquired the same ideas of philosophy, physical science, and history taught in the schools, learned by heart the same 'selected passages' . . . dreamed the same revolutions, loved from afar the same actresses, cheered the same singers or the same sports champions, haunted the same cafes, were bewitched by the same colors rendered by their favorite painters, discovered Wagner or Ravel together.[3]

Events occurring in later life may also leave lasting impressions on the mind of a generation. Young men, for instance, are sometimes profoundly affected by new ideologies or grand causes—liberalism, nationalism, communism, the crusades for civil rights or world peace. And people of all ages may be marked for the rest of their lives by great nationwide or international catastrophies. Thus such words as "depression" and "appeasement" have specific connotations and emotional overtones for those who were mature men and women in the 1930's which cannot be felt

3. Henri Peyre, *Les Générations littéraires* (Paris, 1948), p. 198.

by those born since. From childhood well into adult life, the group mind of a social generation is created by cultural conditions and by the impact of events.

The resulting generational mind expresses itself in many ways, and helps in its turn to shape history. A generation is united at least in its definitions of the problems confronting it, if not on solutions. Members have a more or less common set of presuppositions about the world. They share common tastes in literature and art, or at least agree on the aesthetic framework within which to dispute. They agree in a general way on a hierarchy of values. And in all these matters they may disagree violently with preceding and succeeding generations, who grew up in a different time and have lived through (or will live through) a different period of history. In crises members of a given generation tend to act together, or at least similarly—as radicals of the right and the left, for instance, united in their radicalism if in nothing else. The social generation, like the national group or the social class, may thus be a powerful force in history.

So runs the basic theory of social generations. There have, however, also been some empirical studies of the phenomenon, accounts of particular social generations rather than of theoretical models. In general these have been the work of concerned observers of twentieth-century civilization, attempting through analyses of their own generations to understand the cataclysmic events of these times.

In two important ways this empirical generational literature both supplements and goes beyond the work of the theorists. In the first place, these essentially autobiographical studies of twentieth-century generations usually focus their attention on the youth of the generation in question. It is apparently in this early period of growth that generational consciousness is most highly developed—the result perhaps of inevitable conflicts with a still-vigorous older generation. More important, it seems that a social generation is most likely to have its great adventure, to make its unique cultural discovery, or to embark upon its glorious crusade, during its youth. In this emphasis upon youth, the empirical generational literature makes a real contribution to the theory of generations.

Most of the autobiographical generational writers also stress the decline into pessimism and the reversion to conservatism of the typical social generation in its old age. Ralph de Toledano, for example, thus describes the crusading generation of the 1930's —twenty years after they had set out to save the world: "There was grey in our hair, and the Great Mushroom cast an even greyer light on our faces. We had entered the middle limbo. . . . If we had gained any wisdom, it was to repeat after Montaigne that long life or short it was made all one by death."[4] And Georges Valois, repenting in age the youthful rebellion of the World War I generation, wrote simply: " Our fathers possessed the truth. . . . The dead of the Great War were the victims of the errors of an age."[5] The self-conscious ardor of youth gives way in the end to the gloomy conservatism of old age—this is the message of the empirical generational literature of our own times.

This, then, is the theory of social generations in its simplest form. Scholarly theorists have postulated a developing group mind in people growing up through the same span of history. The resulting unity of outlook is believed to be as real as that which binds members of the same nationality or social class, and may be as powerful in directing the course of history. Astute observers of their own generations have particularly put stress on youth and age, on the generational cohesion and passionate conviction of youth, and on the pessimistic conservatism of old age. It remains for the historian to put this simple theory to the test by applying it to a particular problem in cultural history.

An understanding of Elizabethan ambition in generational terms must begin with an outline of the generational structure of sixteenth-century England as a whole; for, of course, several generations of the Elizabethan ruling class were alive and functioning during the later decades of the reign. In the glorious year 1588, for example, Queen Elizabeth herself was fifty-five; her most recent favorite, the Earl of Essex, was twenty-one. The Cecils, father and son, were on the verge of beginning their administrative partnership, though old Lord Burghley was Robert's senior by more than forty years. The recent Netherlands inter-

4. *Lament for a Generation* (New York, 1960), p. 260.
5. *D'un siècle à l'autre: Chronique d'un génération (1885-1920)* (Paris, 1921), p. 292.

vention and the sea raid on Spain had been commanded by the Earl of Leicester and Sir Francis Drake respectively, both of the Queen's aging generation. But by this time a throng of swash-buckling younger men—Essex, Sir Francis Vere, Charles Blount, the future Lord Mountjoy, and a number of others—had won their spurs in these expeditions, and were already beginning to clamor for commands of their own. Everywhere, young men and old men shared the stage, working together or at cross purposes for individual and national ends. This confusing generational picture must be analyzed and schematized if it is to be of any use to the historian.

A generational analysis in terms of the key quality of ambition must begin by singling out and defining the particular generation with which the study is primarily concerned—the younger generation of Elizabethan courtiers. For this purpose, the younger generation may be defined as those members of the English ruling class who were in their twenties and thirties during the last two decades of Elizabeth's reign, the 1580's and the 1590's. An examination of the dates of the most successful members of this aristocratic generation reveals that almost all of them were born during the fifteen-year span between the birth of Raleigh in 1552 and that of Essex in 1566.[6] Raleigh and Essex, furthermore, competed as equals, as contemporaries, for the favor of the aging Queen—they were, as enemies of the regime put it, her successive *mignons*. Men born before mid-century treated the Essex end of this generational spectrum as their juniors and considered themselves the colleagues of older men than Raleigh. Men born after the middle 1560's, on the other hand, simply played very little part in history until the following reign. For purposes of research into the nature of Elizabethan ambition, then, this group of men, born during the later 1550's and the earlier 1560's, constitute a single social generation. For the sake of convenience, this generation may be called, after a year close to the center of its span of birth, the generation of 1560.

Relative to this Elizabethan younger generation, more than one older generation may be distinguished. To begin with, there are the two generations most prominently represented by Lord

6. A chronological listing of the most prominent members of the Elizabethan younger generation may be found in the Appendix.

Burghley, born in 1520, and by Queen Elizabeth, born in 1533—though these birthdates fall near the beginning rather than at the midpoint of their generational spans of birth. Between Elizabeth's social generation and that of 1560, furthermore, yet another age group must be postulated, one born mainly in the 1540's. Members of Burghley's generation, of Elizabeth's, and of the generation of the 1540's were all alive and influential throughout the youth and young manhood of the Elizabethan younger generation. But since these three generations are important here only insofar as they affected the generation of 1560, specific generational spans need not be assigned them.

Of these three older generations, that of the 1540's requires no separate treatment here. The main function of this generation, relative to the problem under consideration, was simply to reinforce the attitude and influence of the generations of Burghley and Elizabeth, and to provide a few individual heroes, like Sir Richard Grenville, for the younger generation. As for the two older generations which are to be considered in detail, both were molded by the revolutionary decades of the later Henry VIII, Edward VI, and Mary; they therefore tended to think and act alike, and thus to reinforce each other in their impact on the generation of 1560. In fact, as they grew older, they became virtually contemporaries in outlook and in the eyes of the younger generation, and may be so considered in the later chapters of this study.

When this generational scheme is inserted into its historical framework, the following picture of the century emerges. The generations of Burghley and Elizabeth grew up during the revolutionary middle Tudor decades, took over the country in the 1550's, and ran it for the rest of the century—with some help from the generation of the 1540's and, towards the end, with more help than they expected from the generation of 1560. It is within this generational context that the aspiring mind of the Elizabethan younger generation emerged and grew. It is therefore in terms of these generational relationships that an understanding of Elizabethan aspiration is most readily to be found.

But is not this imposition of "generational structure" on the past really rather artificial? Is there any real evidence that interacting social generations played any significant part whatever in the history of the reign of Elizabeth I? As it happens, there is a good deal of testimony to the rise of a significant younger generation in the later years of the reign—enough evidence at least to make the Elizabethan Age seem a likely period for such an experimental study as this.

Many historians of this period have noted the rise of a new generation to prominence in the 1580's and 1590's—the very decades when the generation of 1560 grew to maturity. Pollard, for example, writes: "During these last fifteen years of her reign, Elizabeth seems like an actor lingering on the stage after his part has been played . . . a queen who had outlived all her early friends and ministers. . . ."[7] Neale sees the last years of the reign as a "tragic drama of age and youth" and declares that "the generation coming into power in the 1590's was out of tune with the old Queen and her ways."[8] A. L. Rowse has done some impressionistic generational periodizing of the Tudor century, in which he sees in "Elizabeth's later years" the rise of "a new type, the young men, more brilliant and dashing, unrestrained by the fears of their fathers. . . ."[9] A biographer of one of the most brilliant of these young men has written of the aging Queen: "A generation was pressing on whose thoughts were not her thoughts, nor their ways her ways."[10] Leading political historians have thus noticed the rise to prominence of the Elizabethan younger generation.

Writing from the viewpoint of the history of ideas, an authority on Elizabethan literature says: "The 1590's are the crucial years," the years in which "there occurred a change, a shift of thought and feeling, which led directly to the greatest moment in English poetry: the 'Shakespearean moment. . . .' "[11] Cruttwell goes on to explain that "to think of the Elizabethan age as a solid, unchanging reality is utterly misleading. Within it there were two generations and (roughly corresponding to those generations)

7. A. F. Pollard, *History of England from the Accession of Edward VI to the Death of Elizabeth (1547-1603)* (London, 1910), pp. 458, 479.
8. J. E. Neale, *Queen Elizabeth I* (New York, 1957), p. 364; *Elizabethan Political Scene*, p. 19.
9. *The English Spirit* (New York, 1945), p. 90.
10. Algernon Cecil, *A Life of Robert Cecil, First Earl of Salisbury* (London, 1915), p. 188.
11. Patrick Cruttwell, *The Shakespearean Moment and Its Place in the Poetry of the Seventeenth Century* (New York, 1960), p. 1.

two mentalities. In the 1590's the one 'handed over' to the other."
It is certainly true that almost all the celebrated writers of the
Elizabethan Age were comparatively young men in the 1580's
and the 1590's—were in fact members of the generation of 1560.[12]
The literary production of these talented young men was
prodigious and of enduring significance in English literature,
scholarship, and thought. In a decade and a half an avalanche of
great literature poured from the presses, including such celebrated titles as the *Arcadia, Astrophel and Stella, The Faerie
Queene, Tamburlaine, Doctor Faustus, Richard III, Julius Caesar,
Romeo and Juliet, Hamlet, Every Man in His Humour,* Camden's
Britannia, Hakluyt's *English Voyages,* Hooker's *Laws of Ecclesiastical Polity,* and the first edition of Bacon's *Essays.* It was a
tremendous period of literary experimentation and production,
and many of the young men who made it so, the writers of what
might be called the "university wits" generation, were dead before
the reign was out. To some extent, certainly, the flowering of
Elizabethan literature at the end of the sixteenth century was a
generational phenomenon.

In religion, to take a less familiar example, the impact of the
younger generation was also clearly felt. It was the young men
who swelled the ranks of militant Puritanism and resurgent
Catholicism, the two extremist reactions against the *via media* of
the Elizabethan Settlement. It was said of the Puritans in the last
years of the reign that "none but young men do hear our doctrines," and a famous preacher of the Puritan persuasion declared that "the young men follow Christ, the young men hear
the word, the young men sanctify themselves . . . which made an
old father of this city say . . . that if there were any good thing to
be done in these days, it is the young men that must do it."[13]
At the opposite extreme, competent observers pointed out that
"the greatest number of papists is of very young men," of men
"born since your Majesty's reign."[14] Historically, a new genera-

12. A list of the most prominent Elizabethan writers who were members of the
generation of 1560 may be found in the Appendix.

13. Henry Smith, "The Young Man's Task," in *The Sermons of Master Henry
Smith* . . ., ed. Thomas Man (London, 1611), pp. 215, 228-229.

14. Francis Bacon to Queen Elizabeth, 1584?, in James Spedding, *The Life and
Letters of Francis Bacon* (London, 1890), I, 50; H. B., *Moriemini: A Verie Profitable
Sermon Preached . . . at the Court . . .* (London, 1593), p. 11.

tion of religious fanatics made itself known in the later 1580's with the Catholic-inspired Babington Plot and the Puritan Marprelate Libels. Tides of religious radicalism rolled in once more, until fifteen years later Protestant militants presented their demands to a new king before he had even reached his capital, and Catholic extremists responded by planting gunpowder under the Houses of Parliament. This rebirth of religious passion was also to some extent a generational phenomenon, the work of men too young to remember the awful consequences of religious extremism in the reigns of Edward VI and Queen Mary.

Even more concrete evidence exists for the importance of the Elizabethan younger generation in the political and military spheres, as this book will attempt to show. But surely there is already enough evidence before us to suggest the advent of a new generation on the Elizabethan scene in the later 1580's and the 1590's. The younger generation was in fact so vigorously and ubiquitously in evidence that both intellectual and political historians have been drawn to comment on the fact. For students of cultural developments, indeed, the Elizabethan Age has tended to become synonymous with the romantic extravagance, the cavalier daring, the poetry and music of its closing fifteen or twenty years, the years of the ascendency of these young men. Scholars concerned with the solider if less spectacular political and constitutional achievements of the reign, on the other hand, have tended to lose interest about the time of the Armada, about the time when the older generation began to pass away. Both groups of historians, however, have sensed a significant turning point about the years 1585-1590. It is the thesis of this book that this change in the quality and tempo of Elizabethan life was primarily the result of the rise to prominence of a new generation of Elizabethans.

ii. Ambition in Elizabethan England

It remains to define a little more closely the quality of the Elizabethan younger generation with which this study is concerned—the quality of high aspiration, revealed most commonly in intense personal ambition. A more precise definition will require some explanation of the socio-political framework within which sixteenth-century aristocrats sought success and a brief description of the particular objects of their ambition. In addition, certain distinctions between types of Elizabethan aspiration should be made.

For an understanding of the social framework within which Elizabethans aspired to success, it should be remembered that this social generation was essentially a generation of courtiers. Such qualifications as this are absolutely necessary, particularly when dealing with periods before the advent of modern mass culture. The sharper the class distinctions, the more radically do the formative influences affecting one social group differ from those affecting another. The generation of 1560, most obviously, was a generation of the land-owning English aristocracy; as ambitious men, they were also, and most importantly, a generation of courtiers. Their aspirations were therefore defined by a long-vanished institution, the royal court, and by a political system which may most conveniently be labeled the courtier system of government.

The courtier system was the method by which Elizabethan England, like other strongly centralized monarchies, was governed. The keystone of these early modern governments was the monarchy itself; but the central institution, through which the power of the monarch was exercised, was the royal court. The court was not a place, since it existed wherever the sovereign happened to be at any given time. Nor was it a fixed group of designated officials; for its composition was in a constant state of flux as courtiers, many of whom held no official position at all, came and went. And yet, amorphous and ill-defined though it was, the royal court was the most important political institution of early modern times.

Essentially, the court comprised the most ambitious and talented members of the aristocracy, gathered about the monarch they served. There were basic qualifications for membership, at least in Elizabethan England: birth, education, and a considerable amount of wealth. The highest ministers of state were usually there, and the chief administrative, legal, and even military officials. The leading lights among the nobility were often in attendance, too, as were outstanding members of the gentry. Finally, there was a motley throng of the comparatively base-born but nonetheless ambitious, and of assorted hangers-on, milling about the fringes of the court.

The number of courtiers was actually small, and so was the generation with which we are dealing. The "politically active class" in Elizabethan England included an inner group of perhaps a hundred men. All told, including many younger sons, those eligible for high place cannot have numbered more than two or three thousand, only a minority of whom were at court at any given time.[15] It was a fairly homogeneous little group, many of them related by ties of blood or marriage. Most of them knew each other personally or by reputation; almost all of them must have been known to one or another of the Queen's chief ministers. Through this small ruling class, and most especially through its ambitious courtiers, the sovereign ran her central government and ruled the shires. The court was the living heart of the English government.

For the courtiers and governors themselves, however, the court was most importantly the focus of all their ambitions, the key to their hopes for successful careers. For the courtier system worked two ways: if service flowed up from the bottom, rewards flowed down from the top. "Service" and "reward" are the proper words: in theory at least, all services were freely given out of love for Queen and country, and all rewards were expressions of royal gratitude, not mere wages for work done. In fact, however, just as the Queen's government depended upon the services rendered by her courtiers, so the ambitions of the courtiers depended wholly upon the Queen, the fount from whom all blessings flowed. Ambitious aristocrats therefore eagerly offered their services to the Queen's Majesty; and, in return, they fully expected a fair share of the favor and preferment which she alone could dispense.

The services they offered included the whole range of governmental functions in Tudor England, from administering royal decrees or judging law cases in the Queen's name, to conducting diplomatic missions or leading the Queen's armies and

---

15. Wallace T. MacCaffrey, "Place and Patronage in Elizabethan Politics," *Elizabethan Government and Society*, ed. S. T. Bindoff, J. Hurstfield, and C. H. Williams (London, 1961), pp. 98-99.

navies into battle. In return her Majesty's faithful servants could expect rewards enough to gratify the most ambitious soul. There were the marks of honor which only the monarch could confer—knighthoods, nominations to the orders of chivalry, even titles of nobility. More readily available were a large number of offices, some of which brought real power to their holders—offices in the royal household and the court itself, as well as all administrative, legal, military, and ecclesiastical posts. Finally, there were a miscellaneous conglomeration of royal favors which provided the courtier with sorely needed sources of revenue—monopolies, farms, leases, annuities, and sometimes fabulous royal gifts. These were the specific objects of the ambitions of the Elizabethan ruling class—all the forms of honor, power, and wealth that lay within the Queen's power to grant.

The court was the center of the lives of the young gentlemen of Elizabethan England, and the operation of the courtier system their major preoccupation. High aspiration, manifested most commonly as personal ambition, provided the motive force of their careers. This particular motive, and the qualities of character which it implied, thus held a peculiarly central place in the make-up of the Elizabethan younger generation. A word or two should therefore be said about an interpretative problem which Elizabethan aspiration presents for the modern historian.

The phrase "aspiring mind" in common sixteenth-century usage stood for something very different from the significance it has acquired since. The aspiring mind of Tudor times had nothing to do with an earnest desire to improve oneself mentally, morally, or spiritually. An aspiring mind was simply an ambitious man, and the label had definite pejorative connotations. Cardinal Wolsey, Thomas Cromwell, and the Duke of Northumberland, for instance, were all aspiring minds in the sixteenth-century sense of the term. In the eyes of preachers, social satirists, and other commentators on the Elizabethan scene, the vast majority of courtiers in fact qualified as aspiring minds. The courtier betrayed his own ambitious nature by his very presence at the court, the center of worldly advancement for the Elizabethan ruling class.

Toward the end of the reign, however, the phrase "aspiring mind" acquired a new overlay of associations and emotional significance. In the 1580's and 1590's, there appeared what might be called the Marlovian aspiring mind, the mind of Marlowe's heroes, of Tamburlaine the Great and Doctor Faustus, of Barabas and Guise. These tremendously popular characters were aspiring minds with a passion and a style seldom seen before, and with new or strangely modified goals for their ambitions. They were towering supermen driven by lust for power and glory, for wealth and for knowledge infinite. The novel connotations of the term "aspiring mind" as epitomized in Marlowe's heroes reveal a new attitude toward ambition, and a broader, more positive, and even idealistic concept of the content of ambition itself. For many of the courtiers of the younger generation were themselves aspiring minds in this Marlovian meaning of the term. Like their fathers and grandfathers, they aspired to high honors, to political power, and to the wealth which might secure both—but they aspired with a difference. It is this difference that concerns us here. In investigating the aspiring mind of the generation of 1560, we are trying to understand the meaning of ambition for this generation of Elizabethans.

But as with the generational division of Tudor England, so with the primacy of ambition in the minds of these Elizabethans, the question of evidence arises. In fact, there is considerable proof of the central place of ambition in the lives and busy minds of Elizabeth's courtiers. Economic, social, and even political and constitutional historians have seen the key role of worldly aspiration in this bustling age of change. A great many biographies of Elizabethans, from the multi-volume lives of the great to the thumbnail sketches of lesser men in the *Dictionary of National Biography*, have stressed the prevalence of driving personal ambition in Elizabethan England. Many of these authorities will be cited later, in connection with various special features of the phenomenon. For the present, however, it will be sufficient to glance at some confirmation of this interpretation from two rather different scholarly disciplines: literary criticism and social psychology.

A comprehensive survey of that most revealing of Elizabethan art forms, the drama, shows that the "range of motives" of the tragic protagonists of the period was "very much narrowed."[16] In fact, "ambition and lust . . . are practically the only two which are admitted"; and even lust "may be called a special form of ambition or possessiveness. . . ." Elizabethans, like audiences in all societies, did not attend plays whose characters acted from incomprehensible motives. One of the basic methodological postulates of this study is that popular literature is in some sense a cultural projection of a society, revealing the ideals and basic attitudes of a people, or at least those ideals and attitudes which are of particular interest to them at any given time. The predominance of ambition as far and away the most common motive in the serious drama of the period thus indicates widespread familiarity and concern with the ambitious man in Elizabethan society.

Students of social psychology, also seeking their data in the literary remains of Tudor England, have contrived special techniques for estimating the intensity of psychological "need for achievement."[17] These techniques attempt to measure the extent to which the literate classes of a past culture felt an emotional need for "success in competition with some standard of excellence," for "winning, or doing well or better than others. . . ."[18] The result of the application of these methods to sixteenth-century English society was the conclusion that "the n Achievement [need for achievement] level was high from 1500 through 1625. . . ."[19] As graphed by Bradburn and Berlew, furthermore, the psychological need for success was at its highest pitch between 1550 and 1600: that is, during the five decades of the reign of Elizabeth I.[20] The results of such research into the need for achievement of an epoch have been considered indicative of the desire to "get ahead" that leads to surges of economic progress. Certainly, however, many of the motives that led to business booms in other times also sparked the political and military ambitions of the Elizabethan ruling class. The conclusions of the

16. M. C. Bradbrook, *Themes and Conventions of Elizabethan Tragedy* (Cambridge, 1960), p. 56.

17. David C. McClelland, *The Achieving Society* (New York, 1961), pp. 110 ff.; Norman N. Bradburn and David E. Berlew, "Need for Achievement and English Industrial Growth," *Economic Development and Cultural Change*, X (1961), 8-20.

18. David C. McClelland, et. al., *The Achievement Motive* (New York, 1953), p. 110; McClelland, *Achieving Society*, p. 113.

19. McClelland, *Achieving Society*, p. 140.

20. Bradburn and Berlew, 19.

social psychologists thus support the judgments of historians, biographers, and literary critics that these generations of Englishmen were driven by an extraordinary passion for success—they were, in short, extremely ambitious men.

It is, then, the thesis of this book that during the 1580's and '90's, there grew up among Elizabethan courtiers of the younger generation a Marlovian mood of high aspiration. It is further contended that this new form of worldly aspiration was in fact central to the thought and feeling, as well as to the public careers, of these younger Elizabethans. The aspiring mind is here presented as in a real sense the defining characteristic of the Elizabethan younger generation.

In attempting to prove these assertions, this book will seek also to demonstrate the value of the theory of social generations for the study of cultural history. This detailed examination of a single Elizabethan character trait has been researched as a generational case study. The results will be presented in the form of a generational biography, accompanied by an analytical account of the inner development of the Elizabethan aspiring mind. It is hoped that this approach will reveal more clearly the nature of Elizabethan ambition, a vital sociological and psychological fact of the age. It is also hoped that such a case study will demonstrate the value of the notion of social generations for the historian.

*The aspiring mind of the Elizabethan
younger generation*

I. *A burned-out generation*

Musing over portraits of the aging Elizabeth and her venerable ministers, A. L. Rowse observes: "They were a tough lot . . . tenacious and adaptable . . . harsh and treacherous." He compares them to the Parliament of 1918: "hard-faced men who looked as if they had done well out of the war."[1] There was undeniably an air of successful opportunism about these older generations of the Elizabethan ruling class. There was a certain harsh realism in their make-up, and more than a hint of the Italian school of diplomacy. Even in their old age, freighted with years and dignities, they still seemed to be men with a sharp eye out for the main chance. And yet, there was another and strangely contradictory side to the character of these older Elizabethans. Many interpreters of the late Tudor period have stressed the conservatism and undue prudence of many of the rulers of Elizabethan England. And certainly the generations of Elizabeth and Burghley rang the changes repeatedly on the need to maintain established institutions, to observe due order and degree. Certainly too, the older Elizabethans often showed a strong predilection for the safe compromise solution and the middle way.

Such harsh, hard-driving opportunism and such prudent conservatism seem somehow an unlikely combination. The contrast stands out still more clearly when seen in terms of relations between older and younger generations. As successful opportunists themselves, the Elizabethan older generations might have been expected to preach a Horatio Alger gospel of ambition to their children. They ought logically to have urged young men to strive for advancement, to pull themselves up by their own bootstraps as their fathers had done. And yet we know these older Elizabethans as arch conservatives, who swore by the social hierarchy and heaped abuse on "climbers" and "new men." In the England of Elizabeth I, ambition was in fact a vice so universally condemned that almost no Elizabethan ever willingly confessed to possessing it.

The aspiring mind of the generation of 1560 was shaped in

1. A. L. Rowse, *The English Spirit* (New York, 1945), p. 89.

large part by this paradoxical attitude of their parents toward ambition. And the origins of the oddly contrasting opportunism and timid conservatism of the Elizabethan older generations lay in their own past lives, and especially in their youth. For it was during their youth that the traumatic course of English history left an indelible mark on these two generations of English rulers.

i. The web of ambition

What was the past of the generation of Queen Elizabeth, born mainly in the 1530's, and of the still older generation of Lord Burghley, born in the 1520's and earlier? The dates themselves shift our attention abruptly from one end of the century to the other, from the great days of the Armada and Shakespeare's plays to the chaotic years of the Henrician Reformation. For it was during the latter half of the reign of Henry VIII that the older Elizabethan generations grew up; and it was under Edward VI and Queen Mary that Elizabeth and Leicester, Burghley and Walsingham and the other builders of Elizabethan England came of age.

Those were revolutionary times. William Cecil was born in 1520, the year that Martin Luther's three famous tracts against the Pope irrevocably rent the ancient fabric of Roman Christendom. The propaganda barrage thus begun was to divide all Europe before the end of Cecil's long lifetime. Princess Elizabeth, born in 1533, was herself an unwitting cause of England's break with Rome. Then too, by the 1520's and '30's, the work of the English humanists had born fruit, and the pagan classics were winning a central place for themselves in the educational curriculum of the English ruling classes. The future governors of England were no longer trained exclusively in fighting, hunting, and other gentlemanly pastimes; now they were set to parsing their Latin and steeping themselves in the practical wisdom of the ancients. Thus the older Elizabethan generations were exposed in their formative years to the radical new doctrines of Lutheran Protestantism and Erasmian humanism, preached by ardent young converts. These generations grew up in an age of ideological ferment, a ferment that was to be even more intense by the time their children came of age.

But if radical ideologies made the air of the universities electric, the real world of the ruling class—the world of politics and money, of social position and power—was still more tumultuous in the second quarter of the century. Young Cecil's generation was certainly old enough in the 1530's to be conscious of the revolutionary activities of the Reformation Parliament, which then began the institutional transformation of the English church. He and his contemporaries must also have had vivid memories of the wholesale looting of the monasteries of England, and of the Romanist reaction, the bloody Pilgrimage of Grace. Princess Elizabeth's generation came to conscious life in the 1540's, in time to witness the first backswing of the pendulum toward Catholicism. They lived in their childhood through all the erratic economic developments, the increasing social and religious discontent of the nervous forties. Both generations, furthermore, saw confusion reach the throne itself in Henry VIII's shocking series of marriages and sanguinary separations.

After Henry came the deluge: Elizabeth's generation was in its teens, Cecil's in its twenties, when the brief reigns of Edward VI and Queen Mary brought the central crisis of the Tudor period. Under Henry VIII's sickly son and unfortunate daughter, men and movements that Henry's iron hand had barely held in check broke loose in an orgy of extremism and bloodshed. The mid-century years were years of ideological radicalism and reaction, of revolution, war, and economic disaster. Political instability was endemic. There were at least three major shifts in the center of political power during the decade 1547-1558—from Somerset to Northumberland to Mary to Elizabeth. Each change of government was a time of trial and of real danger for England's ruling class. It was a nerve-wracking time to be alive, and the lessons it burned into young minds were never forgotten.

Through the record of these turbulent times runs the red thread of ambition. For contemporaries, the greatest names of that age were synonymous with overweening ambition. King Henry's reign saw Thomas Wolsey and Thomas Cromwell, notorious as the sons of a butcher and a blacksmith, rise to become for a time the mightiest subjects in the land.[2] The earth-shaking falls of these two power-hungry men bracketed the revolutionary 1530's; and for Elizabethans, Wolsey and Cromwell became type figures of the Tudor aspiring mind. Then, under the sickly boy-king Edward VI, the future rulers of Elizabethan England saw two giants of ambition collide head on, with the kingdom itself as the prize. The rivalry of Lord Protector Somerset and North-umberland the Queenmaker became the pivot around which English politics and policies revolved; and to contemporary eyes, ambition was their prime motive. For the older Elizabethans, high aspiration became probably the single outstanding characteristic of the political life of the earlier sixteenth century. Some knowl-edge of the overweening ambition of the 1530's and '40's, par-ticularly as the Elizabethan older generations saw it, is therefore vital for an understanding of the attitude which they adopted toward the aspiring minds of their children.

There were certainly facts enough to lend credence to this sixteenth-century interpretation of their own times. Personal am-bition—for wealth, power, prestige—was common to all classes in the youth of Elizabeth and Burghley. And the origins of this feverish aspiration lay deep in the fluid nature of Tudor society itself.

The tremendous social mobility of those years was not due solely to the institutional revolutions of the 1530's, the economic crises of the 1540's, and the political tensions of the decade 1547-1558. Long-range economic developments had for centuries been throwing up "new men," merchants and country gentry, to finan-cial parity with the ancient aristocracy. And these economic trends had given the newly rich increasing hopes of social and political equality to come. In the later fifteenth and earlier sixteenth cen-turies, furthermore, the pace of social change had perceptibly quickened. The Wars of the Roses decimated the old feudal aristocracy; and the new Tudor polity demanded special talents and training which the rustic baron could not readily supply. The road to social and political success was thus opened up, not only for efficient businessmen and gentry, but for scholarly humanists and lawyers as well.

2. Cf. W. S., *The True Chronicle Historie of the whole life and death of Thomas Lord Cromwell* (London, 1602), sig. A2r-A3r.

By Henry VIII's day, then, the aristocracy of blood had lost its medieval monopoly of place and power, and several new groups were rising to share in the governing of England. Within this already extremely mobile society, the unsettling events of the middle Tudor years had a vigorous catalytic effect. The accelerating pace of social mobility swelled to a crescendo in the sixteenth century—a crescendo of ambitious climbing so furious that by mid-century it seemed to be on the verge of shaking the commonwealth to pieces.

Of course, not all these lawyers and humanistic scholars, merchants, gentry, and newly elevated aristocrats were cynical opportunists seeking only to further their own ambitions. Protestant religiosity, humanist ethics, and the sense of moral responsibility inculcated by the old-fashioned education of the county families helped to guide the lives of many of the most successful of the new Tudor ruling class. But the times favored the man of easy conscience; and complex, dangerous situations dulled the edge of scruple. The Machiavellian methods of a Cromwell rubbed off even on such men as William Cecil, a sincere Protestant and a conscientious official who carried Cicero's *Offices* in his pocket all his life. Increasingly—though this was never publicly admitted—success became the standard, the touchstone by which an ambitious man's life was judged, by himself and by others.

The success of such ambitious climbers could in fact be breathtaking—almost unbelievably so as described in the sixteenth-century history books available to Elizabethans. Thus a London chronicler described the rapid rise of Thomas Cromwell: "Then was . . . M. Thomas Cromwell, temporal man, made M[aster] of the Rolls and the King's secretary, and after that Lord Privy Seal, and after that Vicar General of all England and Knight of the Garter, and after that Lord Chamberlain and Earl of Essex."[3] Coming from nowhere, a man like Cromwell could rise under Henry VIII to the highest offices, the most distinguished honors, indeed to the peerage itself. Such a meteoric rise to place and power must have made old men blink, and young men wonder.

But if a man could rise rapidly under Henry VIII, the ac-

3. Clarence Hopper, ed., *London Chronicle during the Reigns of Henry the Seventh and Henry the Eighth* (Camden Soc. Pub. No. 93; London, 1859), p. 9.

cession of Edward VI, a child of nine, provided the best opportunity since the coming of the Tudor dynasty for ambitious, hard-driving men to seize power, wealth, offices, and honors. John Dudley, Earl of Warwick and Duke of Northumberland, was for Elizabethans the prototype and most successful example of the breed of ambitious opportunist that dominated English politics about 1550. John Dudley's father had begun life as a lawyer with some skill at mathematics and administration; he had risen to become one of Henry VII's chief financial agents— only to be executed for extortion by his successor. Under Henry VIII and Edward VI, however, the younger Dudley climbed far higher than his father had. He became a knight, then an earl, and finally a duke; he rose from the post of Lord Admiral to a place on the Regency Council, and thence to mastery of the Council, the King, and, almost, of the realm itself. As Duke of Northumberland, he apparently aspired to transfer the crown of England from the Tudors to the Dudleys; and, to his contemporaries, it seemed for a time as if he might succeed even in this extravagant ambition.

Nor were Cromwell and Northumberland isolated instances of high ambition in this mobile society. Statistical study shows that under Henry VIII and Edward VI there was in fact "a very substantial turn-over in the English titular aristocracy . . . the great majority representing the elevation of successful soldiers and administrators after 1529."[4] The members of Edward VI's Regency Council provide an obvious example of high ambitions and their reward. Before the young king was even crowned, many of these chief men of the realm had helped themselves to substantial promotions; and the councillors steadily "advanced in station as the new reign progressed."[5] At mid-century, the English government was actually being run by "new men": the senior peerage among the leaders of the Council was Somerset's, and his title of nobility was barely ten years old.

In the train of each of these major contenders for power, there came a throng of clients and followers and relatives, jostling

4. Lawrence Stone, "The Inflation of Honors, 1558-1641," *Past and Present*, No. 14 (Nov., 1958), p. 55.
5. Conyers Read, *Mr. Secretary Cecil and Queen Elizabeth* (New York, 1955), p. 37.

for pride of place in the second rank. Thus knighthoods were also "distributed more freely" at this time, especially during the mid-century wars.[6] Lesser men, ranging all the way from Cromwell's notorious monastery visitors to the scholarly humanist reformers who clustered about Lord Protector Somerset, labored and schemed as ambitiously as their superiors for their own share of advancement. City businessmen and country squires squabbled over confiscated monastery lands. Merchant traders and the new industrial entrepreneurs fought for profits in the booming 1540's. Lawyers, scholars, and even preachers competed for preferment in the hierarchies of church and state. From simple gentleman to knight, from commoner to peer, from earl to duke to Lord Protector, the climbers mounted the ladder of success in mid-Tudor England. It was the hey-day of the aspiring mind, as the older Elizabethans understood that term.

Even those who had no particularly high aspirations of their own were often drawn into this carnival of ambition. If one's patron was involved with an aspiring faction, for instance, one was more than likely to be drawn willy nilly into the struggle for power. The same was true if one's personal rival—for favors at court or simply for prestige in the home county—was involved in some ambitious scheme. Ties of blood or a miscalculated marriage or even a purely professional relationship, like a tutor's or a secretary's post, could involve a man closely in the success of another man's ambition. It was alleged, for example, that Lord Admiral Seymour had entangled as many as four hundred young lords and gentlemen in his ambitious plans to replace his brother the Lord Protector.[7] Princess Elizabeth herself was caught in the web of Seymour's extravagant ambitions—an experience she was not likely to forget.[8]

In addition, personal ambition inevitably bred personal competition; and the ambitious rivalries of great men were particularly likely to involve many more. "My lord," said one of the Duke of Northumberland's allies in the plot to put Lady Jane Grey upon the throne, "if you mistrust any of us in this matter,

6. Stone, p. 49.
7. *C. S. P., Span.*, IX, 340, 341, 332; *C. S. P., Dom., Ed. VI.*, VI, 1.
8. J. E. Neale, *Queen Elizabeth I* (New York, 1957), pp. 18-26.

your grace is far deceived, for which of us can wash his hands clean thereof?"[9] The high aspirations of the mighty were a web that entangled many lesser men. And when the opportunity to rise still higher presented itself, even the greatest seldom refused.

It was in such a mobile society, among men possessed by this sort of intense ambition, that Princess Elizabeth, William Cecil, and their contemporaries grew to maturity. Growing up in this world, their own lives often closely bound up with the careers of such fiercely ambitious men, the older Elizabethans naturally acquired the shrewd opportunism which later distinguished them. Elizabeth herself learned from the time of her involvement with Lord Admiral Seymour, in her teens, to make her way through a fang-and-claw world to the object of her own aspirations. Young William Cecil rose in the service of both lord protectors, and learned before he was out of his twenties to use other men's soaring ambitions to further his own advancement. By 1558 opportunistic ambition had become a way of life for the Elizabethan older generations.

ii. The perils of high aspiration

The opportunities and the opportunism of the mid-Tudor decades provided the generations of Elizabeth and Burghley with a veritable school for ambitious climbing. These formative years, however, also taught the Elizabethan older generations powerful lessons in the dangers of unfettered ambition. For there was danger as well as opportunity in this world of high aspiration—danger for the aspiring mind himself, for his rivals, for the whole ruling class. And it was from the discovery of these perils that the other side of this paradoxical Elizabethan attitude toward ambition, the timid conservatism of the older Elizabethans, developed and grew.

In those times of radical dislocation in so many areas of human life, bloodshed and violent death became, if not commonplace, at least considerably more common than usual. There were peasant rebellions; there were religious martydoms; there were political conspiracies and plots. If England had no Inquisi-

9. Raphael Holinshed, *Holinshed's Chronicles of England, Scotland, and Ireland* (London, 1807-1808), III, 1069.

tion and no Servetus, she had her Marian martyrs and her Saint Thomas More. If the Tudors had no Guises or rebellious German princelings, they had their share of overmighty subjects and civil strife. The Tudor century can only be considered a time of peace and order in a comparative sense, by contrast with the great civil wars of the fifteenth and seventeenth centuries.

An observant Italian, traveling in England in the middle of the sixteenth century, was surprised to discover how many leading English families had lost members to the gallows and the block. The traveler jotted down a bitter jest then current: "Lately a foreigner, having asked an English captain if anyone in his family had been hanged and quartered, was answered, 'not that he knew of.' Another Englishman whispered to the foreigner, 'Don't be surprised, for he is not a gentleman.' "[10] If groups may suffer as individuals do, the Tudor ruling class must have experienced something of a traumatic shock during those later years of King Henry and the brief reigns of his son and elder daughter.

Among the ruling-class casualties of those changing times, it is safe to say that few perished who did not possess a considerable share of ambition. It was ambition that prompted men to seek employment with such dangerous aspiring minds as Wolsey or Northumberland. It was ambition that raised great men in arms against their superiors, knowing well the awful price of failure. Ambition often played a part in the motivation of even the most dedicated champion of the old order, or the new. Ambition, more often than any other motive, raised men to the high places where the lightning struck.

The most dangerous years were the later 1530's, and the later 1540's and early 50's. In the first of these two periods the bloodshed was largely the result of the policies and personality of an iron-fisted king. In the second period it was precisely the lack of a strong ruler on the throne that brought perilous times to the governors of England. In both periods contemporaries saw unrestrained ambition as a prime cause of the death of many talented and highly placed individuals.

The direct impact of the executions of the later 1530's upon generations born in the 1520's and '30's may not have been great. Nevertheless, the fall of so many highborn gentlemen and ladies

10. Neale, p. 7.

surely formed a bloody background to their childhood. And recollections of this dark period, however hazy, undoubtedly reinforced the conclusions about unrestrained ambition that these young people drew from their later experiences in the troubled decade of Edward and Mary. Even a partial list of the gentlemen and nobles, queens and ministers of state who died by the ax or the rope during the later 1530's reveals the scope of the Terror which swept the English ruling class. As chronicled in a popular, if somewhat inaccurate, Elizabethan history of England, the victims for the seven years 1535-1541 included: in 1535, More and Fisher; in 1536, Queen Anne and her brother Lord Rochford, the Earl of Kildare and his uncles; in 1537, the Lincolnshire rebels led by Sir Robert Aske; in 1538, the Earl of Devonshire; in 1539, Sir Nicholas Carew, K. G., and a number of high churchmen; in 1540, Thomas Cromwell, Earl of Essex, and Lord Walter Hungerford; in 1541, Queen Catherine, the Countess of Salisbury, and Lord Dacres.[11] Around these great names a horde of lesser men clustered in the pages of Tudor history books—and in the memories of the Elizabethan older generations. The ambitious climber, they realized even as children, all too often ended on the scaffold.

Among the noble heads that rolled during the later 1540's and the early '50's were those of Lord Admiral Seymour, Lord Protector Somerset, and the Duke of Northumberland. All three were widely believed to have been led to their deaths by their own inordinate ambition. Thus Lord Admiral Thomas Seymour, executed in 1549, provided a type case of extravagant ambition and its evil rewards. He went to the block for allegedly plotting to murder his brother the Lord Protector, to marry Princess Elizabeth, and "following the example of Richard III . . . to make himself King."[12] Protector Somerset himself was soon being accused by his fellow rulers of "pride and ambition, aspiring further than became a good governor or a true subject."[13] At his trial

11. John Stow, *A Summarie of the Chronicles of England* (London, 1598), pp. 230-243; cf. Richard Grafton, *Abridgment of the Chronicles of Englande, newely corrected and augmented* (London, 1572), pp. 154[r] ff.

12. *C. S. P., Span.,* IX, 349-350.

13. The Lords of the Council to Princess Mary and Princess Elizabeth, Oct. 9, 1549, in Patrick Fraser Tytler, *England under the Reigns of Edward VI and Mary . . . in a Series of Original Letters . . .* (London, 1839), I, 248.

in 1551 it was officially charged that "he was ambitious and sought his own glory."[14] Then in 1553, when Edward VI lay dying, it was widely believed that the mighty Duke of Northumberland aspired to the role of Queenmaker, if not of King. As he collected funds and weapons and installed his creatures in key posts, an observant ambassador concluded: "There is no doubt that he is aspiring to the Crown."[15] And when Northumberland died upon the scaffold, Lady Jane Grey, herself a prisoner in the Tower, spoke a bitter valedictory upon him: "Woe worth him! he hath brought me and our stock in most miserable calamity and misery by his exceeding ambition."[16] She spoke for all those of her generation who were caught up in the web of ambition spun by their elders.

How closely destruction dogged the footsteps of high worldly aspiration is vividly clear from young King Edward's own description of the sudden arrest of the Duke of Somerset and his ambitious followers:

The first [to come to Westminster that day, October 16, 1551] was the Duke, who came later than was his wont . . . after dinner he was apprehended; Sir Thomas Palmer, on the terrace, walking there; Hammond, passing the Vice-Chamberlain's door, was called in by John Piers to make a match at shooting, and so taken. Likewise were John Seymour and Davy Seymour. Arundell was also taken, and the Lord Grey, coming out of the country. Vane upon two sendings. He said my Lord [of Northumberland] was not stout, and if he could get home [to his estates], he cared for none of them all, he was so strong. But, after, he was found by John Piers, in a stable of his man's at Lambeth, under the straw.[17]

The aspiring mind of mid-century England lived in the shadow of danger: ruin was as close as an invitation to a shooting match, a walk on the terrace, a hand on the shoulder as one passed an open door.

Each of the men taken into custody that October day had friends, followers, kinsmen to start and shudder at the news.

14. Richard Grafton, *Grafton's Chronicle or History of England* (London, 1809), II, 522.

15. C. S. P., *Span.*, XI, 55.

16. John Gough Nichols, ed., *The Chronicle of Queen Jane and of Two Years of Queen Mary* (Camden Soc. Pub. No. 48; London, 1850), p. 25.

17. Journal of King Edward VI, quoted in Tytler, II, 4.

Thus, though comparatively few actually followed the giants of ambition down to ruin, many more felt the strain of those uncertain times. They were entangled emotionally in the web of ambition; they suffered its dangers psychologically if no other way. Those most closely involved in the perilous plotting of a Seymour or a Northumberland undoubtedly experienced extremes of tension, fear, and sheer mental anguish. Such emotional distress surely left psychological scars as serious as any material loss or physical suffering—and as unlikely to be forgotten in a single lifetime.

Thus it surely was with the adherents of Somerset and Northumberland at the various crises of their ambitious rivalry. The autumn of 1549, for instance, must have been a nightmarish time for the gentlemen and nobles of both factions. The followers of the Earl of Warwick, the future Northumberland, moved inexorably against the Somerset clique in the government. Tension spread, rumors ran through the court and the city; "and suddenly, of what occasion many marveled and few knew, every Lord and Counsellor went through the City weaponed, and their servants likewise weaponed. . . ."[18] There was "a great assembly" of Warwick's adherents at his house in Holbourne; and every man present wagered his future on the decision to rise against the Lord Protector's rule.[19] At the same time, Somerset's own advisors and clients gathered about him; they stood to arms through long days and nights, first at Hampton Court and then at Windsor Castle, till the threats of their enemies—and lack of provisions—at last undermined their courage. Few of these men were imprisoned, and in the final outcome, fewer still perished with their leader and patron. Nevertheless, while the issue hung in doubt, the psychological suffering must have been considerable. Members of both aspiring factions—those who gathered at Holbourne to risk treason charges, and those who assembled under arms at Hampton Court—must have lived for some days on a razor edge of tension and fear.

The agonizing situation of one such ambitious young man who had hitched his fortune to a falling star was eloquently ex-

18. A. J. A. Malkiewicz, "An Eye-Witness Account of the Coup d'Etat of October, 1549," *EHR*, LXX (1955), 605; Grafton, *Grafton's Chronicle*, II, 521-522.
19. Grafton, *Grafton's Chronicle*, II, 522.

pressed by a follower of Somerset who shared the long vigil at Windsor. Writing to a friend who had defected to the Warwick faction, Thomas Smith lamented: "For my part, I am in a most miserable case. I cannot leave the King's Majesty, and him [Somerset] who was my master, of whom I have had all; and [yet] I cannot deny but I have misliked also some things that you and the rest of my lords there did mislike—as ye know, no man better, yourself." He urged his correspondent to show himself "no seeker of extremity nor blood" and to "let Christian charity work with you Sir, for God's love, and the King's, and to the realm's. . . ." And in a pitiful postscript, he begged his friend to write him, "though it be but *two* words of comfort."[20] With Somerset's fall, Thomas Smith's fortunes "crashed in ruins."[21] And though he survived to become one of the most prominent of the Elizabethan older generation, surely he never forgot the crisis of overweening ambition in which he had himself been so intimately involved.

Even more emotional distress among the ruling class must have accompanied Northumberland's effort to deprive Princess Mary of her throne in 1553. Once more the great Lords of the Council armed themselves and their servants; once again there were secret meetings and agonizing decisions.[22] The awful pressure under which these decisions were made—for Mary or for Northumberland—is dramatically illuminated in Chief Justice Montague's account of how England's highest-ranking judges were drawn into the Northumberland Plot.[23] Justice Montague and his fellows at first refused to prepare the legal documents transferring the right of succession to Lady Jane Grey, declaring apprehensively that such an act would be treason. They were forthwith subjected to terrible pressures by Northumberland and his adherents. The Duke himself, "in a great rage and fury, trembling for anger . . . called the said Sir Edward [Montague] traitor; and furthermore said that he would fight in his shirt with any man in

20. Sir Thomas Smith to Sir William Petre, Windsor Castle, Oct. 8, 1549, in Tytler, I, 228-230.

21. Mary Dewar, *Sir Thomas Smith, a Tudor Intellectual in Office* (London, 1964), pp. 4, 59.

22. *C. S. P., Span.*, XI, 49, 57, 66, 67, 71; Tytler, II, 172, 174-175; Grafton, *Grafton's Chronicle*, II, 532-533; Nichols, pp. 11-16.

23. Declaration of Sir Edward Montague, in Thomas Fuller, *The Church History of Britain*, ed. J. S. Brewer (Oxford, 1845), IV, 137-147.

that quarrel. . . ." At court, "all the lords looked upon them . . . as though they had not known them . . . and said if they refused to do that they were traitors." Chief Justice Montague, "in great fear as ever he was in all his life before . . . being an old man, and without comfort," naturally enough "began to consider with himself what was best to be done for the safeguard of his life. . . ."

Surely the young men feared for their lives no less than the old during those tense weeks in the spring of 1553, when the King lay dying. Young William Cecil, for one, "dreaded assassination; he went about armed, contrary to his usual practice; he resorted to London, often under cover of night; he had his money, plate, and evidences out of his house; he meditated flying from the country. . . ." It was, says one scholar, "the most trying crisis of his life. . . ."[24] It is not likely that even the portly, white-bearded Lord Burghley of forty years hence could have forgotten that nervous spring when his very life seemed to hang in the balance of one man's overweening ambition.

Such nerve-wracking experiences as these, even though no material loss or physical suffering might result, undoubtedly left psychological scars upon the young people who were to become the Elizabethan older generations. In many cases, they were facing the first great crises of their adult lives. They ran very real risks, and they knew it: not merely loss of favor, but attainder for treason, imprisonment, even summary execution. In this harsh school, Elizabeth and Burghley and their contemporaries learned the opportunistic techniques of carving out careers for themselves in a jungle of clashing ambitions. At the same time, and perhaps more importantly, they developed a fear and a distrust of unrestrained aspiration that they were to carry with them all their lives.

iii. *The fear of overreaching*

This Elizabethan interpretation of the mid-Tudor period and its leading personalities was evidently somewhat exaggerated. Like Richard III, some of the great men of the sixteenth century were undoubtedly victims of Tudor legend-building. In the

24. Tytler, II, 172, 175.

present case, however, historical truth should not be allowed to confuse the issue. It is precisely these Tudor myths—not the great men of that time as modern historians see them—that are of primary importance here. It was, after all, largely what court gossip and contemporary chroniclers *said* about these aspiring minds that determined the views of the Elizabethan older generation. It is the Elizabethan legends, not the facts, that we are after.

Twentieth-century historiography has actually tended to find much good in most of these ambitious climbers. Thus a recent biographer declares that "no major figure" in English history "has suffered from so many misconceptions and calumnies as Thomas Cromwell."[25] He was in fact no merely selfish career politician, but a truly creative administrator—"a modern type of statesman" in Elton's phrase.[26] The Duke of Northumberland also, according to a recent account, made real contributions to the growth of modern England; and "had his rebellion succeeded, [he] might well have become one of the most revered figures in our history books, an example not only to the patriotic young but to all devout Protestants."[27] No one, however, denies that most of these men were ambitious. The tendency is to qualify admissions that they were eager to get on in the world with commendations of their modernity, higher goals, or contributions to English history. Thus Dickens clearly states that Cromwell had "ambitions for further advancement"; and Lindsay candidly admits that Northumberland was "a cruel selfish grasping rascal."[28]

Tudor chroniclers, however, evaluated such men as these in a rather different context. Even the most prescient of sixteenth-century historiographers necessarily had a limited understanding of the long-range development of modern England. They were generally more likely to base their judgments of historical figures on Christian morality than on amoral institutional developments. And they inevitably saw the recent past in terms of the rather

25. A. G. Dickens, *Thomas Cromwell and the English Reformation* (London, 1959), p. 11.
26. Dickens, pp. 174-185; G. R. Elton, *The Tudor Revolution in Government* (Cambridge, 1953), p. 71.
27. Philip Lindsay, *The Queenmaker: A Portrait of John Dudley, Viscount Lisle, Earl of Warwick, and Duke of Northumberland 1502-1553* (London, 1951), p. 204.
28. Dickens, p. 31; Lindsay, p. 204.

primitive sociology and political theory of their own time. Thus, for Stow, Thomas Cromwell was pre-eminently an example of overweening ambition: "notwithstanding the baseness of his birth . . . he rose to the greatest authority that might be in this realm. . . ."[29] And ambition was at the root of his rise, as Stow's Cromwell frankly confesses—in a speech from the scaffold upon which he is about to die for his presumption. Camden, writing with understandable caution of the Northumberland Plot, pictures young King Edward "exposed to the cruelty of ambitious persons" and sees Mary's rightful claim to the crown threatened by Northumberland's perilous aspirations.[30]

The sharp contrast between historical reality and the half-legendary aspiring minds of Elizabethan history and literature stands out particularly clearly in the case of the notorious Cardinal Wolsey. Pollard admits in his biography that "Wolsey was ambitious," that he was driven by "a hunger and thirst, sometimes after righteousness but always after wealth and power. . . ." On the other hand, he praises the great cardinal for his "superb ability and force," and says that his "service to . . . England . . . redeemed him . . . from baser servitude."[31] No modern scholar would deny that Wolsey was ambitious; few would question that he was a man of talent. Nor would many Elizabethans have disagreed with these basic judgments. But the sixteenth century differed radically from the twentieth on key points of emphasis and interpretation, and it is these differences which divide today's fact from yesterday's myth.

Writers of the latter half of the Tudor century uniformly depicted Cardinal Wolsey as the very type of the aspiring mind that set his sights too high. In the first place, they put special emphasis on the startling contrast between his base birth and the heights to which he climbed. Even the sympathetic biography of George Cavendish, the cardinal's faithful follower, confesses that Wolsey was low-born—"an honest poor man's son"—and stresses his awesome rise, "ascending by Fortune's favor to high

29. John Stow, *The Annales of England* . . . (London, 1592), pp. 978-979.
30. William Camden, *Annales, or the History of the Most Renowned and Victorious Princesse Elizabeth* . . ., trans. R. N. (3rd ed.; London, 1635), sig. D4r.
31. A. F. Pollard, *Wolsey* (London, 1953), pp. 19, 339, 371-373.

honors, dignities, promotions, and riches."[32] Shakespeare, reflecting the hostile account of Polydore Vergil, acidly characterizes Wolsey as the "butcher's cur" that rose till he could correspond with princes—and sign the epistles in his own and Henry's name, *"Ego at rex meus."*[33] Tudor authors also made it clear that this phenomenal ascent was no mere matter of good service well rewarded. "Ambition led the way" to riches, honors, and unique political power; for Wolsey was a proud and greedy man, unable to break "ambition's hold" upon his soul.[34] Finally, they insisted, his reward was that which awaited all who aspired too high: all the wealth and honors and authority heaped up over twenty years were lost in one.[35]

Shakespeare followed this popular interpretation of the career of Cardinal Wolsey religiously. In the earlier portions of his *Henry VIII*, where the predominant viewpoint is bitterly hostile to the cardinal, the central sin attributed to his eminence is clearly high aspiration. The first mention of his name on the stage elicits—from a future victim—the angry response: "The devil speed him! no man's pie is freed / From his ambitious finger."[36] Nor do later acts, based on Cavendish's biography and much more friendly to the disgraced favorite, exonerate him from the fearful crime of overweening ambition. Rather, Wolsey is made to repent his sin in some of the most famous lines in the play:

> Farewell! a long farewell to all my greatness!
> This is the State of man: today he puts forth
> The tender leaves of hopes; tomorrow blossoms,
> And bears his blushing honors thick upon him;
> The third day comes a frost, a killing frost. . . .
> And then he falls, as I do.
>   . . . O, how wretched
> Is that poor man that hangs on princes' favors!
> There is, betwixt that smile we would aspire to,
> That sweet aspect of princes, and their ruin,

32. George Cavendish, *The Life and Death of Cardinal Wolsey,* in *Two Early Tudor Lives,* ed. Richard S. Sylvester and Davis P. Harding (New Haven and London, 1962), pp. 4-5.

33. *King Henry the Eighth,* I, i, 120; II, ii, 314, in *Complete Works,* ed. Hardin Craig (Chicago, 1951).

34. Thomas Storer, *The Life and Death of Thomas Wolsey, Cardinall* . . . (Oxford, 1826), pp. 8-9, 11; Stow, *Annales of England,* p. 941; Cavendish, p. 193.

35. Cavendish, pp. 192-193; Storer, *passim.*

36. I, i, 52-53.

> More pangs and fears than wars or women have:
> And when he falls, he falls like Lucifer,
> Never to hope again.[37]

These were lessons that the Elizabethan older generation well knew. High aspiration could bring greatness indeed, could carry a man up from the dunghill to rival the might of kings. But ambition that aimed too high would surely precipitate even a Wolsey back into the dung again. To grow too fast, to overreach—there was the fatal crime.

The ambivalence of the attitude of the older Elizabethans toward ambition was clearly revealed in the career and occasional writings of Secretary of State Sir Francis Walsingham. In a brief essay, "Of Ambition," Walsingham revealed the extent to which he had come to accept political aspirations as legitimate motives for a statesman's conduct. "Ambition, in itself, is no fault," he wrote: "Those only offend in their Ambition who . . . settle their minds only upon attaining Titles and Power" for their own sakes, rather than as deserved rewards for "doing honorable and good Acts."[38] Such opportunistic climbers, Walsingham declared, were headed for disaster. Adam's fall, for instance, should be a warning to those who aspired beyond their just deserts. And though Aesop's unworthy log became king of the frogs, it soon came to be so despised by its subjects that "every young Frogling presumed to leap up and down upon it." In practice, the line between legitimate aspiration and that lust for power and position that led to destruction was very fine. What then was the proper course for an honest man? "Honesty," he admitted in a companion piece, consisted not in performing "brave eminent Acts," but simply in "the quiet passing over the days of a Man's life without doing Injury to another Man."[39] Even the most vigorous and ambitious of the other Elizabethans carried this contrasting quietist strain in their battle-scarred souls.

Walsingham himself, like many of his contemporaries, had risen far beyond his father's modest success. Throughout his career as diplomat and spy-master, he received his share of crown

---

37. III, ii, 351-355, 366-372.
38. "Sir Francis Walsingham's Anatomizing of Honesty, Ambition, and Fortitude," in John Somers, *A Collection of . . . Tracts* (London, 1748), IV, 391.
39. *Ibid.*, IV, 389.

lands from the Queen. He bought pretentious town houses on the Strand; he kept a hundred horses at his various estates. His good service surely merited a peerage, and on at least one occasion, rumor said that it would be forthcoming. But when no title of nobility materialized, Walsingham prudently concealed any disappointment he may have felt. He had been a kinsman of Northumberland; his relatives had been involved in the plot itself; and his own flight from England at Mary's accession may not have been purely a matter of religious differences.[40] At any rate, he knew better than to aspire too high: a knighthood was good enough for a country gentleman's son.

Walsingham urged the readers of his essays to learn this lesson of prudent humility from his testament. He himself had learned from experience in those troubled mid-Tudor years when, as Camden wrote:

ambition and emulation among the nobility, presumption and disobedience among the common people, insulted so insolently, that England seemed to be as it were in an outrageous frenzy, inwardly miserably languishing of rebellions, tumults, factions . . . and all mischiefs which are wont to happen under a child King.[41]

This description of the reign of Edward VI clearly reflected the Elizabethan image of those times when the older generations came of age. Nor was that the end of the story. High aspiration had also been common, if less violent, in Mary's brief reign and in the first decade of Elizabeth's, when these maturing generations came to dominate Tudor society. By this time, of course, they themselves were leading actors in the tragedy of high aspiration at which they had been spectators since they first became conscious of the world around them.

Ambition they did not lack, these older generations of Elizabethans; and yet the overweening, extravagant ambition of the true aspiring mind sent shivers down their spines. Though their children found it hard to see the distinction, there was for these older Elizabethans a real difference between the ambition of Lord Burghley and that of Cardinal Wolsey. Wolsey's aspirations were

40. Conyers Read, *Mr. Secretary Walsingham and the Policy of Queen Elizabeth* (Cambridge, Mass., 1925), III, 418-420, 430-432; I, 22; Karl Stahlin, *Sir Francis Walsingham und seine Zeit* (Heidelberg, 1908), pp. 89-90.
41. Camden, sig. d3ᵛ.

boundless, they said, his ambitions insatiable: he would never be satisfied till he stood higher than the crown itself. Burghley climbed as far as any man during his forty years of service to the Queen—but he always remained, in word and deed, a faithful servant of her Majesty. Elizabeth's generation, however high they rose, always knew their place. Four noble graves, ranged side by side before the high altar in the Tower of London—Anne, Somerset, Northumberland, Catherine—were reminder enough of the fate that awaited those that aspired too high.[42]

New men themselves, the older Elizabethan generations were as opportunistic and almost as egotistically ambitious as the Henrician generations had been—only much more prudent, much more willing to move slowly and carefully. *Prudens qui patiens* was one of Lord Burghley's watch words.[43] Craftily, cautiously he and his contemporaries accumulated wealth and wormed their way into high places. They knew the fatal error which had destroyed their mighty predecessors: to fly at the sun was to plummet into the abyss. They themselves would never aspire too high for safety, and by reaching for all, lose all. Thus their road to power was the tortuous middle way of devious, precarious compromise. If these generations had a motto, it was: Moderation in all things.

Hardened opportunists though they were, the Elizabethan older generations had no Horatio Alger gospel of high aspiration for their children. The concept of ambition which they sought to inculcate in the generation of 1560 was at most a conservative doctrine of cautious advance toward strictly limited goals. And in the propaganda of their day, their moderate, cautious attitude was most often transformed into a simple negation. Doctrines intended for wide dissemination in society seldom retain subtle distinctions or delicate overtones. And the more important it is that an idea be generally accepted, the more likely it is to be simplified for public consumption. Thus the fallen Wolsey of the play advises Cromwell, whose great days lie ahead, not merely to avoid overreaching, but to reject all personal aspiration:

> Mark but my fall, and that that ruined me.
> Cromwell, I charge thee, fling away ambition:

42. Holinshed, IV, 4.
43. Edward Nares, *Memoirs of the Life and Administration of the Right Honorable William Cecil, Lord Burghley* (London, 1829-1831), III, 518.

> By that sin fell the angels; how can man then
> . . . hope to win by it?[44]

It was therefore not only extravagant, insatiable ambition that the older generation condemned in Elizabethan England. Rather, it was ambition *per se* that was denounced, loudly and at great length, as a terrible social evil. In support of this generalization, furthermore, an impressive set of sanctions was assembled, sanctions based on the generally accepted scientific and religious truths of the time, and expressed in vivid poetic language and imagery. It will be well now to turn to this orthodox condemnation of ambition as the Elizabethan younger generation received it from their elders.

44. III, ii, 439-442.

II. *The orthodox view of ambition*

The Elizabethan older generations had learned their lesson, and they did their best to teach it to their children. It was in the 1550's and '60's that Queen Elizabeth and William Cecil and their contemporaries came to dominate and direct English society. Certainly in the course of the latter decade, they began the complex process of educating the youth of the nation in the evils of unrestrained ambition.

This broad educational effort brought together a loose natural alliance of governing officials, teachers, preachers, translators, and writers on moral philosophy. Many of these molders of the public mind had lived in the upper ranks of Tudor society during the nerve-shattering years of Edward and Mary; many others had been close enough to the top to feel the wind of the ax. For in the days of crusading "commonwealth men," of the radical Edwardian Reformation and the violent Marian counter-reform, scholars and preachers had sweated out every change of government almost as nervously as had the Tudor governors themselves. If their lives did not hang in the balance, their livings did; budding careers had been blighted by the inordinate ambition of a patron, or the successful ambition of a patron's rival. These generations of Elizabethan rulers and Elizabethan intellectuals had shared a harrowing experience: it is not surprising, then, that the policy of the former and the propaganda of the latter agreed perfectly in condemning overweening ambition.

The basic tools of indoctrination available in sixteenth-century England were the school, the university, the pulpit, and the printing press. All these media of mass communication were largely controlled by the relatively small ruling and educated classes. Teachers and preachers were required by law to have royal or ecclesiastical licenses, and the government prescribed certain textbooks and official homilies for their use. The universities of Oxford and Cambridge were run according to royal statutes and operated under the general supervision of high government officials or great nobles. Government censorship of books and pamphlets increased as the reign wore on, and the phrases "seen and allowed" or "published by authority" soon became common on Elizabethan title pages. The governors of Elizabethan England thus did everything in their power to prevent the corruption of the youth by subversive doctrines, and to see to it that orthodox views were as widely disseminated as possible.

More important than these essentially coercive measures, however, was the voluntary co-operation of the intellectual leaders of the nation with its political managers. Elizabethan schoolmasters, university professors, preaching clergymen, moral philosophers, literati, Latin scholars, and vernacular translators willingly collaborated in the effort to convince the nation of the wrongheadedness of unrestrained ambition. Much of what these molders of the mass mind taught, preached, wrote, or translated about the horrors of rampant ambition had been said before. But these traditional ideas received new emphasis in the hands of men who knew the truth of doctrines older than Plato from bitter personal experience.

As the reign of Elizabeth began, with the generation of 1560 just beginning to toddle, these sadder, wiser men were already creating the climate of opinion in which their children would grow up. They taught many lessons—lessons of the wisdom of compromise, of prudent moderation, and of expedient conformity. Among the maxims they dwelt upon with particular insistence were those that attacked the evils of overreaching ambition. Ambition, according to classical scholar and itinerant preacher alike, according to Christian truth and ancient wisdom, was the bane of the commonwealth, a deadly sin against God, an unnatural rebellion against cosmic order, a futile passion doomed to inevitable failure.

i. A social evil

The primary message was of course the simple statement of the crimes against society spawned by unrestrained ambition. This thesis, as the Elizabethans expressed it, was essentially two-fold: it declared that aspiring minds made poor governors; and it insisted that ambition was a prime cause of revolution, the ultimate crime against the commonwealth. These two related condemnations should therefore be examined separately and in some detail.

Writing in the 1550's, William Baldwin, a leading poet and intellectual under four Tudor sovereigns, dedicated the famous *Mirror for Magistrates* to the nobility and royal officials of England. He began his dedicatory epistle in impeccable humanist form with a quotation from Plato—a quotation which contained, in a few authoritative words, the message of his book:

Among many other of his notable sentences concerning the government of a common weale, [he] hath this: 'Well is that realm governed in which the ambitious desire not to bear office.'

And he proceeded to point the moral:

Whereby you may perceive (right honorable) that offices are, where they be duly executed: not gainful spoils for the greedy to hunt for, but painful toils for the heedy to be charged with. . . . For the ambitious (that is to say prowlers for power or gain) seek not for offices to help other, for which cause offices are ordained, but with the undoing of other, to prank up themselves.[1]

This was the essence of the charge of bad government leveled at ambitious courtiers and counselors. Concentrating all their energies on personal advancement, they would perforce neglect, and if necessary even subvert the welfare of the commonwealth. Aspiring minds would resort to any means to gain their end: they would indulge freely in bribery and flattery; they would even resort to crime to destroy a rival. Nor could a prince ever trust the advice and counsel of such men; for climbers became mere yes-men in order to win royal favor, the key to success at court. No discussion of the qualities of the ideal counselor or governor was complete without such injunctions against ambition.

Authorities as diverse as Solomon, Thucydides, and Guevara's Marcus Aurelius were cited as insisting that the good counselor should be a man who put his country's welfare above his personal well-being.[2] Cicero himself, the patron saint of Latin humanism, whose stately periods every school boy memorized

1. William Baldwin *et al., The Mirror for Magistrates,* ed. Lily B. Campbell (Cambridge, 1938), pp. 63-64.

2. Bartolome Felippe, *The Counseller: A Treatise of Counsels . . .,* trans. John Thorius (London, 1589), pp. 22-36, 38-39; Antonio de Guevara, *The Golden Booke of Marcus Aurelius . . .* (London, 1586), chap. xliii.

copiously, and whose advice mature statesmen treasured, stressed the incompatibility of ambition and public service:

But when one begins to aspire to public eminence, it is difficult to preserve that spirit which is absolutely essential to justice. The result is that such men . . . only too often prove to be bribers and agitators in public life, seeking to obtain supreme power and to be superiors through force. . . . Then too, the higher a man's ambition, the more easily he is tempted to acts of injustice by his desire of fame.[3]

Every sixteenth-century writer on the subject emphatically agreed with this diagnosis.[4] Robert Greene, on this point as perfectly indoctrinated as Shakespeare himself, summed up the official dogma at the conclusion of a play in which evil, ambitious counselors, after bringing Scotland to the brink of ruin, get their just reward:

Exile, torment, and punish such as they;
For greater vipers never may be found
Within a state than such aspiring heads,
That reck not how they climb, so that they climb.[5]

Far worse than bad government, however, was the possibility of no government at all—of a nation rent by civil broils between rival factions of ambitious nobles. In the sixteenth century the English people were apparently regarded as particularly prone to rebellion. Lord Burghley's generation alone could remember four waves of popular revolt in its own lifetime (in 1536, '49, '54, and '69). Each of these uprisings, furthermore, had been accompanied by a flood of diatribes against rebellion from press and pulpit. Long after the severed heads and hanging corpses had rotted away, this anti-revolutionary literature kept alive a fear of civil disturbance that became almost a national neurosis.[6]

3. M. Tullius Cicero, De officiis, trans. Walter Miller (Loeb ed.; New York, 1928), I, xix, 64-65.

4. E.g., Joannes Ferrarius, A Work . . . touchynge the good orderynge of a common weale, trans. William Bavande (London, 1559), pp. 30r-30v, 31v-32r; Fadrique Furio Ceriol, A verie briefe . . . Treatise declaring . . . what maner of Counselers a Prince . . . ought to have, trans. Thomas Blundeville (London, 1570), sig. H4r-H4v, K1v-K2r.

5. Robert Greene, The Scottish History of James the Fourth . . . (London, 1598), ll. 2413-2416, in Plays and Poems of . . ., ed. J. C. Collins (Oxford, 1905), Vol. II.

6. Cf. James K. Lowers, Mirrors for Rebels (Univ. of Calif. Pub. in Eng. Stud., No. 6; Berkeley and Los Angeles, 1953), pp. v-vi, 35-65.

It was common knowledge that presumptuous, proud ambition was a primary cause of rebellion. It was particularly obvious —though modern scholarship, with its concern for larger causal factors, sometimes loses sight of the fact—that aspiring members of the ruling classes provided the leadership in these insurrections. Thus in 1586 a famous preacher, listing the rebels detected and destroyed since the beginning of Elizabeth's singularly peaceful reign, denounced such aristocratic aspiring minds as the Duke of Norfolk, the Earls of Northumberland and Westmoreland, the Irish Earl of Desmond, the notorious Tom Stukeley ("the Pope's Irish marquess"), and a number of lesser gentlefolk driven by overweening ambition to disturb the peace of the commonwealth.[7]

For further evidence that proud, greedy, ambitious men were the makers of rebellion, Englishmen had only to be referred to their own history, particularly to the civil wars of York and Lancaster during the preceding century. The stern lesson of the Wars of the Roses was made clear to the educated ruling class in Hall's chronicles, and was subsequently spread broadcast in the popular history plays of Shakespeare. For a contemporary example, the enemies of ambition could point across the Channel to France, ravaged during Elizabeth's reign by long decades of fratricidal strife. The chief cause of the French Wars of Religion—besides the perennial machinations of the Papists—was believed to be the vaulting ambition of the Guises, who strove to overthrow the government and seize the crown for themselves.[8] Other examples, past and present, of the intimate relationship between ambition and revolution could of course be adduced.

To clinch their case, the humanist-educated older generations naturally turned to the authority of the ancients. They could even cite the master of those who knew, whose stranglehold on university curricula remained unbroken in the sixteenth century: "Aristotle gathereth many grounds of sedition, but in espe-

7. John Rainolds, *A Sermon Upon Part of the Eighteenth Psalm* . . . (Oxford, 1586), pp. 21-25.
8. *An Advertisement from a French Gentleman, touching* . . . *the house of Guise* . . ., (n. p., 1585), pp. 2-3, 57; King Henry III, *Directions from the King* . . . *concerning the Death of the Duke of Guise*, trans. E. A. (London, 1589), sig. A2ʳ, A4ᵛ; Antony Colynet, *The True History of the Civill Warres of France* . . . (London, 1591), pp. 1-3.

cial ambition and covetousness. . . . This is certain, whoso once be desirous of empire, glory, and honor, do quite forget justice, as Tully writeth."[9] In fact, as one preacher told his congregation in the middle 1580's, "the wisest men of all ages" had seen that proud ambition was the root of all disorders of the commonwealth. So testified Moses, David, and the Prophets, the Greeks and the Romans. And, the preacher demanded—

. . . did ever any man harden his heart here in England against lawful regiment, which hath not been full of pride and ambition? Can the sober minded man, resting and taking his felicity in his base and low calling, lift up his hand and pluck the regal crown from the head of the lawful governor? No, no, dearly beloved. . . . It is the light head and the aspiring mind which through pride and ambition flieth into the Prince's palace.[10]

This twofold condemnation of ambition as a terrible danger to society was calculated to be an extremely effective deterrent. For there is no doubt that misgovernment and rebellion were social evils much feared in Tudor England. Flattery, jealous backbiting, and selfish personal ambition were notorious features of court life under Elizabeth, as they had been under her predecessors. And ambitious rivalries did in fact impair the efficiency of the government and distract attention from its central concern with the public weal. Elizabethans also frequently expressed their terror of civil discord, and they were undoubtedly sincere. Many of them had their own grisly memories of the mid-century rebellions in the West and North, of the Northern Earls in arms and of Wyatt's horde encamped before the walls of London. And if their memories faded with the years, numerous contemporary examples of the horrors of civil war were ready to hand. All around the nervous little island, in France, in the Netherlands, in Scotland and Ireland, rebellions flared up again and again or raged on for weary years, leaving a trail of atrocities and ruins. The miseries of misgovernment and the disasters of civil war were believed to be the bitterest fruits of uncontrolled ambition. These social evils were living realities in the late Tudor world, and Elizabethans wanted no part of them.

9. Ferrarius, pp. 142ʳ-142ᵛ.
10. A fruitfull Sermon upon . . . the Epistle of S. Paule to the Romanes . . . (London, 1586), pp. 23-24.

ii. *A religious sin*

Religious sanctions against ambition were uncompromising, and social critics made no bones about invoking them. For any right-thinking Christian Englishman of those times, it was sinful to be ambitious. Woe, cried the moralist, to him who deliberately seeks to advance himself at court or in the wars,

> But leaves God's blessing far behind,
> And lives upon an aspiring mind.[11]

For it was well known that

> . . . the ambitious, to advance their might,
> Dispense with heaven and what religion would.[12]

Not only was the ambitious man certain to turn to immoral means to attain his ends, but his high aspiration was in itself a sin. Classical and Christian authorities agreed in condemning ambition and its attendant vices as sins against Divinity.

There was some disagreement between moralists and preachers as to the exact nature of the sin of ambition. In Aristotelian ethical terms, ambition was a vice of excess, an exaggerated desire for lands, offices, honors, and dignities.[13] A stock example of the extravagant madness of ambition was Alexander the Great, who wept that he could find no more worlds to conquer and ended by declaring himself a god.[14] Julius Caesar was often pictured as a monster of ambition in the Aristotelian sense, aspiring to make himself king of the Romans and "master of the whole world": Cicero questioned the sanity of anyone who could find such insatiable ambition morally defensible.[15]

As good Christians saw it, however, ambition was sin pure and simple. The theological point was clear and uncomplicated by Aristotelian questions of degree: "An ambitious man, by attributing honor unto himself goeth about to defraud God

11. Thomas Churchyard, *A pleasant Discourse of Court and Wars* . . . (London, 1596), sig. A3ᵛ.
12. Samuel Daniel, *The First Fowre Bookes of the civile wars between* . . . *Lancaster and Yorke* (London, 1595), p. 18ᵛ.
13. Thomas Floyd, *The Picture of a perfit Common wealth* . . . (London, 1600), p. 282.
14. Ferrarius, pp. 19ʳ-19ᵛ, 88ᵛ.   15. Cicero, III, xxi, 83.

of his due."*16* All honor was, of course, due to God alone. This Christian condemnation, however, often contained more passion than theology; and such vitriolic denunciations as St. Bernard's undoubtedly impressed Elizabethans, with their taste for good invective style: "Ambition," declared the Saint, "is a lurking plague, a secret poison, a subtle mischief, a mother of hypocrisy, the forger of deceit, the nurse of envy, the well-spring of vices, the moth of devotion, the blinder of arts. . . ." and so on for two more blistering paragraphs.*17* Had not the devil himself been cast into hell for ambition, for wanting to be sovereign rather than subject?*18*

The religious denunciations directed against ambition were also aimed at its attendant vices—pride, avarice, and envy. The three were closely bound up together as causes and effects of ambition, and were frequently grouped with ambition in the attacks of preachers and moral philosophers on the aspiring mind. Some effort should therefore be made to understand the complex relationships between these concepts in the Elizabethan mind.

Ambition and pride stood in a close, yet strangely ambiguous relationship to each other. Theoretically, ambition was an offshoot or extension of pride: it was the swelling humor of pride that most often made men ambitious. But in common usage, the two vices seemed more like twins, so closely did descriptions and condemnations of them tally. The proud man, like the aspiring mind, was characterized as sinning directly against God by claiming for himself some share of the honors due only to the All High.*19* It was for pride as much as for ambition that Satan fell from grace. Pride was in fact the besetting sin of all the great aspiring souls. It had been the sin of Nebuchadnezzar who exalted the towers of Babylon against heaven, and it was the sin of all the proud climbers who followed in his footsteps down the centuries:

16. William Vaughan, *The Golden grove, moralized in three Bookes* (London, 1600), Bk. I, chap. xxvi.

17. *The Garden of Prudence . . . touching the vanities of the world* (London, 1595), p. [44].

18. *Ibid.*, p. [43].

19. Samuel Gardiner, *Portraiture of the prodigle sonne* (London, 1599), pp. 32, 34; Philip Stubbes, *Anatomy of the Abuses in England . . .*, ed. F. J. Furnivall (London, 1877-1879), pp. 28-29; Ludowick Lloyd, *The Pilgrimage of Princes, penned out of Sundry Greeke and Latine authors* (London, 1573), p. 185^r.

. . . when they behold their buildings, or open their coffers, or look upon their train swinging after them, they think as Nebuchadnezzar thought, Is not this great Babel? Is not this great glory? . . . Nebuchadnezzar hath children yet alive which build as high as he, go as brave as he, spend as vainly as he, and are as proud as he, although they be not kings, nor dukes, nor earls, nor knights, nor yet good squires. . . .[20]

After all, lacking the arrogant presumption and bloated self-esteem of pride, what man would aspire beyond his allotted place? But when a man was consumed with pride, ambition was sure to follow; in practice, the two vices were almost indistinguishable.

Closely associated with pride as props for ambition were the sins of greed and envy. Greed, or covetousness, was considered second only to pride as a cause of ambition. The man who coveted this world's goods would never rest content with what he had, but, from the very nature of his vice, would aspire to possess infinite wealth and power. The covetous man was sometimes compared to a peacock "that climbeth up to the highest places, as the rich man aspireth to honor and pre-eminence."[21] Envy, on the other hand, might be considered the chief of the lesser sins that clustered about ambition, pride, and covetousness. Envy, strife, revenge, flattery, prodigality, and other vices were among the evil effects of ambition: they followed inevitably in the train of the aspiring mind and its cohorts, pride and covetousness. But envy was perhaps pre-eminent among these lesser sins, for envy was the mother of strife and revenge, and was more immediately dangerous than flattery and prodigality. A perilous sin was envy, "for thou canst not come nearer the Devil any way, than to be envious . . . . and he that is possessed with envy, is possessed with the Devil."[22]

Pride, greed, envy, flattery, strife, revenge—the whole evil constellation of sins that hovered about the idea of ambition in Elizabethan minds—these set the aspiring mind squarely in opposition to fundamental Christian teaching. And in the days

20. Henry Smith, "The Pride of Nebuchadnezzar," in *Sermons*, ed. Thomas Man (London, 1611), p. 175.
21. Richard Barclay, *A Discourse of the Felicitie of Man, or His Summum Bonum* (rev. ed.; London, 1603), p. 119.
22. Henry Smith, "The Way to Walk in," in *Sermons*, p. 164.

of Elizabeth I, Christian ethics were still firmly rooted in a Christian universe whose center was the pit of hell.

Thus the religious sanction, like the social sanction, was likely to prove a powerful deterrent to would-be aspiring minds. For most Elizabethans sincerely believed that the sinner was doomed to eternal hellfire. As a famous preacher told the Queen and her court in the 1590's:

... our ears are dainty, and the matter melancholic, and we little love to hear it stood on so long. But Chrysostom saith well, of that fire: *Nunquid, si tacuimus, extinximus?* "If we speak not of it, will it go out?" No, no: *sive loquamur, sive taceamus, ardet ille:* "speak we, or keep we silence, it burneth still, still it burneth." Therefore let us speak and think of it . . . for if to hear of it be painful, to feel it will be more so.[23]

The truth of the Christian religion had been impressed upon Lancelot Andrewes' illustrious congregation by their parents, by their schoolmasters or tutors, by the catechisms they had memorized and parsed in three languages, by the theologically saturated air of the universities, by the sermons they had attended all their lives, by the universal public acceptance of its dogmas. Most men of Elizabeth's and Burghley's generations died in the hope of salvation; how many lived in fear of hellfire, we cannot really say. It is certain, however, that most of the opinion molders who appealed to religious sanctions against ambition believed in them, and expected their audience to believe.

iii. An unnatural rebellion

Across the path of the aspiring mind lay the serried ranks of the social hierarchy, the fundamental sociological fact of life in Elizabethan England. This fixed, divinely ordained caste system, in turn, reflected and participated in the immutably stratified structure of the universe itself. The ultimate authority on this world, Aristotle, thus described the hierarchic natural order of things:

23. Lancelot Andrewes, "A Sermon Preached in the Court in Richmond . . . A. D. 1596," in *Ninety-Six Sermons* (Oxford, 1899), II, 86.

Authority and subordination are conditions not only inevitable but also expedient; in some cases things are marked out from the moment of birth to rule or be ruled. . . . because in every composite thing where a plurality of parts, whether continuous or discrete, is combined to make a single common whole, there is always found a ruling and a subject factor, and this characteristic of living things is . . . an outcome of the whole of nature, since even in things that do not partake of life, there is a ruling principle. . . .

Aristotle presented a convincing series of illustrations of his thesis, and drew significant conclusions about the structure of society:

. . . it is natural and expedient for the body to be governed by the soul. . . . Again, the same holds good between man and the other animals. . . . between the sexes. . . . And the same must also necessarily apply in the case of mankind as a whole; therefore all men that differ as widely as the soul does from the body and the human being from the lower animals (and this is the condition of those whose function is the use of the body, and from whom this is the best that is forthcoming)—these are by nature slaves, for whom to be governed by this kind of authority is advantageous. . . .[24]

To aspire to a higher station in life was therefore to violate the functionally designed natural order of things. To climb was both inexpedient and unnatural, disastrous to ordered society and an impious, wrongheaded defiance of God's natural law.

Elizabethan social critics were still preaching the doctrine of fixed classes in a time of unprecedented social mobility. In fact, the more fluid society became, the more passionately they urged the necessity and naturalness of fixed, hierarchically ordered estates. To the generations of Elizabeth and Burghley, social mobility meant the fang-and-claw competition of the dangerous years of their youth. They were firmly convinced that the only hope for a stable society lay in a return to normal class relationships, to recognition of due order and degree.

The fundamental class divisions and the duties of each estate were traditional, and they were reiterated throughout the sixteenth century with little attempt to bring either the classes or their duties up to date. The basic organizing principle of this analysis of the good society was that of subordination, and it was

24. Aristotle, *Politics*, trans. H. Rackham (Loeb ed.; London and New York, 1932), I, ii, 8-13.

in terms of superior and inferior, governor and governed, that these class relationships were defined. Masters and servants; parents and children; princes, magistrates, and subjects; churchmen, aristocrats, merchants, craftsmen, and farmers—all had their prescribed places in the social hierarchy and their prescribed duties to society and to each other. This orthodox image of a normally functioning society based on order and degree seemed impressively logical to sixteenth-century minds. Nor was the aesthetic appeal of this vision of an ordered society lost on Elizabethans:

What can be of greater dignity and worthiness than for all the people of God scattered through the face of the world, having so diverse gifts and offices, being so far distant in place, by an humble, sober, and discreet judging of their gifts, ability, and callings, to serve and worship in the unity of spirit and truth . . . . according to their age, strength, gifts, place and callings. . . .[25]

Elizabethan social theory was both logical and appealing; and it stood foursquare against personal ambition.

As commonwealths are held together by voluntary co-operation of social classes, sixteenth-century social theorists contended, so they "perish and be undone" when insolent ambition is allowed free rein.[26] For to violate the social hierarchy was to strike the keystone from the arch of society. Classical and Christian authorities could be found in abundance to support this basic position— that the good Christian and the good citizen would keep to his own estate and never aspire to a higher place. A moral commentator thus commended the advice of Democritus, that every man should "be contented with the present, and with that portion and measure which it hath pleased God to yield unto him, never coveting the menuage of any greater affair than appertaineth to his own estate. . . ."[27] Elizabethan England's best-selling preacher, the Reverend Henry Smith, affirmed that not only do all good Christians renounce ambitious climbing, but "for the most part, the best worthy do refuse proffered promotion, and on their part well deserved. . . ."[28] In line with this extreme view, a popular play-

25. *Fruitfull Sermon upon St. Paule*, pp. 11-12.
26. Ferrarius, pp. 16ʳ-17ʳ.
27. Martin Coignet, *Politique Discourses* . . . (London, 1586), p. 180.
28. Henry Smith, "A Memento for Magistrates," in *Sermons*, p. 533.

wright represented his commoner hero virtuously refusing a knighthood, though offered as reward for great services to king and country:

> . . . let me live and die a yeoman still:
> So was my father, so must live his son.[29]

But there was more than authority to support the contention that the aspiring mind was an unnatural rebel in a universe of order and degree. The theory of the hierarchic society provided both practical and philosophical objections to ambition. Practical objections arose from the nature of the social order as Elizabethans conceived it. Philosophical objections were raised by the nature of the cosmic order of which human society was a part.

The composition of the fixed estates was determined, according to Elizabethan social theory, not by individual talent for performing a particular task, but by birth into a family and an environment devoted to the performance of a given social function.[30] Such a combination of inheritance and environment would usually produce a man fit only for the tasks assigned to his estate—and fitter for them than any outsider. To attempt to move from one class into a higher one was thus doubly foolish. It meant abandoning a place one was fitted by nature and education to fill, and it generally meant failing miserably in a position for which one had no aptitude.[31] Society also suffered both ways—from the loss of a good farmer or merchant, and from rank misgovernment by a would-be gentleman.

The assertion that only the ruling class was capable of governing the commonwealth effectively was dinned into the ears of the Queen's loyal subjects. The people were sheep, they were constantly reminded, "a weak and unwise cattle, far unable to guide themselves."[32] Only under the staff of their wise shepherds, born and bred to rule, could they find security.[33] Let the lower orders keep their place, and Elizabeth and her ministers, with the

29. Robert Greene, *A Pleasant Conceited Comedy of George a Green, the Pinner of Wakefield* (1599), ll. 1196-1197, in *Plays and Poems*, Vol. II.

30. Ruth Kelso, *The Doctrine of the English Gentleman in the Sixteenth Century* (Urbana, Illinois, 1929), pp. 22-23.

31. *Ibid.*, pp. 35-37.

32. Lancelot Andrewes, "A Sermon Preached Before Queen Elizabeth at Greenwich . . . A. D. MDXC . . .," in *Ninety-Six Sermons*, II, 28.

33. *Ibid.*, II, 29.

help of the gentry and nobility, would bring peace and prosperity to the nation.

But within the ruling classes themselves there were also important distinctions of degree, and here violations of caste were much more common. And precisely because high aspiring minds were more common in the upper ranks of society, they were more frequently and bitterly attacked. The "upstart courtier," the merchant or yeoman's son trying ludicrously to be a gentleman, was a stock subject for satire in Elizabethan literature. His extravagant costume, his efforts to match the majestic airs of his superiors, and his new-bought title of gentility were endlessly sneered at and passionately condemned. The theme was as old as the problem: it could be found in Greek and Latin literature, as well as in contemporary continental satirists like the widely popular Aretino. Nevertheless, the English sneer was reaction to a real English situation. The "new man" was within the gates of the aristocracy: satirist and sermonizer collaborated to make him wish he had kept his place, and to discourage others from following.

There was more literature on the general subject of the estates in the sixteenth century than in the preceding two centuries combined, and the folly of ambition was "a constant refrain" in these popular works.[34] It is true that, during the turbulent middle decades of the century, a few practical humanists and "commonwealth men" wrote treatises recognizing the fact of social mobility without deploring it. Most of these realistic analysts seem, however, to have been men connected with the ambitious Somerset circle—men like Hales, Starkey, and Sir Thomas Smith. And under Elizabeth, following the apparently catastrophic failure of the commonwealth men, there came a definite resurgence of social conservatism. The prolific preacher-printer Robert Crowley, such poets as Gascoigne and Barnabe Googe, these and others stressed the necessity of remaining content with one's estate.[35] Popular poets and serious authorities on the estates joined forces in these early Elizabethan years to propound "a conservative restatement of the philosophy of estates

34. Ruth Mohl, *The Three Estates in Medieval and Renaissance Literature* (New York, 1933), pp. 143, 332.
35. *Ibid.*, pp. 185-194, 199-209.

that survived from the days of medieval feudalism."[36] The wickedness of trying to rise above one's natural estate, and the ludicrous failure of those who tried, were commonplaces in the England in which the generation of 1560 grew up.

But it was not only these practical objections that set the minds of Elizabethans against ambitious social climbing. The hierarchic organization of society reflected and participated in the natural order of the cosmos, and this cosmic hierarchy held a strange fascination of its own.

The principle of hierarchic order was as old as Plato's *Republic* and had for centuries been the foundation of constitutional and social thought in western Europe. This fundamental principle of order in turn depended on two basic metaphysical assumptions. The first of these was a rather complex set of cosmological ideas that was almost universally accepted by serious thinkers in Elizabethan times. This was the view that the universe itself was hierarchically structured, with the best and most real at the apex of the pyramid; that this was the natural and right way for it to be; and that human society naturally and rightly reflected this universal hierarchy. The second assumption, equally basic, was seldom stated and rather vague in content. It boiled down to a belief in permanence and immutability, not only as good qualities, but as metaphysically basic characteristics of the highest truths. Beneath apparent flux lay absolute, eternal reality; beneath all apparent change lay permanence.[37] The first of these axioms made it clear that society was *necessarily* organized in a hierarchy of authority and importance. The second assumption required that the cosmic hierarchy, and the social hierarchy imbedded in it, were permanently and unalterably *fixed*. The aristocratic society of Elizabethan England was therefore no mere

36. *Ibid.*, p. 212.

37. To put this view in proper perspective, it might be compared to eighteenth-, nineteenth-, and twentieth-century trends of thought. Since the eighteenth century, particularly since the French Revolution and the ascendancy of Hegel, thinkers in many fields have sought ultimate explanations in some aspect of change, rather than of permanence. The nature of the universe and the human condition are now described in terms of "progress" or "revolution" or at least "historical development," of Darwinian evolution or Marxian dialectical movement. The search for eternal verities was once the preoccupation of most serious intellectual endeavor; today, only religious mystics and an occasional poet continue to seek the still center of the turning world.

human construct, but an integral part of the eternal grand design of God's universe.

Modern scholars have described this Elizabethan world view in great detail, with its graduated ranks of matter and spirit, its ordered hierarchies of plants, fish, birds, and beasts, of elements and stars, of angels and men. Tillyard and others have pointed out the extensive influence of this view on the thought and expression of the later sixteenth and early seventeenth centuries.[38] In particular, these scholars have analyzed the close relationships between the cosmic and social worlds, pointing out the complex system of correspondences which bound the one to the other.[39] From our twentieth-century point of view, these correspondences are simply analogies, resemblances often inaccurate and fanciful, which to our ancestors somehow implied a real connection. We must not, however, underestimate the intense intellectual satisfaction Elizabethans derived from analogical reasoning. We may even say that an intellectual satisfaction as deep as that which a modern mind derives from discovering causal relationships came to Elizabethans from noting analogical relationships. The fact is, of course, that analogies were not mere analogies for sixteenth-century minds: for them, similarity implied "participation" in a common essence. And for that age, such essences, forms, or Platonic Ideas had a reality attained by no comparable set of abstractions within our experience—with the possible exception of the laws of classical physics.

Furthermore, this Greek philosophical concept of the hierarchically organized cosmos had been infused with religious feeling during the centuries of Christendom, when the universal order was believed to be divinely decreed. And the original concept must have been further reinforced by the normal human longing to find order and design in the world. The resulting world view, the majestic image of the great chain of being, was almost irresistible to Elizabethans.

Society was a part of God's universe, its ordered structure fitting neatly into the eternal order of the cosmos. The grandeur of this world view kindled Tudor imaginations as did few other

38. Arthur O. Lovejoy, *The Great Chain of Being* (Cambridge, Mass., 1936), pp. 67-143; E. M. W. Tillyard, *The Elizabethan World Picture* (London, 1943).
39. Tillyard, pp. 81-93.

commonplaces of their time. This image of the world moved such men as Sir Thomas Elyot, the dean of classical popularizers in the youth of Burghley and Elizabeth, to pious eulogies of "order: which in things as well natural as supernatural hath ever had such a prominence that thereby the incomprehensible majesty of God . . . is declared to the blind inhabitants of this world."[40] And of course the very term "order" denoted hierarchy and subordination to the Elizabethan mind. As the most popular Elizabethan book of moral philosophy put it, "all order standeth in ruling and obeying. . . ."[41]

To defy the social hierarchy by aspiring to rise above one's station in life was thus unnatural in a way that amounted almost to impiety. Ambition was nothing less than rebellion against the divine system of the world. The complete naturalness of the social hierarchy was most clearly expressed in the familiar analogy of the body politic, whose functionally designed estates corresponded to the limbs and organs of the human body. According to this famous metaphor, it was as unnatural for a mere farmer, no matter how well off economically, to aspire to rule the nation, as it would be for the stomach, no matter how well filled, to usurp the brain's function of ruling the human body. Outright rebellion—the ultimate expression of inordinate ambition—was constantly characterized as "unnatural." Such political insurrection against the head of state was likened to violation of the sacred ties of family, as when a child turns against his parents.

This essentially metaphysical sanction, like the social and religious sanctions against ambition, seemed well calculated to turn Elizabethan youth away from high aspiration. No one, of course, could expect the generation of 1560 and its successors to be unduly impressed with the philosophical subtleties behind the theory of the hierarchic society in the chain-of-being universe. Nor could any but the most naïve advocates of the humanistic education have expected the views of Aristotle and Plato to deter ambitious young men from trying their luck. But the general idea of hierarchy, of order and degree, could be planted in their minds

40. Thomas Elyot, *The Boke named the Governour*, ed. Henry Herbert and Stephen Croft (London, 1883), I, 3.

41. William Baldwin, *A Treatyce of Moral Philosophy* . . . (London, 1564), p. 109.

as firmly, for example, as the notion of equality could be implanted in the minds of the Jacksonian generations of early nineteenth-century America. Elizabethan preachers would set children to their catechisms at a young and pliable age:

M[aster]. What is thy duty towards thy neighbor? S[cholar]. My duty towards my neighbor is to love him as my self. . . . To honor and obey the Queen and her Ministers. To submit myself to all my governors, teachers, spiritual pastors, and masters. To order myself lowly and reverently to all my betters.[42]

Tutors would indoctrinate the young with "fear of God . . . obedience to their parents, reverence to their superiors. . . ."[43] Students would fill a page or two in their commonplace books with maxims on order and degree. All their lives they would see the caste system in operation all about them, in every aspect of upper-class life, from the family circle to the highest court circles, from ceremoniously served banquets to endless bickering about precedence at formal functions. And young minds eager for truth and beauty could perhaps be impressed by the magnificent vision of an orderly cosmos in which every king and country squire had his place.

iv. A futile passion

Finally, if warnings of the terrible social consequences of ambition, if invocations of religious sanctions and indoctrination in the nature of the fixed society failed to discourage the aspiring mind of youth, there remained one more powerful deterrent. The ultimate sanction was the threat of certain failure, the melancholy assertion that all ambition was futile.

This was the least tangible of all the objections to ambition, a compound of traditional ideas, recent examples, and hazy emotional tones. Yet this attitude probably provided a more effective reinforcement for fear of the evil social consequences of ambi-

42. Fragment of an Elizabethan ABC book, quoted in H. Anders, "The Elizabethan ABC with the Catechism," *The Library*, 4th ser., XVI (1935), 34.

43. John Walsal, "Epistle Dedicatory," "A Sermon Preached at Paul's Cross . . . 5 October, 1578," in Virgil B. Heltzel, "Young Francis Bacon's Tutor," *Mod. Lang. Notes*, LXIII (1948), 484.

tion than did either religious prohibitions or belief in the hierarchic society. This condemnation of ambition as a futile passion,
doomed to inevitable failure, found two extremely popular forms
of expression in the sixteenth century. The first of these was an
ancient symbol—the image of the fickle goddess Fortune and her
wheel. The second, equally important, was the poetic expression
of this view in the still more venerable voice of the Preacher,
Ecclesiastes. It must be admitted, however, that both symbol and
poetry probably derived much of their effectiveness as deterrents
to ambition primarily from the fact that they embodied truths
which the Elizabethan older generations had learned from first-
hand observation. If they were to carry their message to the
younger generation, they would have to depend much more completely on their own merits—on the concreteness and flexibility
of the symbol and the appeal of the poetry—and of course on constant repetition of both. It is these intrinsic qualities of the wheel
of Fortune and the voice of Ecclesiastes that must therefore be
analyzed here.

Dame Fortune had a long and notorious history when she was
adopted by Tudor enemies of ambition. A goddess in Augustan
Rome, an allegorical figure in the Middle Ages, she attained a
status somewhere between the two in Elizabethan England. Poets
constantly made use of Fortune as an allegorical figure, so clear
and simple in its basic symbolism, yet capable of endless elaboration. A few finicky preachers tried to substitute Divine Providence
for the goddess Fortune in the public mind—perhaps fearful of
the fascination of the pagan divinity—but they had no notable
degree of success. Social critics and moral philosophers continued
to refer to Fortune quite naturally as the mistress of man's
earthly life.

Fortune was commonly described by the adjective "fickle."
More accurately, her distribution of favors in this uncertain
world might have been described as capricious, or even whimsical.
Thanks to her, a country clod might become Lord Mayor of
London, and a king might live to beg in the streets. Yet there was
a pattern to her capriciousness, a pattern often and elaborately
lamented by her disillusioned victims: first she smiled, and the
world was yours; then she frowned, and disaster swept you away.

This was the eternal trajectory of ambition—the often spectacular rise followed by the inevitable fall. In the Fortune allegory, this process of rise and fall was generally depicted as taking place on the rim of a wheel turned by the hand of the fickle goddess. The image of the wheel of Fortune powerfully expressed the inevitability, the inexorableness of the process: as surely as the wheel went round, he who rose on it must come down.

The lesson of the tale was clear. But, if they were successfully to discourage ambition in the youth, Elizabethan moralists had also to demonstrate the appositeness of the allegory to real life. For this purpose, the basic myth was therefore filled out with realistic, contemporary detail, calculated to be both psychologically and sociologically convincing. The result was an apt, believable fable of Fortune and the aspiring mind. As recounted in whole or in part by countless unfortunate climbers in Elizabethan poetry, prose, and drama, this famous myth went something like this: An ambitious man, driven by a burning thirst for fame and sovereignty, a passion to outstrip others and stand above them, aspires to some higher place than his own—perhaps even to the throne. He fights his way to the summit of his ambition, toppling others as he climbs, and never hesitating to employ the most unscrupulous means to attain his end. Fortune smiles: the aspiring mind succeeds and triumphs—it is the moment of hubris. But his triumph is bitter, for he wins only weariness, suspicion, fear, the uneasy pillow of the tyrant. Then Fortune frowns, the wheel turns once more, and the climber falls, utterly and disastrously, to an ignominious end. The moral was only too obvious: Be content with your estate, for the higher you rise on Fortune's wheel, the farther you fall at last.

This myth was most effectively dispensed to the Elizabethan Age by the writers of the celebrated *Mirror for Magistrates*, first published in the 1550's, and reprinted, added to, and borrowed from frequently in the last half of the century. William Baldwin and the other moral poets of the *Mirror*, most of them among the literary lights of their day, were typical of the voices who spoke for the older generation against uncontrolled ambition. They had lived and written under four sovereigns, in years of unparalleled social turbulence and political conflict; they knew the most likely end of high aspiration from personal observation, as well as from ancient authority. They therefore set out to warn the nation of the uncertainty of high estate through a series of brief biographies of famous men from English history. The stated aim of Baldwin and his colleagues was "To show the fall of such as climb too high."[44] And most of the lives illustrated the same discouraging moral; as the aspiring Duke of Buckingham, brought low by Richard III, phrased it:

> . . . who in court will bear the sway alone,
> And wisely weigh not how to wield the care,
> Behold he me, and by my death beware:
> Whom flattering Fortune so beguiled
> That lo! she slew, where erst full smooth she smiled.[45]

Collections of such tales of Fortune's aspiring victims were not uncommon in Elizabethan England; and as usual, classical antiquity furnished its share of anecdotes and sententious counsel.[46]

This apt, colorful myth was part of the mental bric-a-brac of every educated Elizabethan. The smiling goddess, one hand resting speculatively on her golden wheel, stood full across the path to success and fame. Her beckoning finger was perhaps a greater deterrent to ambition than all the thundering of the preachers.

If, however, the assertion that they would inevitably fail to attain their goals did not discourage the ambitious, there remained one ultimate sanction: the declaration that the goals themselves—wealth, power, fame—were valueless. If the goals toward which they labored, in spite of common sense, divine prohibition, and the very structure of society, were utterly without value— then surely ambitious climbing was as futile a passion as Folly herself ever devised. In the sixteenth century there was in fact a considerable body of literature which asserted precisely this: that all the objects of worldly ambition were dust and ashes, that all human aspiration was vain. It was the voice of the Preacher,

44. Baldwin, *Mirror for Magistrates*, p. 120.
45. *Ibid.*, p. 318.
46. E.g., Baldwin, *Treatyce of Moral Philosophy*, pp. 156r-158r; Lloyd, pp. 1r-5v; Thomas Fenne, *Fennes Fruites . . . wherein is decyphered . . . the reward of aspiring mindes* (London, 1590), pp. 6v-16r.

speaking words that countless older generations had learned to accept with a sigh:

> Vanity of vanities, saith Ecclesiastes, vanity of vanities, all is vanity.
> What profit remaineth to a man of all his labor, in which he laboreth under the sun?
> One generation passeth away, and another cometh, but the earth abideth forever. . . .
> That which hath been, is the same that shall be, and that which hath been done, is the same that shall be done, neither is there any new thing under the sun.[47]

The Preacher spoke not only in parables, but directly to their own time:

> In running it helpeth not to be swift, in battle it helpeth not to be strong; to feeding it helpeth not to be wise; to riches it helpeth not to be subtle; to be had in favor it helpeth not to be cunning, but that all lieth in time and fortune.[48]

The words of Ecclesiastes—so the reverend Gifford averred, and many another Elizabethan moralist with him—proved the futility of the aspirations of "those who take such pains to heap up riches, to climb to honors. . . ."[49] And certainly these ancient verses, with their melancholy assertion of the cyclic view of human history and the mutability of all things human, with their stress on the fruitlessness of human effort, would be likely to undermine the confidence of the most enthusiastic climber. But this was by no means all that the somber verdict of Solomon, *Vanitas vanitatum, et omnia vanitas,* meant to the sixteenth-century reader. For the vanities Ecclesiastes listed as profitless and futile were also Christian sins, the sins of worldliness rooted in the corruption of the human condition. All human efforts, according to this view, were tainted with human depravity; and this mortal coil was in its innermost nature a vale of sin and misery. Finally, the stern doctrine that all this world's goods were vanities re-

47. George Gifford, *Eight Sermons upon . . . Ecclesiastes* (London, 1589), pp. 1ʳ-1ᵛ.
48. T. Cogan, *The Well of Wisdome . . .* (London, 1577), p. 35.
49. Gifford, p. 8ᵛ.

minded Elizabethans of another metaphysical truth about this chain-of-being universe: that the world at this material end of the chain of being was in fact largely an illusion. According to the stream of thought that flowed from Plato to Augustine and on into the theology of the Reformation, matter was not only less good than spirit, it was also less real. Thus the material goals of high aspiration were really little more than illusions—costly illusions, since a man could lose his soul in seeking them. The mutability, the wretchedness, and the illusory nature of the objects of worldly ambition made high aspiration seem a futile passion indeed. Each of these implications of the message of Ecclesiastes deserves further examination.

The fact of mutability made a deep impression on the Elizabethan mind; many and various were the expressions of this sixteenth-century commonplace. A poetic moral philosopher put it in jog-trot verse:

> And therefore with a loathsome heart
> I forced am to say
> That everything is vain because
> It comes to vain decay.

and concluded, by way of choral comment:

> And yet their labor frustrate is
> And travails be in vain.[50]

And a West Country schoolmaster carefully inscribed the same melancholy sentiments in his private commonplace book:

Omnium rerum vicissitudo est. The world changeth every day. everything hath his course. . . . in this world is nothing stable, permanent, nor durable, but like as the sea doth continually flow and ebb, so do all things in this world daily change, now up, now down, now merry, now sad, now friend, now foe, now accepted and anon out of favor, today, who but he? and tomorrow shut clean out of doors.[51]

This was the message with which moralist and preacher sought to quench the flames of ambition: "today, who but he? and to-

50. Edmund Elviden, *The Closet of Counsels* . . . (London, 1573), pp. 94ᵛ, 75ᵛ.
51. John Coneybeare, *Letters and Exercises of the Elizabethan Schoolmaster, John Coneybeare* . . ., ed. F. C. Coneybeare (London, 1905), p. 23.

morrow shut clean out of doors." For what were "transitory riches," "honor and promotion," but vanity? "Vanity it is to love those things which do pass away with incredible swiftness. . . ."[52] Catalogues of the vanities were common, and always the moral was the same: these are the highest goals of worldly aspiration, and they are all transitory and profitless.[53] Everything attainable under the sun was mutable, and therefore—as Elizabethans saw it—valueless.

Not only did these sought-after goals have no positive value— they were in fact tainted with the misery and sin which were inherent in all human things. This obvious Christian truth was vividly illustrated by a slim volume called *The Mirror of Man's Life* which appeared in the book stalls when the generation of 1560 was in its teens. On the title page, a plumed, gorgeously clad young gallant sat proudly in the saddle of a rearing, elaborately caparisoned steed; but at his feet a skeleton lay, with a skin-clad hermit pointing at it, and the motto: "O Worm's Meat: O Froth: O Vanity: Why Art Thou So Insolent?"[54] The book was a recent translation of a celebrated tract on the miseries of the human condition by the greatest of medieval churchmen, Pope Innocent III. Its many chapters were disturbing essays on the feebleness, misery, vileness, corruption, griefs, misfortunes, vices, and hideous pains of hell which flesh was heir to. Fifteen chapters were devoted to the misery of the proud man and the wretchedness of the ambitious.[55] Whatever he did, man sinned and suffered; but most especially did he suffer when he committed the deadly sins—which no ambitious man could avoid.

The punishment of the sins of ambition was not altogether deferred to the other world. The stereotypes of the ambitious man's suffering in this world were well known; they were in fact identical with the stereotyped victims of Fortune's wheel. There was Wealth, crouching over his money-bags in suspicion and fear.

52. Thomas à Kempis, *The Imitation or Following of Christ, and the contemning of worldly vanities*, trans. Edward Hake (London, 1567), pp. 1ᵛ-2ʳ.
53. E.g., Henry Smith, "The Trial of Vanities," in *Sermons*, pp. 356, 360-364; Fenne, pp. 1ʳ-1ᵛ; S. I., *Bromleion, A Discourse of . . . Divinity . . .* (London, 1595), pp. 40-41, 44-45.
54. [Innocent III], *The Mirror of Mans Life . . .*, trans. H. Kirton (London, 1577), title page.
55. *Ibid.*, chaps. xxiv-xxxviii.

There was Power, enthroned always under a Sword of Damocles, sleepless with the anxiety of high place and responsibility. There were Honor and Fame, nervously eyeing their rivals in the tense ballet of the court. That ambition was a delusion, leading only to an even greater portion of this world's miseries than was man's normal lot, was a moral truism, too ancient and well known to be disputed.

And always there was death, ending all the petty plots and pitiful heroics of men on earth. On death, Elizabethan poets and preachers waxed eloquent:

Though man for awhile seem never so honorable and mighty, never so rich and wealthy, never so young and lusty, never so beautiful and comely, never so fortunate and happy, yet . . . he shall die, and the finger of God shall suddenly write . . . Thy days are numbered and cometh to an end: and thy pomp and thy pride shall be laid into the grave; worms shall lie under thee, and worms shall be thy covering.[56]

Death was the unanswerable argument: no earthly power, no worldly fame could buy one extra hour of life. Whatever path a man might follow, whether he fought his way to the heights of power and glory or trod the humble road of simple righteousness, all men came in the end to the same destination. How futile then was the compulsive climbing of the aspiring mind.

Behind the mutability and misery of this world, reinforcing their message of despair, lay a final tremendous commonplace of sixteenth-century thought: the Platonic-Christian view that this world itself was an illusion. There were two worlds, said the philosophers—this world of gross matter and imperfect things, and the higher spiritual realm of pure essence and divinity. And the higher realm, invisible to sensual man, was nevertheless not only far better, but also far more real than this mortal coil. For no Elizabethan needed to be steeped in Platonic or Neoplatonic metaphysics to know that in the great chain of being, the spectrum of existence, this world was the farthest link from God. The godhead was perfect being; this wretched world was hardly there at all.

56. H. B., *Moriemini: A Verie Profitable Sermon Preached . . . at the Court* (London, 1593), p. 19.

The popular literature of the sixteenth century reiterated endlessly the belief in this invisible world, and the illusory nature of this material world. That this other world existed was a dogma which Christians were not at liberty to doubt; for the current of thought ran from Plato and Plotinus through Paul and Augustine to the humblest Elizabethan preacher. But it was as poetry, not as dry theology or metaphysics, that this view permeated Elizabethan thought and expression. In this unreal material world, men were shadowy actors on an insubstantial stage, playing at kings and courtiers through a brief afternoon, to be heard from no more thereafter. The shadows on the wall of Plato's cave still capered through the pages of Elizabethan books, an even more common metaphor than the stage to express the unreality of this world. "This our mortal and miserable life," said the Elizabethan moralist, "is none other but the likeness of a shadow, and a birth unprofitable to the earth."[57] He who pursues the good things of this world "followeth a shadow, which, when he thinketh he is surest of it, vanisheth and is nothing."[58] Thus the reduction was complete: The successful aspiring mind with all his power and glory was actually tottering on the brink of inevitable disaster, sure to fall to an ignominious end; in fact, his earthly fame and sovereignty were utterly valueless and even sinful; and finally, neither he nor his successes were real at all, for he was but a strutting shadow in the insubstantial pageant of this world.

This was the attitude toward ambition with which the generations which grew up in the reeling world of the 1530's, '40's, and '50's sought to indoctrinate the Elizabethan younger generation. Much of what these spokesmen for the older generations had to say was not new; but seldom had it been said so often, or with such intensity. The older Elizabethans repeated like a litany the lesson of their own lives: that the ambitious courtier or counselor was the most dangerous of public enemies. To this basic denunciation of a great social evil, they added still more impressive warnings, supporting their empirical knowledge with religious, scientific, and poetic verities. They pointed out that

57. William Phiston, *The Welspring of wittie Conceites* . . . (London, 1584), p. 52.
58. Baldwin, *Treatyce of Moral Philosophy*, p. 85v.

ambition, accompanied always by the mortal sins of pride, avarice, and envy, was a terrible sin against God, which would surely be punished by an eternity of hellfire. They reminded the nation that the ambitious climber was violating the established order and degree of the social hierarchy, which in turn reflected the eternal hierarchic structure of the universe—a monstrous, unnatural crime. And they stressed the certainty of failure—and hence the futility of aspiring—by giving new life to the ancient image of Fortune's wheel, and by repeating the timeless words of Ecclesiastes, that in this vale of tears all achievement is vain. An observable fact—that ambition was a real social evil—was thus reinforced by religious sanctions, by accepted metaphysical truth, and by poetic clichés as old as Herodotus and Solomon. The doctrine of the sinfulness and foolishness of ambition, so impressively supported by the eternal truths of the age, was calculated to convince any educated, Christian Elizabethan.[59]

This in fact remained the orthodox view of ambition throughout the reign. Even such a typical member of the generation of 1560 as Robert Greene, whose works have been quoted above, piously repeated his elders' condemnations of the aspiring mind. And yet, if there was one quality in which this younger generation abounded, it was extravagant ambition. The very names of its leading lights—Sidney, Essex, Raleigh, Cecil, Bacon, Coke— are synonymous with high aspiration. To understand this paradox, we must look more closely at the world in which the generation of 1560 grew up, and examine an entirely different set of intellectual influences from those which molded the character of the generations of Elizabeth and Burghley.

59. Two excellent summaries of the orthodox view of ambition in Elizabethan times may be found in Floyd, pp. 281-288, and Baldwin, *Mirror for Magistrates*, pp. 168-171.

III. *A generation of phoenixes*

In practice, the Elizabethan younger generation all but ignored orthodox denunciations of ambition. This is not surprising: their parents had done so too. The significant difference
between the generations was that the younger Elizabethans rejected orthodox condemnations of ambition in spirit as well as in
fact. These young men accepted high aspiration wholeheartedly,
not only in practice, but internally, at the level of thought and
emotion. For the prudent compromise and *politique* evasion of
their parents, the generation of 1560 substituted a passionately
affirmative mood—the aggressive, extremist mood of the Marlovian aspiring mind.

Two processes seem to have operated simultaneously in the
development of this Elizabethan younger generation during the
1570's and early 1580's. First, there was a gradual process of
alienation from the ideals of their fathers. Among the consequences of this alienation was an emotional rejection of the older
generation's strictures against ambition. Secondly, there was a
restless search for new values in a world of new and changing
facts. Among the results of this quest for new ideals was the
growth of a mood of high aspiration so intense and so all-pervad-
ing as almost to constitute a secular religion. These comple-
mentary processes and the resulting mood of high aspiration are
the subject of this chapter.

In attempting to understand the early development of the
generation of 1560, it will be well to begin with a brief outline of the upbringing of a fairly typical member of that generation. Such a biographical approach will have a number of advantages. In the first place, it will provide a few concrete facts
about the youth of these young men to balance the heavy
theoretical emphasis inevitable in such a study as this. In addition, a biographical profile will make possible a much closer
examination of an exemplary member of this generation, a detailed analysis which should make much clearer some of the
generalizations to follow. Most important, this approach will bring
us into closer contact with the lives of these young aristocrats of

four centuries ago than any set of generalizations, no matter how incisive, can do.

i. The upbringing of an Elizabethan governor:
Sir Robert Sidney

It is clear that the Elizabethan younger generation was early indoctrinated in a morality which condemned ambition in no uncertain terms. Paradoxically, however, these future governors of England were simultaneously given a thorough training in the fine art of getting ahead. An excellent example of this practical training in courtiership will be provided by an account of the early life of Robert Sidney—his youth, his education, and his apprenticeship as a governor of the commonwealth. For Sir Robert Sidney, younger brother of the celebrated Sir Philip, was himself the pattern of the perfect courtier and successful aspiring mind. His education and upbringing closely followed the recommended program for the training of future governors: he received an almost ideal preparation for a successful career at the court of Elizabeth. He had, in addition, every advantage of family, influence, and natural ability. Finally, he was innately ambitious enough to make eager use of all his opportunities for advancement. In his youth, Robert Sidney was thus a model of the aspiring mind of the Elizabethan younger generation.

The career of the younger Sidney—like that of most of his contemporaries—began not with his childhood, but with his ancestors. Few indeed made good at Elizabeth's court who could not point to some distinction or gentility in their family trees. The Queen was extremely sensitive to sneers that her court was filled with upstarts, and no merchant's son or rude mechanical was likely to enjoy her graces long. Robert, therefore, began life with a considerable inherited advantage—the honorable name of Sidney.

The Sidneys were certainly gentlemen—but, like many other great houses in the last half of the sixteenth century, they were distinctly Tudor aristocracy. The grandfather of Philip and Robert Sidney had fought for Henry VIII, notably at Brest and Flodden Field, and had been well rewarded with lands and offices.[1] Their father, Sir Henry Sidney, had grown up with Prince Edward and had become a personal favorite of the boy king. Sir Henry had further advanced his fortunes—or so it seemed—by marrying a daughter of the mighty Duke of Northumberland; but when the wind changed, Sir Henry had been one of the first to go over to Mary.[2] Having thus survived the troubled decade of the lesser Tudors by shrewdly shifting factions at the opportune moment, the elder Sidney had gone on to become one of the most energetic builders of the Elizabethan state. Altogether, he had served the last three Tudor sovereigns on several diplomatic missions, as President of Wales, and three times as Lord Deputy of Ireland. Sir Henry was a model of successful aspiration for his sons. He also had the money to educate them as future governors, and the court influence to further their careers. The same was true of the Bacon brothers, of hunchbacked little Robert Cecil, of the dazzling young Earl of Essex, and of many other future aspiring minds of this generation. Their fathers' achievements provided them with inspiration and advantages for their own careers.

In his brother Philip, nine years his senior, young Robert Sidney probably found another source of inspiration during his early years. Sir Philip Sidney was apparently quite fond of his "sweet Robin," and was of very material help to the younger man.[3] It was he, for instance, who saw to it that enough money was forthcoming from their father so that Robert might make his European tour—a necessary part of his education—in proper style.[4] At the same time, Sir Philip Sidney may have made an important, if unintended, contribution to his brother's success simply by being his splendid self. For it is not unlikely that Robert felt a competitive urge to assert his own individuality against the oppressive weight of his older brother's perfection and popular success. Sir Philip Sidney was known as a paragon of all the courtier's virtues long before his premature death elevated him to the rank of patron saint of the aspiring younger

1. Arthur Collins, ed., *Letters and Memorials of State in the Reigns of Queen Mary, Queen Elizabeth, King James* . . . (London, 1746), I, 76-82.
2. H. R. Fox Bourne, *Sir Philip Sidney, Type of English Chivalry in the Elizabethan Age* (New York and London, 1891), pp. 11-14.
3. Philip Sidney to Robert Sidney, Oct. 18, 1580, in Collins, I, 283.
4. *Ibid.*, I, 285.

generation. It is not surprising that Robert, throughout the years of his youth, was constantly referred to as Sir Philip's younger brother.[5] The highest praise Robert could receive was to be compared to Philip. Their father urged Robert to emulate his brother: "Imitate his virtues, exercises, studies, and actions; he is a rare ornament of this age, the very formular that all well-disposed young gentlemen of our Court do form also their manners and life by."[6] Under these trying circumstances, the younger man may well have felt a sense of competition, at least with his brother's awesome reputation. At any rate, the older brother, like the father, certainly served as a patron to Robert's ambition; they both may well have provided models of aspiration for his developing mind; and the elder brother perhaps whetted ambition by being, all unconscious, an object of emulation.

In these relationships with his father and older brother, Robert was probably typical of young Elizabethan courtiers. The model of a father's successful ambition must in many cases have more than outweighed the teachings of moralists and preachers. It has been suggested, for instance, that Francis Bacon developed in his youth an "inner drive to emulate his father," the great Lord Keeper Bacon, by rising to the same high post.[7] Competition with an older brother, resulting in the further intensifying of an ambitious nature, was also perhaps not uncommon. Parental encouragement of "emulation" between talented brothers was apparently a fairly standard educational procedure.[8] It is notable that a surprising number of the most successful aspiring minds of this generation were in fact younger brothers: the list includes such outstanding names as Sir Walter Raleigh, Robert Cecil, and Francis Bacon. And of course in the background of any such fraternal competition lay the grim fact of primogeniture. This fundamental law of inheritance condemned many a younger son to social inferiority, and compelled him to win back by his own efforts the honor and authority his elder brother would simply inherit. The formation of the Elizabethan aspiring

5. E.g., *C. S. P., For., Eliz.*, XV, 362; XIX, 202, 595.

6. Sir Henry Sidney to Robert Sidney, March 25, 1578, in Collins, I, 246; cf. Malcolm William Wallace, *The Life of Sir Philip Sidney* (Cambridge, 1915), p. 208.

7. Paul H. Kocher, "Francis Bacon and His Father," *HLQ*, XXI (1958), 149.

8. Francis Bacon, "Of Parents and Children," in *Selected Writings*, ed. Hugh D. Dick (New York, 1955), p. 21.

mind, therefore, probably depended to a significant extent on such psychological and sociological factors as the model of the father's success, competition with the older brother, and the fact of primogeniture.

Young Robert Sidney went up to Christ Church College, Oxford, as early as 1574, when he was barely into his teens. He was never the student that his brother was, however, and he was often truant from Oxford, much to his father's chagrin.[9] He does seem to have been an avid student of history, which in those simpler days was still the story of statesmen and generals. He took no degree until much later, when, his career well under way, he was ceremoniously granted the honor of a master's degree. Neither early matriculation nor a late degree was particularly uncommon for young Tudor governors. The probable impact of such formal education will be discussed later in some detail.

The next step in the education of an Elizabethan aristocrat was likely to be the grand tour, or at any rate some travel in foreign lands; and so it was for Robert Sidney. From approximately 1578 through 1582 he was traveling on the Continent, particularly in Germany and France. Such trips were primarily educational in two senses. Young future governors were expected to pick up some smattering of European languages and some knowledge of the current situation in the nations of Europe. The grand tourists were, however, also expected to keep up their more formal studies and to complete the process of "finishing" themselves as well-rounded courtiers. On all these things, Robert had the invaluable advice of his brother, whom he had dutifully asked for guidance in the matter of how best to make use of his time on the Continent. "Your purpose," Philip reminded him, "is, being a Gentleman born, to furnish yourself with the knowledge of such things as may be serviceable to your country and fit for your calling. . . ."[10] He went on to mention languages and what amounted to geopolitical knowledge of other nations, both of which we may assume Robert did attempt to acquire. In a subsequent letter, Philip advised him on his studies and accomplish-

9. Mona Wilson, *Sir Philip Sidney* (London, 1950), p. 111; Sir Henry Sidney to Robert Sidney, March 25, 1579, in Collins, I, 247.

10. Quoted in Frederick S. Boas, *Sir Philip Sidney, Representative Elizabethan* (London, 1955), p. 165.

ments.[11] Among the former, he stressed mathematics and decent Latin, though on the subject of Latin he spoke for a generation that was thoroughly bored with the classical passions of their parents: "So you can speak and write Latin, not barbarously, I never require great study in Ciceronianism, the chief abuse of Oxford. . . ." As for accomplishments, Philip advised Robert on such courtier-like skills as music and horsemanship, and reminded him to be careful of his diet, in order to care for his complexion. Robert presumably heeded this practical advice. He also apparently met the right people in the course of his travels, including such celebrities as the Prince of Orange, the celebrated soldier François de La Noue, and the famous Protestant educator, Dr. Sturm.[12] Finally, there is evidence that he saw some military service in the Low Countries; and this is not unlikely, since experience at the wars was highly desirable for a young gentleman.[13] The impact of the grand tour will require some further discussion.

There were great expectations of young Robert's success; his father was actually pressing suits on his behalf as early as 1577, when the boy was only fourteen.[14] In 1584 Robert's cousin, Ambassador Stafford, writing from Paris, suggested his name for a delicate mission to Henry of Navarre.[15] But that fall twenty-one-year-old Robert Sidney was deeply involved in complex and secret negotiations of his own: he was getting married.

Marriage for an aspiring courtier in those times was essentially a business proposition.[16] True love, for example, probably had little to do with the marriage of Arthur Gorges, whose bride was only thirteen years old.[17] Nor is it likely that Sir Christopher Blount was carried away by pure passion when he married the mother of his own close friend and contemporary, the Earl of

11. Philip Sidney to Robert Sidney, Oct. 18, 1580, in Boas, pp. 165-166.

12. Hubert Languet to Philip Sidney, March 16, 1579, in Philip Sidney, *The Correspondence of Sir Philip Sidney and Hubert Languet*, ed. and trans. Stuart A. Pears (London, 1845), p. 159; C. S. P., For., Eliz., XVIII, 484.

13. Hubert Languet to Philip Sidney, Feb. 6, 1580, and Robert Sidney to Sir Henry Sidney, Nov. 1, 1580, in Sidney, *Correspondence*, pp. 171, 171 n.; C. S. P., For., Eliz., XVIII, 780.

14. Collins, I, 187, 194, 247.   *15*. C. S. P., For., Eliz., XIX, 108.

16. Lewis Einstein, *Tudor Ideals* (New York, 1921), pp. 245-247.

17. Helen Estabrook Sandison, "Arthur Gorges, Spenser's Alcyon and Raleigh's Friend," *PMLA*, XLIII (1928), 648.

Essex.[18] The attitude of the time towards matrimony is illustrated by John Chamberlain's report of the death of Arthur Gorges' own daughter a dozen years later, when Gorges was on the verge of marrying her off in her turn: "Sir Arthur Gorges had a shrewd windfall the last week. His daughter the great heir (for whom he should have had eight thousand pound of the Earl of Pembroke, or as others say ten thousand of the Lord Thomas) died on Friday. . . ."[19] A good wife, with proper connections and a sizable inheritance, was a material asset for an ambitious young man.

The marriage of Robert Sidney to Barbara, daughter and heir of John Gamage of Coity, Glamorganshire, has all the earmarks of such a typical alliance of expediency. The last words of a letter from a servant of Sir Philip Sidney's reveal the general attitude toward the match: "I hear from England that my master's brother, Mr. Robert Sidney, is married to Mr. Gamage's daughter and heir."[20] The last three words clearly reveal the basic Elizabethan attitude toward such a marriage. In arranging the match, furthermore, much pressure and influence was apparently brought to bear by relatives and other interested parties: the betrothal seems to have been something of a court intrigue.[21] Some interested individuals, including Sir Walter Raleigh and Lord Admiral Howard, apparently resented the secrecy of the negotiations, and felt that their special interests in the Gamage heiress had been ignored.[22] Raleigh, for instance, complained bitterly that his "kinswoman" had been "bought and sold" without his being consulted; and in fact, the Sidney faction did put up a bond of £6,000 to seal the bargain.[23] The ethical level of the whole affair is perhaps indicated by the fact that efforts were later made to recover the bond.

Equally important for the career of young Robert Sidney was his election to the Parliament of 1584—a symbol of increased prestige, certainly, though the Lower House was not yet gen-

18. Sidney Lee in *DNB*, s.v. Blount, Christopher.
19. John Chamberlain to Dudley Carleton, Oct. 15, 1600, in John Chamberlain, *The Letters of* . . ., ed. Norman Egbert McClure (Philadelphia, 1939), I, 109.
20. *C. S. P., For., Eliz.*, XIX, 202.   21. Wallace, pp. 311-312.
22. John Montgomery Traherne, ed., *Stradling Correspondence . . . in the Reign of Elizabeth* (London, 1840), pp. 9-10, 20, 22-24, 29-30.
23. *Ibid.*, pp. 22-23, 10, xii.

erally recognized as a path to political eminence. Interestingly
enough, he sat for Glamorganshire, where the estates of his new
bride's father lay. His election—or better, selection—was in fact
due to the influence of some of the same people who had arranged
the marriage.[24] Robert's choice of a wife was thus the first step
towards the realization of his political as well as his financial
ambitions. He was still only "a younger brother . . . more stored
with discourse than money," and perhaps too given to elegant,
expensive clothes.[25] But these were common weaknesses in the
growing generation of 1560, idle young courtiers who had as yet
found no challenge to try their metal. And from the younger Sidney's earliest youth there had always been "great expectation" of
his success. By the middle 1580's he had taken the first big step up
the ladder; he must have been happy, if not surprised, to learn
that his marriage was "generally well liked" at court.[26]

Robert Sidney in 1585 thus stood out as a well-rounded future
governor of England. Certainly he was ambitious: he had "an
eye for the main chance," and already in the early 1580's he was
busily and efficiently suing the Queen for public office.[27] He was,
however, not so dedicated to politics and diplomacy as was the
elder of the Bacon brothers, Anthony, whose delicate health alone
seemed to stand between him and a brilliant career. Nor was he
so exclusively preoccupied with the military traditions of his
class as was, for example, George Clifford, who was to make his
name as the "buccaneer Earl" of Cumberland. Robert Sidney
considered himself equally fit for civil and for military service;
he aspired to succeed in both these main fields of endeavor open
to the Tudor ruling class.

ii. *The failure of the humanist education*

By 1585, then, young Robert Sidney had obviously profited
from the more practical aspects of his training in the arts of the

24. *Ibid.*, pp. 21-22, 77.
25. Philip Sidney to Robert Sidney, Oct. 18, 1580, in Collins, I, 283; *C. S. P., Dom., Eliz.*, CL, 85.
26. Sir Francis Walsingham to Sir Edward Stradling, Sept. 27, 1584, in Traherne, p. 30.
27. Wallace, p. 310; Robert Sidney to Molyneux, 1582, in *ibid.*, p. 311.

courtier. But the other, more formal aspect of his education probably had no more impact on him than it did on most of his contemporaries. And it was this other, primarily humanistic side of his upbringing which was charged with the task of discouraging overreaching ambition in the younger generation. There is a good deal of evidence and even direct testimony of the failure of the much-admired Christian humanist education to produce the race of Platonic governors and Christian magistrates it was intended to create. Certainly the new Tudor education failed with the generation of 1560. Certainly, too, this failure of the educational process contributed largely to the deeper spiritual alienation of the younger generation from the ideals of their elders. Thus the failure of the humanist education played a real, if negative, part in the development of the aspiring mind of the 1580's and '90's. It will therefore be worthwhile to look more closely at the fundamental nature of the humanist education, as actually experienced by young Elizabethans, and at some related factors which contributed to their rejection of the official morality of their parents.

To begin at the beginning, it is probable that there were few close family ties between the older and younger generations of the Elizabethan aristocracy. There were a number of reasons for this lack of strong emotional ties between parents and children. In the first place, the young gentlemen of those days quite commonly grew up in broken homes. Death was as efficient as a divorce court in those uncertain times, and two or three marriages almost seem to have been the rule rather than the exception. Furthermore, since most marriages were arranged with an eye to dynastic and property interests rather than to personal compatibility, unhappy home life must have been at least as common then as now. A writer on marriage thus described many such matches in the 1560's: The unfortunate couple "curse their parents even unto the pit of hell for coupling them together. . . . what frowning, overthwarting, scolding, and chiding is there between them, so that the whole house is filled full of those tragedies. . . ."[28] Children raised in such broken, loveless, or

28. Thomas Becon, *Book of Matrimony*, quoted in Chilton Latham Powell, *English Domestic Relations, 1487-1653* (New York, 1917), p. 125.

turbulent homes were not likely to develop a great deal of respect, much less affection, for their elders.

Nor were the orthodox relations between parents and children calculated to create filial affection. If the conduct books are to be believed, children were to be seen and not heard in Elizabethan households. Family relationships were matters primarily of duty, and the "duties of children to parents [were] to be subject and obedient. . . ."[29] Such strict obligations were part of the daily life of Elizabethan children, and were often severely enforced.[30] Allowances were not made for precocity, and even the most talented youth had to subject himself absolutely to the will of his father.[31] Discipline, duty, and proper conduct were the keynotes of life in the Elizabethan aristocratic household; surely high-spirited, talented adolescents were likely to chafe under such a regimen.

Finally, the simmering rebellion which such rigid discipline must have created in many aggressive and gifted youths was provided ample opportunity for development by the educational routine itself. For in their late teens and twenties, young gentlemen were released from parental control and allowed to live unsupervised in London and even at the royal court. As Ascham wrote in 1570:

Indeed, from seven to seventeen, young gentlemen commonly be carefully enough brought up; but from seventeen to seven and twenty (the most dangerous time of all a man's life, and most slippery to stay well in) they have commonly the rein of all license in their own hand, and specially such as do live in the Court.[32]

This sudden release quite likely led to just the sort of rejection of the injunctions of the older generation which Ascham lamented. Bear-baiting, play-going, and court entertainments now occupied their time; and gambling, whoring, and drinking exhausted the

29. Powell, p. 129.

30. Carroll Camden, *The Elizabethan Woman* (Houston, New York, London, 1952), pp. 134-135; Wallace Notestein, "The English Woman, 1580 to 1650," in J. H. Plumb, ed., *Studies in Social History: A Tribute to G. M. Trevelyan* (London, New York, Toronto, 1955), p. 84.

31. John Stockwood, *A Bartholomew Fairing for Parents*, quoted in Powell, p. 131.

32. Roger Ascham, *The Scholemaster*, ed. John E. B. Mayor (London, 1863), p. 39.

substance of many a squire's son come up to London. For those of more talent and finer metal, the pursuit of their own high ambitions became the absorbing problem of these first years of freedom.

It is of course unlikely that all parents obeyed the injunctions of the conduct books. These guides to child-rearing and household management were essentially digests of Biblical and classical authority, with embellishments based on immemorial custom.[33] Nevertheless, parental laxity in matters of moral indoctrination was not unheard of in Elizabethan times. In such easy-going homes, where no serious attempt was made to inculcate morals in the younger generation, it was even easier for young men to escape the commandments against ambition. They did not rebel, but only because there were no parental injunctions and discipline to rebel against; and where they had the talent and the drive, they simply went their naturally aspiring ways. But it may well have been that the most fiercely ambitious natures were molded in the strictest homes.

If parents did little to inspire affection in the younger generation, Elizabethan schoolmasters and tutors often dealt so tyrannously with their charges that they aroused lifelong dislike— for themselves and for the doctrine they had attempted to inculcate. These humanistically trained teachers did make sincere efforts to instruct their students in Christian morality as well as in Ciceronian Latin. They sought seriously to instil in the sons of the Elizabethan aristocracy and gentry "a composite of all the ideals which the history of Western Europe has recorded."[34] Children and youths committed to memory whole commonplace books full of "flowers" from the Greeks and the Romans, not only for style, but for the wisdom they contained.[35] Everything that could be done to raise a generation of governors imbued with the ideals of Christian humanism was attempted by teachers often dedicated to their calling.

33. *Ibid.*, p. 46.

34. Ruth Kelso, *The Doctrine of the English Gentleman in the Sixteenth Century* (Urbana, Illinois, 1929), p. 12; cf. Hugh Rhodes, *The Book of Nurture . . .*, in Frederick J. Furnivall, ed., *Manners and Meals in Olden Times* (E. E. T. S., orig. ser. No. 32; London, 1868), p. 63; Ascham, pp. xxii, 268-280.

35. Statutes of Eton, Westminster, Rivington, and Shrewsbury Grammar Schools, in Foster Watson, *The English Grammar Schools to 1660: Their Curriculum and Practice* (Cambridge, 1908), pp. 332-333.

But any hope there might have been that the young gentlemen would take all this moralizing seriously was effectively dispelled by the brutality of their instructors and by the unappetizing format in which this wisdom was presented. These and other practical aspects of the humanist education seem to have effectively sabotaged the best efforts of the English humanists to produce a race of Platonic guardians and Ciceronian magistrates for their country.

The severity of Elizabethan schoolmasters was proverbial. Richard Mulcaster, the famous headmaster of Merchant Tailors' and of Paul's School, laid down the dictum that "the rod can no more be spared in schools than the sword in the hand of the prince."[36] And he lived up to his rule: "The prayers of cockering mothers prevailed with him as much as the requests of indulgent fathers, rather increasing than mitigating his severity on their offending child."[37] Ascham pointed out the futility of the common practice of trying to indoctrinate young aristocrats by force: "they carry commonly from the school with them a perpetual hatred of their master, and a continual contempt of learning."[38] And a young gentleman of the generation of 1560 wrote of his contemporaries: "In those days . . . you might have seen, among schoolboys of genteel circumstances, few who were not repelled from literary discipline, either by the severity of the teachers or the delight of playing."[39] The result, he continued, was a "distaste and a kind of contempt for knowledge and duty."

Nor was the form in which the wisdom of the ancients was presented calculated to be excessively palatable to the young. The humanist reformers, in their determination to revive the excellences of classical Latin, had merely succeeded in making classical studies such a chore that few students could have had much enthusiasm for what Roman moralists and philosophers had to say.[40] Anyone who has examined Lily's exhaustingly com-

36. Richard Mulcaster, *The Educational Writings of* . . ., ed. James Oliphant (Glasgow, 1903), p. 113.
37. Thomas Fuller, *The History of the Worthies of England*, ed. John Nichols (London, 1811), II, 431.
38. Ascham, p. 30.
39. Thomas Moffet, *Nobilis or A View of the Life and Death of Sidney*, ed. and trans. Vergil B. Heltzel and Hoyt H. Hudson (San Marino, Calif., 1940), p. 72.
40. C. S. Lewis, *English Literature in the Sixteenth Century, Excluding Drama* (Oxford, 1954), pp. 18 ff.

plete, scholastically complex *Grammar*—with its seven genders of nouns, for instance—can understand the lack of enthusiasm of the average Elizabethan student.[41] If such a paragon as Sir Philip Sidney could object to Oxford Ciceronianism, what must the reaction of his far less gifted—and less interested—fellow students have been? The generation of 1560 made their discoveries in the vernacular literatures, especially in French and Italian, as their parents had discovered the Latin and Greek classics.[42] And they found much less sententious moralizing against ambition in the most popular modern writers than in the carefully selected and edited maxims of the ancients.

University training succeeded no better than the home and the school in the moral education of these young men. The ruling class did send their children to the universities in increasing numbers during the last half of the sixteenth century, to prepare them for social and political success. It was apparently expected that they would pick up at least enough quotable aphorisms and enough of a nodding acquaintance with Latin literature to make them socially alert at Elizabeth's euphuistic court. It was probably hoped that they would also imbibe some of the prudent wisdom and morality of Seneca and Cicero. But the Elizabethan universities could not compel healthy young men with no clerkly instincts to concentrate on Aristotle, and probably few did. Complaints about this state of things and reforms of the university statutes and administration occurred periodically throughout the century, but without apparent effect. Most young gentlemen still went up to Cambridge or to Oxford primarily for social background.

The studiousness of the Bacon brothers was thus much more the exception than the rule among aristocratic university students. The hawking and the dancing lessons of the young Earls of Essex and Cumberland were much more typical.[43] The latter, who matriculated at Cambridge at the age of thirteen, seems to have spent thirteen pence for his *Orations of Tully*—and ten

41. [William Lily], *A Short Introduction of Grammar, Generally To Be Used . . .* (Oxford, 1651); Watson, pp. 261-264.

42. Cf. Gabriel Harvey, *Marginalia*, ed. G. C. Moore Smith (Stratford-upon-Avon, 1913), *passim*.

43. Charles Edward Mallet, *A History of the University of Oxford* (New York, 1924), II, 120, 127, 142-144.

shillings for a "gittern lute."[44] The proportion was extreme, but indicative of the basic focus of the interests of this younger generation.

There were, however, quite adequate reasons for the tendency of these young people to reject what the universities had to teach them. The fact was that "the courses they found provided for them were quite remote from the affairs of . . . a world in which the realms of politics, science, commerce, and industry were seeing tremendous changes of which the traditional university studies failed to take cognizance."[45] Even so good a student as Francis Bacon condemned this antiquated curriculum and urged a modern, practical course that would help prepare a young governor for service to the state.[46] Charles Blount, the future Lord Mountjoy and conqueror of Ireland, came away with little profit from his Oxford years—"not well grounded," a contemporary admirer admits. But he soon accumulated considerable practical knowledge of languages, mathematics, and geography, simply by "spending his vacant hours with scholars best able to direct him. . . ."[47] He and others like him felt—quite rightly—that the university course in rhetoric, logic, and metaphysics was not likely to be of much direct help to them in their future careers. The Earl of Essex declared frankly that "the most of the noblemen and gentlemen of our time have no other use of their learning but in table talk. . . ."[48] The result was "a late sixteenth-century protest against the inadequate curriculum of the universities."[49] This protest took a variety of forms, including the Ramist movement at Cambridge, the establishment of Gresham's College in London, and a number of projects for a "court education" which would produce, not a logic-chopping

44. G. C. Williamson, *George, Third Earl of Cumberland (1558-1605), His Life and His Voyages* (Cambridge, 1920), p. 9.

45. Kenneth Charlton, "Holbein's 'Ambassadors' and Sixteenth Century Education," *JHI*, XXI (1960), 103.

46. *The Advancement of Learning*, in *Works*, ed. James Spedding *et al.* (London, 1864), VIII, 399.

47. Fynes Moryson, *An Itinerary Containing His Ten Yeares Travel* . . . (Glasgow, 1907), II, 265.

48. Earl of Essex to Earl of Rutland, Jan. 4, 1595, in Walter Bourchier Devereux, *Lives and Letters of the Devereux, Earls of Essex* (London, 1853), I, 331.

49. Charlton, p. 104.

debater, but "a man fit for the wars and fit for the peace, meet for the court and meet for the country."[50]

The final stage in the preparation of a young governor was travel in Europe, "to see countries abroad, to mark their singularities, to learn their languages, and to return thence with an equipment of wisdom that will serve the needs of one's own country."[51] This part of the training of the gentry and aristocracy also helped to alienate the youth from the moral outlook of their elders, and that in a more direct and positive way than any earlier stage of the educational process had done. Parents and teachers had aroused the resentment of the younger generation, and had presented them with moral maxims that they found irrelevant to their own lives. But travel in Europe offered them for the first time actual alternatives to the conventional wisdom of their fathers. The danger of such moral and religious infection was repeatedly and vehemently asserted by the older generation in the later sixteenth century.[52] An impressionable young man had only to cross the Channel to be exposed to all the glamorous temptations of the church of Rome, with its saints and incense and splendor. To cross the Alps was to be subjected to the subtle deceptions of an older, more sophisticated culture —and to the doctrines of the wily Machiavel. Everywhere there were new customs, different attitudes, strange ways of life that made their own island home seem narrowly parochial and provincial. And even if a young gentleman did not return a Papist or a Machiavellian, Italianated or Frenchified, he was more than likely to have developed a good deal of skepticism about any set of absolute precepts.

Unhappy childhoods, rigid dsicipline, and severity on the part of parents and teachers were not new in the later sixteenth century. But the difficulty and pragmatic irrelevance of the humanist education were new; and so was the infliction of such an education upon the unscholarly sons of the ruling class. The

50. *Institution of a Gentleman,* quoted in Kelso, p. 39.
51. Mulcaster, p. 74.
52. Lords of the Council to Lord Admiral Howard and Lord Buckhurst, Dec. 31, 1593, in Henry Ellis, ed., *Original Letters Illustrative of British History . . . Second Series* (London, 1827), III, 171; Ascham, pp. 68-79; Bartolome Felippe, *The Counseller . . .* (London, 1589), p. 46.

high hopes of the university reformers of the early Tudor period that they might train true Christian humanist magistrates for England were thus doomed to inevitable disillusionment. England continued to be ruled by an aristocracy of birth rather than one of brains; and the attempt to treat the former as if they were the latter could only lead to frustration, indifference, and resentment. A young aristocrat, forced to memorize and parse an ancient maxim on the evils of ambition which was in difficult Latin, and was moreover utterly irrelevant to his own future career, was more than likely to shrug it off as platitudinous nonsense, or even to reject it as rank hypocrisy.

iii. The deeper spiritual alienation

This negative reaction was particularly probable in view of the deeper spiritual alienation which undergirded the younger generation's specific rejection of humanistic moral precepts. That there was such an alienation should be evident from a simple comparison of the two generations. Surely a vast gulf yawns between the generation of Burghley and Walsingham on the one hand, and that of Essex and Raleigh on the other. A generation of administrators, religious reformers, and humanistic commonwealth men contrasts sharply with a generation of adventurers, playwrights, and poets. The many Tudor historians who have sensed this spiritual cleavage between Elizabeth and her younger subjects provide sufficient indication that such an alienation in fact took place.[53] It would be difficult to overestimate the profundity and pervasiveness of this reaction of the ardent younger generation against their cool, cautious, *politique* elders. Both the causes and the nature of this inner alienation must be studied in more detail, for this psychological factor played a vital part in the growth of the Marlovian aspiring mind.

During the 1570's and early '80's, when members of the generation of 1560 were in their teens and early twenties, England basked in the peace and prosperity of the middle years of Elizabeth's long reign. The older generations, born in the revolutionary times of Henry VIII, had come through the storms and

53. See Introduction, pp. xvi-xvii.

shoal waters of mid-century to safe harbor in the long Elizabethan peace. Middle-aged and older, they had had enough of extravagant causes and reckless adventures. They sought the prudent middle way, avoiding danger and even action wherever possible and cheerfully compromising high ideals for security and peace. They were not conscious of hypocrisy—only of common sense. Their motto was that which Lord Keeper Bacon caused to be inscribed over the door of his mansion at Gorhambury: *Mediocria firma.*[54] And they raised their children on the prudent but unexciting precept of Aristotle: "Virtues be found in things that have a mean between extremities, which are either too much or too little."[55] Moderation in all things was the watchword of the older generation.

For in the youth of Elizabeth and Burghley, the middle way had been the only safe road, a narrow, twisting path through a jungle of clashing ambitions and rival fanaticisms. For them, prudence and moderation were not an ethical choice so much as a practical necessity of life in their troubled world. But their children, born about the time Elizabeth ascended the throne, had not seen overweening ambition's inevitable end upon the scaffold, or passionate extremism consumed by the fires of Smithfield. To the aspiring minds of the younger generation, the middle way of their parents was the well-paved high road of safety and sloth. It was an uninspiring avenue where strolled portly, pusillanimous men too faint-hearted to hack their way through the wilderness to the golden mines of America or the gleaming walls of the New Jerusalem.

The young generation of 1560 vibrated with a new intensity, the new intensity of life and thought which produced the flowering of Elizabethan England. The burst of energy and creativity that filled the last two decades of the reign of Elizabeth was thus, at least in part, a generational phenomenon. This explosion of creative energies was, to begin with, the product of the extravagant passions and restless idealism natural to youth. But it was more than that: it was the result of the further intensifica-

54. Quoted in Sidney Lee, *DNB*, s.v. Bacon, Nicholas.
55. Aristotle, *Ethiques of . . .*, tr. John Wylkinson, quoted in Lily B. Campbell, *Shakespeare's Tragic Heroes, Slaves of Passion* (New York, 1961), p. 95; cf. pp. 95, 98, 101.

tion of this natural, passionate idealism by reaction against the cautious negativism and apparent hypocrisy of a spiritually burned-out older generation. This was the basic generational mechanism at work—the emotional and intellectual intensity of youth, heightened still further by a reaction against the abnormal prudence and conservatism of their elders. Only a psychologically burned-out generation like that of Elizabeth could have produced the extravagantly aspiring mind of the generation of Essex.

This rejection of the ideals of their fathers was given impetus and direction by general trends of thought in the sixteenth century and by the facts of life in Elizabethan England. It will be worthwhile, then, to review some of these intellectual tendencies, and to look more closely at these facts of Elizabethan life.

The general direction of sixteenth-century thought was away from the dogmas of the past. The men of genius who molded the mind of this early modern period may have sought guidance in the classical and biblical past; but they presented their contemporaries with a lengthening list of radical new ideas to digest. There were new arts, new literatures, new religions, a new world beyond the seas, and a new heaven above. Perhaps never before had men faced such rapid and radical changes in the intellectual climate; nor would they do so again until the late nineteenth and twentieth centuries—until our own time. Then as now, the process of digestion of so much novelty was not easy. "More than a century of 'innovators' had left thoughtful men . . . dizzy and bewildered, the traditionalists utterly confused. Authority and tradition in all fields of human thought and endeavor had . . . been challenged."[56] For the young Englishmen of the 1570's and '80's, this trend away from past ideologies revealed itself as the failure of the ideals of their forefathers. The consequence of this failure was a deeply felt need for a new set of values, a new code of conduct, in this strange new world.

The authorities to which scores of generations had turned for guidance, classical antiquity and the Christian church, had been tumbled from their lofty eminence by a troubled century of discovery, confusion, and conflict. This crumbling of ancient verities and established standards of course contributed some-

56. Hiram Haydn, Introduction to *The Portable Elizabethan Reader* (New York, 1955), pp. 4-5.

thing to the relapse of the generations of Elizabeth and Burghley into timid compromise and coolness towards grand causes. But the older Elizabethans did not feel the vacuum of ideals as their children did. They could not, because the primary effect of the collapse of authorities and values had been a numbing of the moral faculties, a psychological retreat to the standard of expediency which left them incapable of feeling their own lack of higher values. Furthermore, the older generation did not feel the normative and metaphysical vacuum for the paradoxical reason that, despite their lack of enthusiasm, they did retain a certain confidence in some standards. Protestantism and human- ism were the crusades of their youth, and many members of the older generation never lost faith in Cicero and Scripture. They hastened to compromise whenever controversy arose, but they kept enough of the faith to satisfy their attenuated emotional needs.

But the young generation of 1560 did not share their parents' advantages in dealing with the new world of the sixteenth century. For the younger generation, orthodox Protestantism was not a crusade, but a matter of lengthy catechisms in three languages. For them, the classics were no discovery, but a long purgatory over Lily's scholastic *Grammar*. And for many of them, the au- thority of both Christianity and the classics was too controversial, even too doubtful, to provide a psychologically satisfying basis for a system of values. During their formative years, the pulpit and the press seethed with religious controversy. As students, they saw the universities rocked by the Ramist assault on Aristotle, the master of those who knew. Under such conditions, it is hardly surprising that many young Elizabethans should grow up sorely confused and in need of new authorities. This need led the generation of 1560 along many strange paths of thought and feel- ing; in particular, it led them to the cult of high aspiration.

Equally important for the development of the aspiring mind, however, was the apparent hypocrisy and obvious irrelevance of their parents' Christian humanist code to their own young lives. How could Anthony and Francis Bacon take seriously their father's motto, *Mediocria firma*, when old Sir Nicholas himself had begun life as a sheep reeve's son and died Sir Nicholas Bacon,

K.G., P.C., Lord Keeper of the Great Seal of England?[57] How could Charles Blount take a lofty, disinterested view of material wealth when his own father had devoted most of his life and almost ruined himself and his family to possess it?[58] Even Robert Cecil's father, old Lord Burghley, whom many considered the real master of England, was a "new man" who had climbed high and fast under three sovereigns. Under such circumstances, the young future governors of England must have seen the sententious piety of moralists and preachers as naïve at best, hypocritical at worst.

And when these models of successful ambition sought to bar the progress of advancing young talent with hoary phrases about the evils of overweening ambition, the charge of hypocrisy was inevitable. This was not, of course, the sort of thing an aspiring courtier talked about in public, or left in writing for posterity to study.[59] On the rare occasions when they did commit their resentment to paper, it was usually in the form of some such oblique reference as Spenser's lines, probably about Lord Burghley:

> O grief of griefs, O gall of all good hearts,
> To see that virtue should despised be
> Of him, that first was raised for virtuous parts,
> And now broad spreading like an aged tree,
> Lets none shoot up, that nigh him planted be. . . .[60]

Nevertheless, the feeling of falseness and hypocrisy was surely there—the feeling that in later years Raleigh spat out in "The Lie":

> Tell men of high condition,
>   that manage the estate,
> Their purpose is ambition,
>   their practice only hate:

57. Lee, *DNB*, s.v., Bacon, Nicholas.

58. Cyril Falls, *Mountjoy: Elizabethan General* (London, 1955), pp. 17-19.

59. The inherent difficulty of gathering evidence about real attitudes and states of mind is not lessened by the prudent reticence of these Elizabethan courtiers. When they discussed important matters, including the progress of their ambitions, they frequently wrote each other in private codes. Important letters were probably often burned, as is indicated by the instructions to do so on some surviving letters. Most often the type of revealing discussion we are interested in was probably carried on orally and without witnesses.

60. Edmund Spenser, "The Ruines of Time," in *The Poetical Works of . . .*, ed. Ernest de Selincourt (Oxford, 1909-1910), I, 141.

> And if they once reply,
> then give them all the lie.[61]

The orthodox view of ambition, when expressed by such men as these, must have seemed a sham and a deception to the younger generation.

Most devastating of all, these aspiring sons of the Tudor aristocracy undoubtedly saw all this pious moralizing as utterly irrelevant to their own careers. These young men were the future governors of England, and they knew it. They were going to rise as fast and as high as they could, and all the threats and laments of Puritanical preachers and sententious Poloniuses were no more to them than the faintly irritating buzz of a bee somewhere out of doors. For the fact is that, despite the tremendous volume of sententious literature that issued from Elizabethan presses, the moralist remained a pathetically lonely figure among the hustling ruling class of England. He preached status quo to an exuberantly progressive nation; he extolled the virtues of a poverty-stricken, pray-and-bear-it culture to a jubilantly affluent society. Everything in the lives of these young gentlemen pointed one way: it is not surprising that they had short shrift for the sleeve-tugging moralizer who pointed the other.

These young courtiers were themselves being raised and trained to be successful men, to acquire wealth and power, prestige and honors. The "Ten Precepts" which old Lord Burghley provided for his son Robert Cecil are extremely revealing, coming as they do from a model of public probity:

Let the kindred and allies be welcome to thy house and table . . . and father them in all honest actions. For by this means . . . thou shalt find them so many advocates to plead . . . for thee. . . . Be sure to keep some great man thy friend, but trouble him not for trifles. Compliment him often with many, yet small, gifts, and of little charge. And if thou hast a cause to bestow any great gratuity, let it be something which may be daily in sight.[62]

This is not the morality of Seneca, nor the teaching of Scripture. These are practical maxims for the man who wants to get ahead

61. Walter Raleigh, "The Lie," in *The Poems of . . .*, ed. Agnes M. C. Latham (Cambridge, Mass., 1951), p. 45; cf. Walter Oakeshott, *The Queen and the Poet* (London, 1960), pp. 51-52.

62. Quoted in Algernon Cecil, *A Life of Robert Cecil First Earl of Salisbury* (London, 1915), pp. 10-11.

in a fiercely competitive world. Burghley himself made clear the reason for this advice to his son: "Otherwise," he concluded, "in this ambitious age, thou shalt remain like a hop without a pole, live in obscurity, and be made a football for every insulting companion to spurn at." And Robert Cecil surely knew that in the career that lay ahead of him, his father's practical advice would be far more valuable than the more idealistic but infinitely less practical precepts of that Cicero whose *Offices* the old man so admired. For the aspiring mind, many of the orthodox Christian and classical ethical standards, and most especially the orthodox condemnation of ambition, were simply irrelevant.

The alienation of the younger generation from their elders was thus a profound one. Young aspiring minds rejected the moral indoctrination to which they were subjected, and felt a deep-rooted dissatisfaction with the broader ideals of the older generation. But the generation of 1560 was essentially positive in outlook; they were not satisfied with merely rejecting old ways. Thus even while they progressively abandoned the standards of their fathers, they were searching for new values. And one of the values they discovered was the cult of high aspiration.

iv. The search for new values

The search for new values, like the renunciation of the old, was powered by the new intensity of thought and feeling which permeated the younger generation. But their search for values was the result of the new intensity operating in a different frame of reference, in the context of a world of almost unlimited possibilities. The new intensity, the new context, and the new values which resulted all deserve further examination.

The surging ardor and aggressiveness, the feverish new intensity of the Elizabethan younger generation have not been easy for less enthusiastic generations to appreciate, or even to understand. It is all too easy for the popular biographer to conceive of Raleigh and Essex and their fellows as "romantic" in some nineteenth-century sense. Even serious scholars have thrown up their hands and dismissed these incomprehensible young men as "children" playing at Knights and Saracens about the throne of a wise old queen. That the new intensity existed, however, there can be little doubt; something of its nature will come out in this and subsequent chapters.

The difference between the burned-out older generations and the ardent young generation of 1560 was clear even to contemporaries. Elizabethan England's best-selling preacher, silver-tongued Henry Smith, characterized the older generation as a race of exhausted old men, spiritually worn out. He lamented the survivors of the Reformation agony, the builders of Elizabethan England, "they that wear the furs and scarlets, as though they were all wisdom and gravity. . . ," declaring "that if there were any good thing to be done in these days, it is the young men that must do it; for the old men are out of date, their courage stoops like their shoulders, their zeal is withered like their brows. . . ."[63] Around the Council table the Queen and her white-bearded ministers faced the economic facts of life and fretted over the expenses; with the fleet outside Lisbon harbor, Sir Walter Raleigh shouted from a small boat, *"Entramos!"* and Essex, on the bridge, whooped for joy and flung his hat into the sea. This was the great difference: the older generation lived in a world of difficulties and dangers; the young men lived in a world of possibilities.

The generation of 1560 in fact grew up in a world of apparently unlimited possibilities. There was more wealth in Elizabethan England than ever before, and most of it went into the coffers of shrewd members of the ruling classes. "Never in the annals of the modern world," a great modern economist has said, "has there existed so prolonged and so rich an opportunity for the business man, the speculator, and the profiteer."[64] The land market had seldom been so busy, and agriculture generally prospered. Trade was expanding beyond the imagination of earlier times, extending by the end of the century even to Russia and the Levant, and beyond to the Far East and the New World. Even industry and mining were booming, for the country was in the grip of an industrial revolution that, in the course of Elizabeth's long reign and that of her successor, made England perhaps

63. Henry Smith, "The Young Man's Task," *Sermons*, pp. 228-229.
64. Lord Keynes, *Treatise on Money*, quoted in A. L. Rowse, *The England of Elizabeth* (New York, 1961), p. 109.

Europe's greatest industrial power.[65] Material wealth, the key to the honors and power the generation of 1560 sought so zealously, seemed to be there for the taking.

For those who aspired primarily to rank and political power, horizons were also apparently unlimited. The rank of gentleman was still comparatively easy of attainment in England throughout the second half of the century. The ascents to power of such spectacular giants of ambition as Wolsey, Cromwell, and even Burghley had mellowed over the years from the ruling-class nightmares they had been into inspiring success stories in the minds of the young.[66] In such times any ambitious country squire with a talent for affairs or for fighting could imagine himself as another Francis Walsingham or Francis Drake. And any man of spirit, born to rank or to even moderately good connections, would expect at the very least an important secretaryship or a company to command.

The possibilities seemed unlimited for such young men, the sometimes ungrateful beneficiaries of Elizabethan peace and prosperity. There were, for instance, the celebrated Abbot brothers. They were born sons of a clothworker of Guildford, yet George Abbot rose to the exalted estate of Archbishop of Canterbury, and his brother Maurice became Governor of the East India Company and Lord Mayor of London.[67] In an age when even the lower orders could rise so high through sheer talent and energy, the great expectations of young aristocrats and gentlemen, with their special training and family connections, are quite understandable. And did not the immediate results seem to justify such bright hopes for the future? Elizabeth was always ready with encouraging words where she could give nothing else; and the great court magnates, the patrons of youthful ambition, never discouraged a client. Robert Sidney's father was a very important man, and his splendid brother a great favorite of the Queen's. The Queen herself had promised, at their very first meeting, to do something for handsome young Charles Blount, saying warmly: "Fail you not to come to the Court, and I will bethink

65. John U. Nef, *Industry and Government in France and England, 1540-1640* (Ithaca, New York, 1957), p. 1.

66. Harvey, pp. 141, 192.

67. Sidney Lee, *DNB*, s.v. Abbot, George, and Abbot, Maurice.

myself how to do you good."[68] The Bacon brothers were Lord Burghley's nephews; Robert Cecil was his son; the impoverished Earl of Essex was Leicester's stepson. These young men were born and grew up close to the seat of power, the Queen's court, where honors and authority seemed available for the asking. In their gilded little world, no future was too incredible to be hoped for, no hope too extravagant to inspire action.

The possibilities, like the new intensity, extended into every sphere of life. No man knew, for instance, what wonderful kingdoms, new Perus and Mexicos, might still lie hidden in the unexplored depths of the New World. Some of these young aspiring minds were eager to find out: a contemporary wrote enthusiastically of Sir Humphrey Gilbert's voyage of 1583: ". . . whereby you may perceive that our long peace doth not breed in us all slothful and abject minds; but that this island is of too strait bounds to contain some of us here."[69] In another sphere of absorbing interest to many of this generation, the profoundest truths of religion seemed still open to a wide range of possible interpretations. The very keys of eternal life might be discovered in the depths of a man's own soul, or in the wisdom and incense of the ancient Roman church, or nowhere at all—so wide was the range of possibility.

There had not for hundreds of years been such a welter of intellectual activity as that which agitated the minds of the sixteenth century. For an understanding of the world he lived in, and of his own place in it, the educated Elizabethan did not turn with automatic reverence to the priest or to the scientist. The developing mind of the later sixteenth century had an astounding choice of competing schools of thought about everything of significance. He could pick up in the book stalls in Paul's Yard books by eminent contemporary exponents of a dozen or more living philosophies.[70] There were modern Platonists, Aristotelians,

68. Robert Naunton, *Fragmenta Regalia*, ed. Edward Arber (London, 1870), p. 57.

69. Mr. Faunt to Anthony Bacon, May 6, 1583, in Thomas Birch, ed., *Memoirs of the Reign of Queen Elizabeth . . .* (London, 1754), I, 34; cf. Anthony Esler, "Influence of Social and Cultural Developments and of Traditional Geography on Elizabethan Concepts of the Nature of the American Indian," unpublished M.A. thesis, Duke University, 1958, pp. 142-153.

70. Cf. John O. Riedl, *et al.*, *A Catalogue of Renaissance Philosophers (1350-1650)* (Milwaukee, 1940).

Stoics, Epicureans, and skeptics, to mention only the best represented of the ancient schools. For those with a Catholic bent, there were Thomists and Scotists and the new Jesuit thinkers. For those who sought the truth within themselves, there were mystics, both Protestant and Catholic. There were, of course, humanists and reformers of many types and tendencies. There were exotic "natural philosophers" of various sorts, including astronomers, astrologers, alchemists, and students of the Cabala. And there were those startling individuals which the age produced so prolifically, thinkers whose views were so new that they had as yet no label, from Machiavelli to Montaigne. In literature too—perhaps the most important of the courtly avocations—there were new directions and a multitude of possibilities. The accumulated techniques and insights of ancient and modern times were at the disposal of a generation with a humanistic education in Latin and Greek and a courtly knowledge of Italian and French. They could seek inspiration in Senecan themes and Petrarchan conceits, in the metrics of Vergil and the plots of Belleforest. Into this world of almost infinite possibility, then, the generation of 1560 adventured in search of new authorities and new values.

The restless search for novelty, for something new in every field from sartorial elegance to literature and religion, is well testified to. In the first place, there is the very fact that the age was so energetic in denouncing innovation. The very "practice of listing . . . the men who had upset the universal applecart," to which Elizabethans were so addicted, indicates clear consciousness of the impact of the innovators.[71] But this newness was a fact of life as well as of thought; and rapidly changing ways of living helped to orient men's minds toward the need for a new code of conduct. Toward the end of the sixteenth century, country gentry flocked to the excitement of metropolitan London, to the new theaters, the new luxury goods, to the busy law courts, and to the glittering court of the Queen. Carriages began to replace sedan chairs in the streets of the city, and so rapid was the change that "an infinite number of coaches" owned by English gentlemen

71. Haydn, p. 5.

were available to welcome the new sovereign in 1603.[72] The dangerous practice of dueling became more popular among courtiers, despite the alarmed objections of the older generation. Young men took to smoking tobacco, an exotic vice imported from the New World and much affected by radical thinkers like Sir Walter Raleigh. From the repeated denunciations of innovation, and from direct evidence of the rapidity of social change, something may be deduced of the breadth and depth of the Elizabethan quest for novelty, and of the effect these changes must have had on the intellectual development of the younger generation.

There is, moreover, some direct testimony to the passion for new ideas and novel attitudes which swept the generation of 1560. As early as 1570, Ascham condemned the "quick wits" among his students who were "carried to desire every new thing. . . ."[73] At Cambridge in the 1580's Gabriel Harvey noted the prevailing passion for "news, new books, new fashions, new laws . . . and some after new elements, and some after new heavens and hells too."[74] And an observer in 1603 wrote:

The first question at every stationer's shop is, What new thing? and if it smell of the press, and have a goodly title (be the matter never so base and unprofitable) it is a book for the nonce; but be it never so good, if once the Calendar be changed, that it bear the date of the former year, it is never inquired after. . . .[75]

Among the most significant results were youthful trends towards extremism in religion and the development of a new literary taste and of a new literature by members of the generation of 1560. The quest for new philosophical authorities brought forth a variety of responses from such thoughtful writers of this generation as Samuel Daniel, Fulke Greville, and George Chapman.[76] Here, however, we are concerned only with the new

72. Lady Anne Clifford, *The Diary of* . . ., ed. V. Sackville-West (New York, 1923), pp. 8-9.
73. Ascham, p. 16.
74. Gabriel Harvey to Edmund Spenser, quoted in Haydn, pp. 2-3; cf. Gabriel Harvey, *Letterbook of* . . ., ed. E. J. L. Scott (Camden Soc. Pub., new series, Vol. XXXIII; Westminster, 1884), *passim*.
75. T. Jackson, *David's Pastoral Poem*, quoted in Alan Fager Herr, *The Elizabethan Sermon* . . . (Philadelphia, 1940), p. 71.
76. Cf. Douglas Bush, *Themes and Variations in English Poetry of the Renaissance* (Claremont, Calif., 1957), pp. 38-41.

secular code of conduct which the younger generation adopted to replace the unrealistic imperatives of the orthodox ethics they had been taught.

The code of the Elizabethan younger generation was new in spite of the obvious fact that most of its principles were neither new nor original. In the first place, this courtly ethic was a recombination and an elaboration of a number of old or borrowed notions of aristocratic conduct, and thus represented, in a real sense, a new creation. In the second place, this code was permeated by the peculiar new intensity of this young generation of courtiers. As a mixture of old and borrowed principles, it was a ramshackle affair; to the extent that it depended on the special emotional intensity of a particular generation, it was unique. It is not surprising that only portions of this system of values and mores survived even into the next century.

The code of the Elizabethan younger generation was a bizarre and exotic affair, a thing of rags and patches collected from many times and lands. There were, for instance, elements of Italian courtesy—in the primary sense of courtiership—imported directly from the trans-Alpine city-states where the new age had first taken shape. In striking contrast, there was a romantic revival of chivalry that brought back some of the gaudier aspects of the Gothic world for a final flowering in the tiltyards of Elizabethan England. There was also an important element of patriotism in this patchwork code, and a good deal of secular humanism. The perfect courtier of the generation of 1560 thus possessed Italian manners and knightly skills; he was a lover in the traditions of Petrarch and the Court of Love; he hated his country's enemies and eagerly served his Queen; he was an educated man and a poet, or at least a patron of poets.

But the typical young courtier of this generation was more than all this: he was an aspiring mind, and that of a new and unique sort. Perhaps the most important element of the new code of conduct—though certainly the least clearly articulated aspect of it—was this pervasive Marlovian style of high aspiration. It is to the Marlovian mood that we must turn next.

v. The religion of high aspiration

The ideal young Elizabethan courtier was an ambitious man, but the quality of the soaring passion for honor and power that consumed him differed subtly but vitally from the ambition of his father. To define this difference will occupy most of the following chapters. To begin with, however, two quotations from the private jottings of Gabriel Harvey will perhaps serve as the best possible introduction to the Marlovian aspiring mind:

An iron body; a silver mind; a golden fortune; a heavenly felicity upon earth. But ever excell more and more. . . .

A perfect disposer and dispatcher of private occasions; a bold solicitor of public persons; a resolute practitioner in judicial or extra-judicial causes. *Ad omnia Quare, resolute et prudenter.* In all attempts, enterprises, actions, negotiations, affairs, adventures, practices, whereinsoever you may happen to be employed more or less, contrive for life to dispatch and perform it most excellently: the sooner to grow and shoot up higher and higher.[77]

This was the sum and substance of Marlovian aspiration: "ever excell more and more . . . the sooner to grow and shoot up higher and higher." The passionate intensity of this thirst for success made the ambitions of their fathers seem tame and pallid by comparison—and contrasted sharply with the timid conservatism of their parents' later years.

The Marlovian mood of high aspiration was thus in no sense the *Zeitgeist* of Elizabethan England: it was, for a number of years, the mood of a generation. Both before and after the Armada, the dominant older generation feared the worst and prudently counted the charges of every project that youth could conceive. But for a time, in the 1580's and the '90's, the younger generation was possessed by a new, only vaguely articulated configuration of ideas and emotions which may be accurately characterized as a Marlovian mood of high aspiration. High aspiration it surely was— these young men aspired for the moon and more; Marlovian, be-

77. Harvey, *Marginalia*, pp. 196, 156.

cause no member of this generation expressed their aspirations better than Kit Marlowe.

This new mood remained partially submerged throughout the period of its dominance; it was far too subversive for public or even private expression. The orthodox view of ambition continued to dominate all serious thought on the subject, and even to appear as a commonplace in the elegant writings of the poets and pamphleteers of the younger generation. But even a cursory examination of the careers of the leading courtiers of the generation of 1560 reveals a very different attitude toward worldly aspiration. And a closer comparison of their deeds and their words—as well as of the more characteristic works of the writers of their generation—provides convincing evidence that these young men had indeed formulated a new view of ambition.

The nature of the new view was determined to a considerable extent by the nature of its origins. The new attitude toward ambition began with a complete acceptance of the actual goals of the older generation—economic, political, and social advancement. Like their fathers and grandfathers, these younger Elizabethans aspired to possess a multitude of specific benefits available to their class and time. They lusted after public dignities and popular acclaim. They schemed to acquire offices in the royal household or in the government at large. And they sweated to win the financial rewards that were the *sine qua non* of any sort of advancement at all in Elizabeth's England. Honor, power, and wealth—these were the primary objects of the worldly ambitions of older and younger generations alike. But in the minds of this gilded youth, born to prosperity, the last of these goals became, perhaps more than for their predecessors, merely a means to other ends. A perceptive contemporary observer thus summarized the true objects of these ambitious courtiers: "their thoughts, actions, endeavors are all for sovereignty and honor."[78] Wealth was surely important, but the gold itself flowed like quicksilver through their fingers, lavishly expended on matters of honor or sources of power. Reputation and dominion— these were the ultimate objectives of the aspiring minds of the young generation of 1560.

78. Robert Burton, *The Anatomy of Melancholy* (New York, 1924), p. 186.

The younger generation thus rejected the orthodox condemnation of ambition in practice, just as their fathers had done
in their day. But the generation of 1560 went further: the pursuit of these worldly ends was infused with the ardent idealism
of their youth and the expansive outlook of their generation.
Their new intensity elevated the quest for worldly advancement
to a plane of high idealism. Their sense of the infinite possibilities of their world enlarged the scope of their ambitions till
they came to encompass the most extravagant projects conceivable.

These two fundamental enlargements of the worldly ambitions of their predecessors took concrete form in the 1580's
and '90's, and affected both of the primary goals they had inherited from their elders. Their youthful idealism was channeled
mainly into a veritable cult of honor, an unquenchable thirst
for reputation and acclaim which blossomed forth particularly
with the coming of the Spanish War in the middle of the 1580's.
The feeling of infinite possibility opening up revealed itself
primarily in an uncontrolled and sometimes unlimited lust for
dominion and sovereignty, a passion for power which was stimu-
lated by the frustrations of the 1590's, the political bottleneck
years of the reign. Aspirations for honor and power were thus
elevated to unparalleled levels of intensity and extravagance by
the new idealism and the feeling of infinite possibility which
possessed these young men.

These basic aspects of the aspiring mind will be examined
in detail in later chapters. Here, however, it remains to point
out the essentially religious quality of the high aspiration of these
young courtiers, for only by appreciating this quality can we
adequately explain the passionate intensity of their quest for
honor, or the extravagant sense of infinite possibility behind their
lust for power.

The Marlovian mood of high aspiration may be seen as an
early attempt at formulating a secular religion, following the
faith-destroying cataclysm of the Reformation. The three decades
preceding 1560, the years of the youth of the Elizabethan older
generations, had seen no less than four sweeping changes in the
allegedly eternal religion of Christian England. As a result,
several generations of the English ruling class were left with a

sadly attenuated, definitely cool, even expedient attitude toward Christianity. The generations of Elizabeth and Burghley certainly accepted the fundamental dogmas of salvation through Christ, and tried to pass them on to their children. But they did so without enthusiasm, without passion, and above all, without stressing the relevance of these dogmas to the practical and emotional lives of young courtiers. A psychological void was left in the younger generation by this thinning out of the emotional and the practical content of religion. To fill this void, these young men turned to what were all too obviously the real goals of their fathers' lives—honors, political power, and the wealth necessary to attain them. These goals became imbued with some of the emotional and idealistic overtones of the religion that was denied them.

Many young men feel such a psychological need for high ideals. In Counter-Reformation Europe religion was the primary orthodox channel for idealism; hence what the Elizabethan younger generation sought was a new religion. They sought an emotionally satisfying set of ideals; in their society, the great institutionalized idealism was the Christian religion; it was, quite naturally, on this religious form of idealism that their own code was modeled. There was, after all, no other model of comparable prestige and pervasiveness available to them. The generation of 1560 sought a substitute religion—and found it in high worldly aspiration.

Growing up in the burned-out *politique* world of the Elizabethan aristocracy, these young men developed their own faith to live by. The god of the aspiring mind was, evidently, himself; it was each man's capacity for stupendous accomplishment— in short, human power. His ethic was his own courtier's code of values, with all its grandiose trappings and idealistic overtones, of which the most important was what he called his honor. But in this secular religion, both human honor and human power were raised to the level of the superhuman. These young men lived like gods in the paradise of Elizabeth's court, while the poets of their own generation hymned their praises in extravagant eulogies. They actually lived by their own fantastic code of honor; they attempted prodigious deeds; no goal was too high for their soaring aspiration. And when they failed to achieve the impossible, the angels fell again: in the private mythology of this generation, Essex was Lucifer.

The Marlovian mood of high aspiration may, then, be considered as a secular religion. The critical reader, however, may well snort at the comparison. Did not these younger Elizabethans remain at least as good Christians as their parents, as the average Christian of any age? Were they not simply spoiled, self-centered young men with a highly artificial code of conduct? Why, then, should we gratuitously label their self-centeredness a "god," their artificial code a "religious" creed?

As to the first objection: it is probably true that most of the courtiers of the younger generation sincerely believed in much of the Christianity of their time. But the fact seems to be—to risk an important generalization—that polytheism has been the rule rather than the exception in human societies. Throughout history, men have worshiped the most fantastic combinations of natural phenomena, gods and demons, saints, heroes, and romantic characters. Nor is this the wilful perversion of the term "worship" that it may seem. The experience of worship differs from one culture to another, from one social class to another, even from one individual to another: its aspects and nuances are almost as various as the objects of its adoration. A religious Roman, for example, could worship simultaneously a number of divinities, including the Stoic World-Soul, the genius of the emperor, his own ancestors and personal household gods, as well as Zeus Pater and the official Olympians. A medieval peasant could focus his religious adoration on God the Father, on Christ the Saviour and Christ the Judge, on the merciful Virgin Mary, and on an indefinite number of angels and saints of particular personal or local interest—and still not forget to leave a bowl in the stable for the Good Folk. In the same way, the younger Elizabethans remained good Christians, at least by their own lights, while channeling considerable religious feeling into high worldly aspiration.

The comparison becomes perhaps more compelling when we remember that Elizabethan England was, even in a material sense, a religiously impoverished nation. The English had lost their

Pope, their saints, their ubiquitous monks and friars; and that at the very time when the Counter-Reformation was successfully re-emphasizing these objects of reverence in Catholic Europe. Not only were the objects of Christian worship fewer in England, but those that remained may well have lost a good bit of their appeal as a result of the eminently practical Elizabethan Settlement. The attempt of the older generation to stress morality while manipulating metaphysics in the interests of expediency surely helped to weaken the appeal of Christian worship for idealistic young people.

Some of this baffled religious instinct was successfully directed into the worship of the Virgin Queen by the older generations. The young courtiers no doubt poured some of their religious feeling into the erotic idealism of courtly love in the Petrarchan and "Platonic" traditions. Some religious passion perhaps spilled over into aesthetic expression in the music and poetry of the age. Some, of course, went into the Puritan upsurge and the Catholic revival. And some, I believe, found an outlet in the secular religion of high aspiration.

As for the second fundamental objection: these were indeed self-centered young men, and theirs was certainly a highly artificial code of conduct—but there is more to their high aspiration than that. Self-centeredness among such a *jeunesse dorée* is certainly not rare in history; but few generations have produced so many colorful megalomaniacs as this one did. Granted that theirs was an artificial, unrealistic code, yet it found young martyrs in plenty, willing to bankrupt themselves and even to die in adherence to its values. In short, it is the very intensity and extravagance of the cult of high aspiration that elevates it from a mere matter of self-centered youth and artificial mores to the level of a secular religion. While dedicated Jesuits risked any danger and scoured the far places of the earth in the consecrated service of God and the Pope, young Elizabethan courtiers ran the same risks and traveled as far in the service of their own egos.

It is, after all, this very quality, the amazing intensity and fantastic extravagance of Elizabethan aspiration, which rings so strangely on the modern ear. Their gorgeous costumes, the yards of costly materials, the grotesque padding and slashing, the prodigal use of lace and jewelry, cosmetics and perfume; their strutting and parading, the swarms of liveried attendants, the drums and trumpets, the sweeping bows and doffing of hats, the pompous ceremonial and Byzantine ceremoniousness of phrase— these are not merely the ways of another time, they are the trappings of another world than ours. Surely the exotic picture makes more sense if we assume that these young men were lavishing upon themselves much of the religious ardor that the continental Counter-Reformation poured into churches, saints, and sumptuous religious ceremonial.

More importantly, the bizarre combination of incredible idealism and ruthless egotism revealed by the behavior of these young Elizabethans baffles us. The gallantry and lofty idealism of the conventions of courtly love contrast strangely with the fierce, ruthless competition for place and power in the dog-eat-dog world of court politics. The chivalric gestures and reckless heroism of Elizabethans at war does not sit well with the thirst for gold that drove these same Elizabethans to church-looting and brutality. But the paradoxical behavior of religious fanatics in many ages—not least among them the sixteenth century—offers clarifying parallels, if we will but admit them.

An analogy is not an explanation—though on this point an educated Elizabethan would surely disagree with us. But at least the conception of a "religion of high aspiration" among young Elizabethan courtiers gives us another, and more likely, explanation for their behavior than the theory that they were just "children" at heart. And more detailed explanations for some aspects of this secular religion will be forthcoming in later chapters.

In rough outline, then, this was the aspiring mind of the generation of 1560 as it had developed by the middle 1580's. These young gentlemen were reared as future governors of England; they knew, or believed, themselves to be men of parts; it was quite natural for them to take the first steps up the ladder of success their fathers had climbed before them. At the same time, growing up in a world of crumbling loyalties and dying traditions, they rejected the orthodox view of ambition internally as well as externally, in theory as well as in practice. Following their own ardent natures in a changing world which to them was a world of endless possibilities, they evolved a code of conduct for themselves, at the heart of which lay a secular religion of high aspiration. The devotees of this cult of ambition were a special breed. For this was a generation of Phoenixes—of men born at a uniquely propitious time, unique in the extravagance of their high aspirations, hailed by the poets as the only Phoenixes of their age. The basic goals of these Marlovian aspiring minds were honor and power, reputation and dominion. It is with these two elements that we shall deal primarily in the following chapters, in which is traced the career of the generation of 1560 in the Spanish War and the political bottleneck years.

IV. *The bubble reputation*

The Spanish War, beginning with the English intervention in the Netherlands in 1585, was the first watershed in the careers of the aspiring generation of 1560. In responding to the opportunities for quick gain and rapid advancement opened up by the war, the younger generation particularly displayed one of the key qualities of the aspiring mind—a consuming passion for "honor." The intensity of this passion as revealed under the pressure of war, and its origins, nature, and consequences form the subject of this chapter. Again, it will be useful to begin with a case history, an account of the experiences of an Elizabethan gentleman in the early years of the war with Spain. There could be no better example of the Elizabethan cavalier in search of honor in the wars than Robert Devereux, the dashing young Earl of Essex.

i. An Elizabethan cavalier at the Spanish War:
the Earl of Essex

For clues to the character of this strange man, we should glance briefly at his childhood and upbringing. The famous Earl of Essex was apparently a quiet, studious, even shy little boy. Like many of this generation of the ruling class, Robert Devereux came from what we would probably call a broken home. Walter Devereux, the gallant first Earl of Essex, died young in 1576, leaving his title—and little else—to his nine-year-old son. The boy's mother soon remarried, taking as her second husband the Earl of Leicester, the Queen's aging, portly favorite. Robert apparently never liked his stepfather: he rejected Leicester's advice on his career; and he seems to have rejected also the latter's comparative moderation in the pursuit of high honors.[1] One who knew Essex wrote that he was always bitterly jealous of his high place, adding significantly that "herein likewise as in the rest [he

---

1. G. B. Harrison, *The Life and Death of Robert Devereux, Earl of Essex* (New York, 1937), p. 7; Henry Wotton, *A Parallell between Robert Late Earle of Essex, and George Late Duke of Buckingham* (London, 1641), p. 9.

was] no good Pupil to my Lord of Leicester, who was wont to put all his passions in his pocket."[2] Young Essex probably had nothing but contempt for the prudence and moderation of the older generation.

He was fond of scholarship and literature in his youth, and he seems to have been well brought up by Elizabethan standards. He was described as "very courteous and modest, rather disposed to hear than to answer . . . very comely and bashful."[3] Then in 1584, at the age of seventeen, Essex was finally prevailed upon to present himself at court. There his good looks and his attractive personality made a great impression, particularly on the Queen. In a matter of months he found himself one of Elizabeth's greatest favorites, and as such the admired of all her courtiers. It is no wonder this young man, still in his teens, came so extravagantly to life at this first taste of the adulation he was to command for more than a decade. His passion for public honors and popular esteem probably goes back to these early years at court, when his words and deeds were suddenly heeded and praised by all beholders.

During the mid-1580's, while he rose rapidly in royal favor, he also cultivated the chivalric skills and the intense sensitivity to personal honor which were to play such a vital role in his subsequent career. He became an adept and celebrated tilter, one of the best of Elizabeth's practitioners of the courtly sport.[4] His skill with weapons would prove essential to the military adventures by which he won his first and most enduring public distinction.

Then in 1585 came the Spanish War, and with it a golden opportunity for the Elizabethan younger generation to win chivalric honor in plenty. Essex responded as eagerly as any to the challenge of the war; he fought in the Netherlands, in Portugal, in France, in Spain. For most of the next decade, his primary serious concern was with military strategy and chivalric exploits —mostly the latter. The Earl's military career was summarized after his death by the soldier-poet Robert Pricket in a verse biography,

2. Wotton, p. 9.
3. Edward Waterhouse to Lord Burghley, Nov., 1576, in Walter Bourchier Devereux, *Lives and Letters of the Devereux, Earls of Essex* (London, 1853), I, 166.
4. Ray Heffner, "Essex, the Ideal Courtier," *ELH*, I (1934), 11-12.

Honor's Fame in Triumph Riding.[5] The key word was "honor," the first word of the title and the most frequently used word of significance in the text. In this soldier's interpretation, the key to Essex's whole career lay in his life-long quest for honor. As Pricket used the term, honor meant fame and glory—the approbation of the public and of posterity. Essex's career was seen as a long march to glory. In the Netherlands

> Brave troops of horse be bravely led,
> And thus at first his fame was spread.

In Portugal

> How did his deeds his praise to heaven exhale!
> His honor's worth you sacred Muses sing.

In France

> French King and Peers did signify
> This Peerless warrior's Chivalry.

In Spain,

> Let [Cadiz] tell forth the honor of his deeds
>
> .   .   .   .
>
> As dateless time shall speak his fame,
> And blaze the honor of his name.[6]

It was for this that Essex enthusiastically took up arms in 1585— for the praises of his Queen and of his peers, and for "the honor of his name." To understand the forms and intensity of this aspiration for honor which Essex shared with so many of his generation, it will be helpful to trace the earlier adventures of this type of the Elizabethan cavalier at the Spanish War.

Essex went to the Low Countries in 1585, not only to serve his Queen, but to serve with honor, and in a style befitting his dignity. He was to be General of the Horse under his stepfather, the Earl of Leicester, and he was determined to be equipped and followed in a manner becoming his rank and nobility. He spent £1,000 to outfit a private company of horse to follow him, an unnecessary expense that only put him deeper in debt than his

5. Reprinted in *Honors Fame In Triumph Riding (1604)* [and] *A True Coppie of a Discourse written by a Gentleman, employed in the late Voyage of Spaine and Portingale . . . 1589*, ed. Alexander B. Grosart (Manchester, 1881), pp. 1-33.
6. *Ibid.*, pp. 8-9.

courtier's life had got him already. His grandfather, old Sir Francis Knollys, wrung his hands at what was to him a pointless extravagance, but for Essex this was an obvious necessity: his "private followers . . . must be handsomely equipped for nobility's sake. . . ."[7] His honorable reputation as a nobleman demanded this medieval extravagance, a personal following of gorgeously caparisoned men at arms.

Essex's introduction to the wars, and that of a whole generation of cavaliers, was nothing if not glorious; unfortunately, it was also utterly unrealistic. The first month after the landing of the English expeditionary force in the Netherlands was given over to a sort of "royal progress" through the chief cities of the United Provinces.[8] Leicester and his glittering corps of officers were hailed in every town as conquering heroes, with allegorical pageantry and artillery salutes and cheering crowds. On St. George's Day there was a gala tournament at Utrecht, at which "the Earl of Essex behaved himself so valiantly, that he gave all men great hope of his noble prowess in arms."[9] But the fighting was all in fun: nobody suffered more than a bruise or two, there was equal praise for all contestants, and afterwards "there was a sumptuous banquet prepared with sugar meats for the men of arms and the Ladies. . . ."

Then, as the spring of 1586 came on, brute reality began to intrude upon the festivities. The Prince of Parma moved in the spring and suddenly startled the allies out of their celebrations by capturing the Dutch stronghold of Grave. Meanwhile, the English troops were pushed to the verge of starvation for lack of pay, and their captains fell to bickering among themselves. At the same time the young English gentlemen began to see some actual service and to learn that war could be real and sometimes fatal.

The most sensational skirmish—it could hardly qualify as a battle—was the fight at Zutphen on a misty day in September, 1586, an action which Leicester enthusiastically described as "the most notable encounter that hath been in our age."[10] Essex,

7. Sir Francis Knollys to the Earl of Essex, Nov. 14, 1585, in Devereux, I, 178-179; Harrison, p. 9.
8. Harrison, p. 11.
9. John Stowe, *The annales of England . . .* ([London], 1592), p. 1215.
10. John Bruce, ed., *Correspondence of Robert Dudley, Earl of Leicester . . . in the Years 1585 and 1586* (Camden Soc. Pub. Vol. XXVII; London, 1844), p. 416.

Lord Willoughby, Sir Philip Sidney, Sir John Norris, and many other heroes of the Elizabethan younger generation were in the thick of the hand-to-hand fighting that developed around an English ambuscade of a Spanish supply train. According to a contemporary historian, Essex flung himself joyously into the fray, avid for honor. " 'For the honor of England,' " he shouted, " 'my fellows, follow me!' and with that he threw his lance in rest, and overthrew the first man, and with his curtle axe so behaved himself, that it was wonder."[11] It was a glorious day, and Essex was made a knight banneret for his impetuous heroism.

But it was a tragic day, too, for it saw Sir Philip Sidney's last gallant gesture—a piece of chivalric derring-do as brave as it was foolish. Sir William Pelham, the marshal, was unable to wear his thigh armor into battle because of a recent wound; Sir Philip Sidney, that no man's courage might be greater than his own, chivalrously cast aside his own thigh pieces.[12] The fatal musket ball struck Sidney in the thigh, shattering the bone, and leaving him three weeks of intense pain before he died. His generation was shocked by the tragedy of his death—but not by the folly of such honorable recklessness as that which killed him. Essex was in all probability much less moved by the spectacle of his comrade's painful death than by the fact that Sir Philip bequeathed to the "much honored Lord, the Earl of Essex, my best sword."[13] "To one of Essex's temperament," says his best modern biographer, "no relic could have been holier or more symbolic."[14]

This, then, was the Earl of Essex's first encounter with the Spanish War. Harrison has pinpointed the significance of the Earl's adventures in the Low Countries: "In his most impressionable years"—he was not yet twenty—"he was infected with the romance of war. . . ."[15] For him, as for many of the young gentlemen of the generation of 1560, "the soldier's profession" became "a religion, older than the oldest, with its own code, ritual, and ecstasies." The glamour of the military profession was to beguile Essex and his generation for years to come.

11. Stow, p. 1252. 12. Harrison, p. 20.
13. Will of Sir Philip Sidney, in Arthur Collins, ed., *Letters and Memorials of State in the Reigns of Queen Mary, Queen Elizabeth, King James . . .* (London, 1746), I, 112.
14. Harrison, p. 21. 15. *Ibid.*, p. 331, note to p. 21.

Essex found opportunities in plenty to feed his boundless appetite for honor on the great Portugal expedition of 1589. It was, as Pricket judged, his "forwardest" service; and it revealed clearly "how infinitely a romantic spirit of knight-errantry surpassed all other passions in his breast. . . ."[16] The very fact that he joined the expedition at all revealed his willingness to risk all else for military honor; for he went against the express commandment of the Queen. Wotton summed up the boldness of Essex's decision: "all his hopes of advancement had like to be strangled almost in the very Cradle, by throwing himself into the Portugal Voyage without the Queen's consent . . . whereby he left his friends and dependants near six months in desperate suspense what would become of him."[17] But though his already considerable power at court might have been lost at a stroke, Essex seems to have been too ardent in his quest for honor to care.

While his dependants agonized over his political future at home, Essex stormed ashore in Portugal, leading the troops in under the guns of Peniche. With his usual impetuosity, he seized the honor of being literally the first man ashore, leaping into the breakers and wading in shoulder-high through roaring seas that drowned a score of lesser men.[18] Throughout the campaign, until the Queen's peremptory order summoned him home, Essex conducted himself with notable courage and impeccable form. Standing before the walls of Lisbon, he drove his pike into the city gates and shouted a chivalrous challenge, daring any Spaniard of rank to meet him in single combat for the honor of his mistress.[19] During the English withdrawal from the siege of the city, when General Sir John Norris—also of the younger generation —sent a final challenge to the Spanish commander to meet the English army in a pitched battle, Essex, "preferring the honor of the cause . . . before his own safety, sent a particular cartel, offering himself against any of theirs, if they had any of his quality. . . ."[20] Even an ordinary ambuscade was not undertaken primarily as a tactical move, with some military advantage in view, but as a chivalric exploit that might secure honor for the

16. Devereux, I, 194. 17. Wotton, p. 3.
18. Devereux, I, 202.
19. Heffner, "Essex, the Ideal Courtier," 12-13.
20. *A True Coppie of a Discourse* . . ., in Pricket, *Honors Fame*, p. 84.

Earl of Essex. And Essex did indeed return to England with a full measure of military renown. His disobedience had not seriously damaged his high place in royal favor, and his heroic deeds in Portugal were widely celebrated in print.

Then came the French intervention, opening up still more new fields for a knight in search of chivalric honor. Essex was an enthusiastic admirer of Henry IV, the renowned "white plume" of Navarre, and had been a passionate advocate of aid for the French King. Naturally, Essex hoped for a command on this enterprise; and in the end, he had his way. The command of the first English expeditionary force, which was sent to Brittany, went to Sir John Norris, another ambitious—and more experienced— champion of the younger generation. But when a second, smaller force was sent to Normandy, it was given to Essex, his first independent command. He sailed for France full of confidence and high hopes that "your Majesty shall presently have great honor by the service of your little troop. . . ."[21]

As in the Low Countries five years earlier, the English military operations left time for a good deal of chivalric pageantry, pomp, and circumstance. The French Huguenots were astonished and not a little amused at the English knights, "armed and costumed like the antique figures shown on old tapestries, with coats of mail and iron helmets . . . going into battle to the sound of bagpipes and trumpets."[22] The young gentlemen wandered about the country like knights errant in search of adventure; and there was many a chivalrous exchange between the young Earl and the King of France and Navarre.

There was also some fighting against the troops of the Catholic League, in which prodigies of valor were performed. The official objective of the expedition was to help with the siege of Rouen, a stronghold of the League which was believed to be the key to Normandy. But this strategic goal does not appear to have concerned these young heroes half as much as their personal honor. The English contribution to the siege developed, not as a military campaign with a specific objective, but as a long

21. Essex to Queen Elizabeth, July, 1591, quoted in Devereux, I, 219.
22. Duc d'Angoulême, *Mémoires*, Oct. 1, 1589, in Georges Ascoli, *La Grande-Bretagne devant l'opinion française depuis la Guerre des Cent Ans jusqu'à la fin du XVIe siècle* (Paris, 1927), p. 175.

series of chivalric exploits in which honor was won and lost by both sides. Describing a good day's fighting before Rouen, Essex typically stressed the personal heroism of individual young officers, discussed the capture of an enemy redoubt as a point of honor, considered a victory won if the enemy was duly disgraced on the field, and mentioned the tactical significance of the day's skirmishing almost as an afterthought.[23] The whole siege, as Essex saw it, had much of the air of the tiltyard about it. And in fact, combat casualties do not seem to have been high: the hot day's skirmishing described above cost no more than half a dozen lives.

Essex seemed to imagine that war, like tilting or dueling, was essentially a sport in which the contestants won or lost honor, depending on their skill and courage. In this, he shared the view of his generation, a view expressed also by other young gentlemen on this expedition. An enemy attack was thus described by a typical young gallant of Essex's command: the enemy sallied forth from Rouen, and, having "shown their worth and valor in all other places," against the troops of Henry IV, presently assaulted the English position. "We were ready to entertain them," continued Robert Carey, "and we held skirmish at the least two hours, and after some killed and hurt on both sides, they fairly retired into the town, and we to our lodging; and so ended that day's sport."[24] Sir Thomas Coningsby exulted in such spectacles and agreed with his fellows that war was grand sport: "It was a most pleasing day to see horse and foot together by the ears on both sides," and to win "great honor" for an exploit which also —almost incidentally—had some real tactical significance.[25]

Essex himself was often to be found in the front ranks, indulging in casually extravagant heroics that would have done a D'Artagnan or a Cyrano proud. Thus, on one occasion, the Lord General of the English force stood "within three pikes of th' enemy's guard, where they have continual shooting," to exchange courtly compliments with one Chevalier Picard, who had once been Essex's guest in England, but now fought on the Catholic

23. Essex to Burghley, Nov. 3, 1591, in Devereux, I, 256-260.
24. *Memoirs of the Life of Robert Cary* . . . (London, 1759), p. 45.
25. Thomas Coningsby, *Journal of the Siege of Rouen, 1591* (Camden Soc. Pub. Vol. XXXIX; London, 1847), pp. 32-33.

side.[26] In this dangerous spot "there passed many fair speeches between them" while "the bullets went apace the mean time" and men fell dead at the Earl's side. This was the sort of performance, combining real courage with courtly grace, that brought honor to an Elizabethan gentleman at the wars. The prudent, practical older generation obstinately failed to understand this. Elizabeth was horrified that her favorite and her general should risk his life "like a common soldier," and the Lords of Council wrote strictly forbidding Essex "for respect of any vain glory, to put in danger *your own person* . . . by any other exploit there. . . ."[27]

Essex's lamentations and pleas when the Queen at length ordered him home made it quite clear that his main concern was rather for his own honor than for the capture of Rouen. He claimed to believe the city would soon be taken, but had no illusions that the tiny English force that remained was indispensable to this strategic victory. What the young Earl wanted, and wanted desperately, was to be in on the final struggle, in order to reap his share of the honor that would surely be won. "If Her Majesty would now revoke me with disgrace, when Rouen were to be won," he wrote in great distress, "I would humbly beseech her that she would take from me my life, and not my poor reputation. . . ."[28] Before obeying the royal commandment, furthermore, Essex made one last bid for special glory: he ostentatiously challenged the Governor of Rouen to meet him in single combat. He suggested in all seriousness that the two commanders should fight a duel over a typically chivalric point of honor: "that the King's cause is more just than that of the [Catholic] League, and that my Mistress is more beautiful than yours."[29] The Governor, of course, replied quite sensibly that his responsible position made a personal duel impossible—exactly the point the Queen's ministers had been trying to explain to Essex. And the French shook their heads over these old-fashioned

26. *Ibid.*, p. 63.
27. Lords of the Council to Earl of Essex, Oct. 3, 1591, in Devereux, I, 245; cf. Sir Henry Unton to Lord Burghley, Jan. 10, 1592, in *Correspondence of Sir Henry Unton . . . In the Years MDXCI And MDXCII*, ed. Joseph Stevenson (London, 1847), p. 261.
28. Earl of Essex to Lord Burghley, Sept. 13, 1591, in Devereux, I, 240.
29. Quoted in Devereux, I, 273.

English knights errant who wandered the world in search of honor.[30]

In 1592 Essex's most brilliant military exploit still lay ahead of him—the Cadiz expedition of 1596, from which he gained an international reputation as a soldier. At Cadiz he was once again the first man ashore, and the first, or close to it, to scale the walls of the city. His heroism won him great honor, and he could write Burghley with truth that "fame itself" would bring him the news of the glorious victory.[31] Neither his goal nor his style had changed one whit, nor did they ever change. As late as his final disastrous Irish campaign, he was still challenging enemy commanders to single combat.[32]

At home too, the Earl of Essex concerned himself above all things with what he called his honor—the public honors the Queen heaped upon him, and the personal reputation he enjoyed among his contemporaries. Thus, for instance, though Essex saw no action in the glorious year 'eighty-eight, he nevertheless garnered more than his share of public honor. When the troops were mustered to defend the island against the impending Armada, Essex was named General of the Horse, serving again under the command of his stepfather. His most spectacular contribution to the defense of his country, however, appears to have been a morale-boosting display of tilting skill during a grand review of the troops.[33] Nevertheless, when the Queen made her famous visit to the camp at Tilbury, she showed special favor to Essex and his private company of light horse and musketeers, who received her drawn up in brilliant array, resplendent in the Earl's colors of orange and white.[34] Her Majesty, said a contemporary, "much graced him openly in view of the soldiers and people, even above my Lord of Leicester."[35] It was on this glorious occasion that she honored him with England's highest and most exclusive order of knighthood, the Order of St. George. According to Henry Wotton, it was from this time on that Essex's aspiration for high honors became insatiable: "from henceforth he fed too fast."[36]

30. Cayet, *Chronologie novenaire*, in Ascoli, p. 208.
31. Devereux, I, 364-367, 372.
32. Heffner, "Essex, the Ideal Courtier," 15.
33. *C. S. P., Span., 1587-1603*, IV, 423.
34. Harrison, p. 34.   35. Wotton, p. 11.
36. *Ibid.*

About this time too, Essex began to make it clear that he would brook no rivals in his quest for honor. Thus when Sir Charles Blount received a silver chessman from the Queen for his skill in the tiltyard, and wore the favor prominently displayed upon his arm, Essex was infuriated. "Now, I perceive, every fool must wear a favor," the young Earl sneered.[37] A duel of course followed, an affair of honor in the most literal sense. The two youths met in Mary-le-Bone Park to fight with rapiers. Essex came off second best—he received a superficial thigh wound— but the demands of honor had been met, and that was the important thing.

Honor came in many forms, and Essex was fascinated by all of them. He cut a wide swath in his passion for public honors, and in his jealousy of others who possessed them. He competed with Lord Mountjoy for military command, with the Earl of Cumberland for naval command, with Sir Robert Cecil for highest place among the Queen's Councillors. This apparent desire to monopolize high place was partly based on the power such places represented, but more significantly grew from avidity for the public honors these chief places conferred. Thus in 1593, the year after his return from Rouen, young Essex was named one of the Privy Council. From the very beginning of his service on this august body, he developed the infuriating habit of signing official documents so high on the sheet that the names of his colleagues would necessarily be written beneath his, giving him apparent precedence even over his seniors.[38] Men grown old in her Majesty's service could only curse the arrogance of one so sensitive to the honor of his name.

By 1593 Essex had achieved a unique position among Elizabeth's younger courtiers: he had become both the Queen's greatest favorite and a great popular hero into the bargain. To his generation, furthermore, Essex represented above all "the lost enchantments of feudal chivalry," and the ideal "Knight of Courtesy."[39] Such fashionable writers as Spenser, Peele, Daniel, and Chapman

37. Devereux, I, 193-194.
38. P. M. Handover, *The Second Cecil: The Rise to Power, 1563-1604, of Sir Robert Cecil* . . . (London, 1959), p. 136.
39. Patrick Cruttwell, *The Shakespearean Moment and Its Place in the Poetry of the 17th Century* (New York, 1960), p. 35; Heffner, "Essex, the Ideal Courtier," 7.

hailed him as the perfect courtier, and as the perfect knight.[40] They christened him Sir Philip Sidney's successor as the prince of chivalry and courtesy, "Fair branch of Honor, flower of Chivalry."[41]

The Earl of Essex was in fact a notorious cultivator of popularity among his fellows and his inferiors. Courtiers and citizens, Catholics and Puritans, soldiers and scholars—Essex courted them all, and they honored him in return as the soul of courtesy, valor, and justice.[42] His honorable reputation meant everything to him: he was "in ecstasy at praise, almost a glutton for honor."[43] Even on the scaffold "his chief care evidently was, as he had ever lived popularly, to leave a good opinion in the people's minds now at parting."[44]

But there was more to the Earl of Essex's quest for honor than this emotional need for approbation: Essex's passion for honor assumed certain forms, forms dictated by specific conventions of his own time. Essex lived—and died—"by the book," by the codes of his own class and generation.[45] It was the code of honor of the late-sixteenth-century English gentleman that impelled Essex to challenge rival courtiers—or rival commanders—to unlikely duels. It was the same rigid code of honor that drove him to risk his life repeatedly, yet always in certain stylized, often foolhardy ways. He accepted this code of honor completely, and made it the basis of his personal version of the secular religion of high aspiration that stirred within this generation of the English ruling class.

That there was "a 'deep and powerful' religious strain" in Essex, most authorities seem to agree.[46] But this fundamental religiosity could be moved by more faiths and more doctrines than the various versions of Christianity that were available to him. Es-

40. Ray Heffner, "The Earl of Essex in Elizabethan Literature . . .," Johns Hopkins Univ., *Dissertation Collection*, Vol. I, No. 2 (Baltimore, 1934), pp. 5-6.

41. Edmund Spenser, quoted in Heffner, "Essex, the Ideal Courtier," 7.

42. Devereux, I, 279-280; Harrison, pp. 274-275; Heffner, "Essex in Elizabethan Literature," pp. 5-6; Heffner, "Essex, the Ideal Courtier," 20.

43. Harrison, p. 28.

44. John Chamberlain to Dudley Carleton, quoted in Beach Langston, "Essex and the Art of Dying," *HLQ*, XIII (1950), 121.

45. Cf. Heffner, "Essex, the Ideal Courtier," 7-36; Langston, "Essex and the Art of Dying," 109-129.

46. *Ibid.*, 118, 118 n. 20.

sex readily internalized his gentleman's code of honor—an elaborate complex of ideas and practices which will be analyzed in the balance of this chapter. He thus made the honor of his name a matter of personal conscience as well as of public approval. It was then his own passionately held ideal of honor and reputation, popular fame and eternal glory, that Essex sought in the Spanish War. He found such honor in full measure, and his contemporaries worshiped him for his achievement, for their own reasons for following the wars were much the same as his.

ii. The two generations and the war

Never did the generational fissures which divided Elizabethan society show more clearly than in the conflicting natural responses of youth and age to the challenge of the war. Political historians have of course focused their attention on the "peace" and "war" factions which did exist within the generation in power. But few members of the older generation demonstrated anything like the intense, total commitment to the war which sent thousands of young men to fight on distant battlefields and strange seas during the ten or fifteen years after 1585. The Earl of Leicester, for instance, is generally considered to have been a leader of the "war" faction; yet he came home from his ill-fated Netherlands adventure vowing never to return to the wars. While his stepson was looking about for new battles to fight, Leicester wanted only a warm fire and a little peace. This generational contrast became ever clearer in the 1590's, when the cautious party, led by Lord Burghley, achieved virtually complete control of the Council, following the deaths of the leaders of the more belligerent wing of this ruling-class generation—from Leicester in 1588 to Walsingham in 1591.[47] Thus the most conservative element of a timid generation won absolute control of the government just as the vigorous younger generation began to achieve the vantage point of high military commands from which to demand a bolder policy. The result was a heightening of generational tensions based on sharply opposed attitudes toward the Spanish War.

47. A. F. Pollard, *The History of England from the Accession of Edward VI to the Death of Elizabeth* (London, 1910), p. 411.

The response of the younger generation to the outbreak of the war was immediate and unqualified:

> To arms, to arms, to glorious arms!
> With noble Norris and victorious Drake. . . .
> O ten-times-treble happy men, that fight
> Under the cross of Christ and England's Queen. . . .
> All honors do this cause accompany;
> All glory on these endless honors waits. . . .[48]

And the rapture of the poets was answered by swarms of "voluntary gentlemen" who accompanied every expedition on land and sea. The leaders of the generation of 1560, such glittering idols as the Earls of Essex and Cumberland, Sir Philip Sidney and Sir Walter Raleigh, led the way, and lesser aspiring minds flocked after them. Sir Robert Sidney, for example, plunged into the wars that had taken his illustrious brother's life, and soon so distinguished himself that a Dutch official declared "that in Sir Robert Sidney the perfections of the late Monseigneur de Sidney live again.[49] They not only volunteered for the wars, they sought combat with unexcelled ardor and enthusiasm, like men possessed with a strange passion for war.[50] Leicester thus praised two young cavaliers, Sir Henry Unton and Sir William Hatton—knighted for their courage at Zutphen—who had "not failed any journey since they came over hither, either a horseback or foot, and none more forward than they were at the winning of Axell, at the siege of Doesburgh, and in the first rank to give the assault."[51] And always, in every action, in every skirmish, these two heroes had gone forward "as far and as dangerously as the foremost." Charles Blount, the future Lord Mountjoy and conqueror of Ireland, revealed this same spirit in the assault in which he received his first battle wound. He was singled out for special commendation because he had plunged impetuously into an action where he had no charge,

---

48. George Peele, "A Farewell . . . to the Famous and Fortunate Generals of Our English Forces . . .," in *The Works of . . .*, ed. A. H. Bullen (London, 1888), II, 238, 240.

49. *C. S. P., Dom., 1588,* XXII, 213.

50. G. R. Waggoner, "An Elizabethan Attitude toward Peace and War," *Philological Quarterly,* XXXIII (1954), 22; G. R. Waggoner, "The School of Honor: Warfare and the Elizabethan Gentleman," Univ. of Wisconsin, *Summaries of Doctoral Dissertations [1947-1949]* (Madison, Wisconsin, 1950), I, 625.

51. Earl of Leicester to Sir Francis Walsingham, Sept. 28, 1586, in *Correspondence of Robert Dudley, Earl of Leicester . . .*, pp. 415-417.

no official place at all, and in so doing had taken a piece of chain shot in the leg.[52] Overall, the immediate response of the younger generation to the war was one of tremendous enthusiasm.

The dominant reaction of the older generation was fear. All through the later 1580's and earlier 1590's, hardly a springtime came without rumors of impending invasion, scarcely a year passed without mutterings of treason and rebellion. And always there was the unprecedented drain on the government's finances. The carefully hoarded surplus of fifteen peaceful years quickly disappeared; then, for the Queen's weary ministers, came the grinding effort to accumulate more funds with medieval tax machinery, and the growing load of debt. Foreign wars were the occasional sport of the young men; but the protection of England was the life-long responsibility of the older men, and they lived in anxiety and fear while the threat of war hung over their heads.

But the generation of 1560 was off to the wars. How they went and what honor they found has been illustrated in the early career of the Earl of Essex. A more balanced version of this characteristic experience of the young Elizabethan courtier in the Spanish War was brilliantly sketched by one of the leading satirists of the younger generation, Thomas Nashe:

A young hare or cockney, that is his mother's darling, if he have played the waste-good at the Inns of the Court or about London, and that neither his student's pension nor his unthrift's credit will serve to maintain his college of whores any longer, falls in a quarrelling humor with his Fortune, because she made him not King of the Indies, and swears . . . that ne'er a such peasant as his father or brother shall keep him under: he will to the sea, and tear the gold out of the Spaniards' throats, but he will have it, byrlady! And when he comes there, poor soul, he lies in brine, in ballast, and is lamentable sick of the scurvies: his dainty fare is turned to a hungry feast of dogs and cats, or haberdine and poor john at the most, and . . . that without mustard. . . . *Dulce bellum inexpertis.* . . . it is a pleasant thing, over a full pot, to read the fable of thirsty Tantalus; but a hard matter to digest salt meats at sea, with stinking water.[53]

52. *C. S. P., For., 1585-1586*, XX, 85, 120.
53. Thomas Nashe, *Pierce Penniless his Supplication to the Devil*, in *The Works of . . .*, ed. Ronald B. McKerrow, revised by F. P. Wilson (Oxford, 1958), I, 170-171.

Enthusiasm ran as high, and suffering was as great, on land campaigns as on naval expeditions. The constellation of young gentlemen who went to France with Essex learned to ride all a hot and dusty day, broiling in their heavy armor, under constant threat of enemy attack.[54] In Ireland the witty court poet John Harington thanked God for merely keeping him healthy in a castle where sixty "as lusty men as any came out of England" died, and where "eating raw beef at midnight, and lying upon wet green corn ofttimes, and lying in boots, with heats and colds, made many sick. . . ."[55]

What was it that impelled these plumed and eager dandies to risk their lives and their high hopes again and again in Elizabeth's foreign wars? For one thing, as Nashe pointed out, there was the hope of material gain, of loot from the treasure troves of Spain. Then too, this was the great opportunity to shorten by years the climb to fame and fortune, and that through service that was generally more congenial to young courtiers than the paper work of their parents. Both financial gain and official advancement came more quickly to youth in military service than in any other way.

But there was another motive, and one that outweighed all others in the breast of dedicated soldiers like the Earl of Essex. In later years the daughter of one of these Elizabethan heroes wrote of her father, a typical voluntary gentleman in those and later wars:

Pride and covetousness had not the least place in his breast. And as he was in love with true honor, so . . . the large estate he reaped by happy industry he did many times over as freely resign again to the King's service. . . .[56]

And a learned commentator wrote of youth and honor and the wars: "As there is no age which doth naturally more abhor infamy, and is more covetous of honor and prowess than is youth; so there is no age that is so apt . . . to tolerate travails, to support discommodities, difficulties, and wants, that of necessity are

54. Coningsby, pp. 13, 19.
55. Thomas Park, *Nugae Antiquae* (London, 1804), I, 258-259.
56. Lucy Hutchinson, *Memoirs of the Life of Colonel Hutchinson*, ed. C. H. Firth (London, 1885), I, 20.

suffered in wars."[57] Such statements, by comparatively disinterested parties, have a ring of truth, or at least of psychological verisimilitude, about them. Modern scholarship, furthermore, tends to support the opinions of contemporaries. Writing of the Elizabethan drama, which here as in so many things reflected Elizabethan life, one critic declares: "The whole of the enthusiasm that surrounded the notion of war . . . sprang from the belief that war was glorious."[58] "In real life, as in the drama," says another modern writer, "the gentleman was expected to be eager to win honor and fame in war."[59] Courtiers, nobles, and gentry were as "military minded" as the dramatists, and for the same reason—they were "concerned for military glory and personal honor. . . ."[60]

In fact, these young men at war did not act as if their sole interest was in preferment and loot, though these motives were often present. At the siege of Doesburgh, for example, young Roger Williams was wounded in the arm by a musket ball. He received his wound when, ignoring the prudent Earl of Leicester's warnings, he repeatedly exposed himself to enemy fire "with a great plume of feathers in his gilt morion, as so many shot coming at him he could hardly escape. . . ."[61] Such bravura was the stock in trade of the young Elizabethan courtier who followed the wars. At the same time, stark heroism far beyond the call of duty—and seemingly beyond the reach of avarice or mere political ambition—was often displayed on Elizabethan battlefields. There was, for instance, the incredible courage of Edward Stanley during the capture of one of the forts at Zutphen.[62] In the thick of the fighting, this young gentleman, conspicuous in a suit of flamboyant yellow, clambered up into a breach in the walls where his company could not follow; there he stood, high upon the rampart, single-handedly holding the whole fort at bay. First with his pike, then with the broken stump of it, and finally with only his sword,

57. Francisco Sansovino, *The Quintessence of Wit* . . ., trans. Captain Hitchcock (London, 1590), p. 8ᵛ.
58. Richard Lindabury, *A Study of Patriotism in the Elizabethan Drama* (Princeton Univ. Stud. in English, No. 5; Princeton, 1931), p. 49.
59. Waggoner, "The School of Honor . . .," p. 625.
60. Waggoner, "An Elizabethan Attitude . . .," 22.
61. Earl of Leicester to Sir Francis Walsingham, Sept. 4, 1586, in *Correspondence of Robert Dudley, Earl of Leicester* . . ., p. 407.
62. *Ibid.*, pp. 427-428.

he fought alone, before the admiring eyes of both armies, with "at the least 9 or 10 against him continually." The English "gave him up for lost if he had a 100 lives" before his men finally reached him, and the fort was taken. Leicester rushed forward to knight him on the spot, and gave him forty pounds and a pension for life. But any one of the pikes wielded against him, or of the muskets discharged upon him during those long minutes alone on the ramparts could have ended all chance of preferment or pension for Edward Stanley. Such cases as this—and they were not uncommon—make it plain that the generation of 1560 aspired toward something more than material rewards, and aspired ardently enough to risk their futures and their very lives for some higher goal.

Honor was the prime object of these young men at war. It is not an original thing to say, but it is important to establish that this thing called "honor" was a real motivating force in the lives of real people. It was not merely an Elizabethan literary convention, reflecting the values of the dead past. It was not merely one of those "higher" ideals, cherished by every society, which have in fact little to do with the actual conduct of life. It was "something more than a subject of conversation. 'A soldier's honor' would never have become a phrase if it had not previously been a reality."[63] It was still a reality in the England of the 1580's and '90's. This was a generation which could still be stirred to the depths of its chivalric soul by the poet's call to follow the gleam:

> To arms, my fellow soldiers! Sea and land
> Lie open to the voyage you intend . . .
> Whether to Europe's bounds, or Asian plains,
> To Afric's shore, or rich America,
> Down to the shades of deep Avernus' crags,
> Sail on, pursue your honors to your graves. . . .[64]

Pursue their honors they did, though all too often the paths of honor did lead but to the grave. To the generation of 1560 this thing called "honor" sometimes proved more valuable than life itself.

63. Lindabury, p. 150.
64. Peele, "A Farewell," *Works*, II, 239.

iii. The forms of aspiration for honor

The personal honor which the Elizabethan younger generation valued so highly was, evidently, much more than simply being a brave soldier. Honor was won through adherence to a strict code of conduct, a code built around the fundamental virtue of courage, but a code that emphasized the forms of bravery at least as much as the quality itself. To understand the content of the Elizabethan code of honor, then, it is necessary to have a clear idea of the forms which this code prescribed. Courage may be essentially the same everywhere and in all times, as far as its psychological core is concerned; but the forms which it assumes in various societies are much more important to the historian of ideas. Simply to say that the Elizabethan gentleman "sought opportunities to display unusual courage" in battle is not to tell us very much about the inner life of these young Elizabethans.[65] It was the *way* in which they risked their lives that distinguished the Elizabethan cult of honor. To a certain degree, indeed, the forms of Elizabethan aspiration for honor *are* its content. Let us look more closely, then, at the honor of the generation of 1560 from a formal point of view.

The formal molds into which these young men poured their natural desire for distinction were borrowed, like so much else in Elizabethan society, from other times and cultures. The two most important sources of the forms of Elizabethan aspiration for honor were the new Italian courtesy tradition, and the old chivalric tradition of the High Middle Ages.

Italians began to write books about the concept of honor in the middle of the sixteenth century, about the time the generation of 1560 was born.[66] The influence of these new Italian ideas of gentlemanly conduct was soon felt in other lands. Italian was a court language in England, and many young members of the ruling class included Italy in their educational grand tours of

65. Waggoner, "The School of Honor," p. 625.
66. Frederick Robertson Bryson, *The Point of Honor in Sixteenth-Century Italy* . . . (Chicago, 1935), p. 1.

Europe.[67] Thus, in a literal sense, the Elizabethan younger generation grew up with the elaborate formulas and secular idealism of
the Italian code of honor. In addition, these young men undoubtedly found the new code both familiar and congenial in its
basic assumptions. The Italian code of honor was hierarchic and
aristocratic: honor was a virtue which could be possessed only by a
gentleman, and in fact helped to set him off from lesser men.[68]
And though some Italian writers identified true honor with inward virtue, in general the Italian "code of honor was concerned
less with virtue than with reputation."[69] For the aristocratic,
other-directed young Elizabethan who came across this new
gentleman's creed in some Italian courtesy book, or in practice
in Venice or Milan, such a code was ideal.

For most Italian commentators, honor consisted of a reputation for two particular virtues—justice and courage. Honor was in
fact defined as "a general opinion among gentlemen that one has
not lacked either valor or justice."[70] It was the particular virtue
of the soldier, though of course gentlemen who did not choose
to follow the profession of arms might also possess it.[71] But even
the gentleman who was not militarily inclined could, in the last
analysis, prove his honor only through courageous confrontation
of physical danger. For the central practice of the new code of
conduct was the elaborate ceremonial of the duel, the sword-
fight which was the ultimate vindication of one's personal honor.
Along with the complex ritual of challenge and reply that was
essential to the formal duel, Italy exported to England its subtle
fencing styles and even its fencing teachers, to whom English
courtiers flocked for instruction.[72] In England as in other countries, young aristocrats and young gentlemen accepted the Italian
courtier's code of honorable conduct, with its emphasis on courage
and formal correctness on the field of honor.

The most authoritative of the Italian courtesy books, Castiglione's *Book of the Courtier*, stressed both the profession of
arms and the belief that "reputation" was the goal of the hon-

67. E. S. Bates, *Touring in 1600: A Study in the Development of Travel as a
Means of Education* (Boston and New York, 1912), pp. 95-98; Lewis Einstein, *The
Italian Renaissance in England* (London, 1902), pp. 97-107, 70-76.

68. Bryson, p. 15. 71. *Ibid.*, p. 15.
69. *Ibid.*, p. 12. 72. Einstein, pp. 70-75; Bryson, pp. 27-103.
70. *Ibid.*

orable man. The ancient debate as to whether arms or letters was the more suitable occupation for the gentleman was more than once taken up in the pages of Castiglione's famous guide to gentility. But by and large, the victory seemed to go to the view that "the principal and true profession of a Courtier ought to be in feats of arms. . . ."[73] Clearly, too, the overriding goal of this skill was to earn a glorious reputation among one's fellows, and to win public honors from one's superiors. The courtier should develop his martial skills that he might be "seen in open shows," be "known among all men," and be "esteemed among the best."[74] He should seek the "estimation," the "admiration," the "general favor" of his compeers on the one hand, and "favor with such great men as he shall attend upon," on the other.[75] The conduct of the perfect courtier at the wars was clearly prescribed for him:

Yet by our rule it may be understood, that where the Courtier is at skirmish, or assault, or battle . . . he ought to work the matter wisely in separating himself from the multitude, and undertake notable and bold feats . . . with as little company as he can, and in the sight of noble men . . . and especially in the presence and (if it were possible) before the very eyes of his king . . . for indeed it is meet to set forth to the show things well done.[76]

The form at least of many an honorable exploit in Elizabeth's wars was here anatomized for the better understanding of the dullest young gentleman.

Finally, it should be pointed out that the imperatives of the Italian courtly code of honor were uncompromising and absolute. Its demands "were considered inexorable. . . . It is to be preferred to one's father, one's ruler, one's country, and life itself."[77] Even a royal command to refuse a challenge, for instance, should be disobeyed: "a man must risk for a prince life, but not honor." Here was a new code of conduct demanding loyalties which cut across the basic allegiances of the older generation, and challenged some of their most sacred principles. But for the younger generation, this code of personal conduct, developed by

73. Baldassare Castiglione, *The Book of the Courtier*, trans. Thomas Hoby (Everyman Ed.; London and New York, n.d.), p. 35; cf. *ibid.*, pp. 73 ff.

74. *Ibid.*, p. 41.   76. *Ibid.*, pp. 95-96.

75. *Ibid.*, pp. 37, 42, 41, 94.   77. Bryson, pp. 12-13.

the young courtiers of a country that was considerably ahead of the rest of Europe in this phase of social evolution, had a natural appeal. The highly idealistic and sweeping demands of the Italian courtly code of honor were tailored to suit a generation in search of emotionally satisfying values and absolute standards, untarnished by compromise.

Probably more important, however, was the old idealization of the military life which was undergoing a full-scale, if purely romantic revival in England in the 1580's and '90's—the code of chivalry. Feudalism, the soil in which chivalry had originally flourished, died slowly in England: in the North particularly, where such fighting men as the "buccaneer Earl" of Cumberland and Sir John Burgh were raised, the barons still insisted on their prerogatives even into Elizabeth's reign.[78] And despite the new Tudor emphasis on the civil duties of the nobility, they were still considered as the natural military leaders of the country.[79] In issuing orders for musters to meet the repeated invasion scares of the late 1580's, the government assumed "that it was the natural disposition of the nobility without any directions to be armed," and to have armor for their tenants.[80] The sons of England's governors were often given military training, as a matter of course. And since tilting was a popular sport and the tourney a frequent spectacle at Elizabeth's court, young courtiers had ample opportunity to keep their skills and their command of chivalric formulas alive. Edward Somerset, the young Catholic Earl of Worcester, was accounted "the best horseman and tilter of the times," and his skill at these knightly sports was considered a signal distinction.[81] The Earl of Cumberland, who was also hailed by some as the greatest tilter of the age, had the additional honor of being the Earl of Essex's favorite opponent in the lists.[82]

78. Helen M. Cam, "The Decline and Fall of English Feudalism," *History*, XXV (1940), 225-226, 232-233; Pollard, p. 300.

79. Waggoner, "The School of Honor," p. 625.

80. The Council to the Nobility (a circular letter), in Thomas Wright, ed., *Queen Elizabeth and Her Times: A Series of Original Letters . . .* (London, 1823), II, 75.

81. David Lloyd, *The Statesmen and Favorites of England Since the Reformation* (London, 1665), p. 392.

82. G. C. Williamson, *George, Third Earl of Cumberland (1558-1605), His Life and His Voyages* (Cambridge, 1920), pp. 17-18; Heffner, "Essex, the Ideal Courtier," 11-12.

Particularly during the 1580's, the tournament became increasingly ornate, with expensive, gorgeous costumes and elaborate allegorical display.[83] On such a stage, performing before the Queen herself, on whose good will all their futures depended, these young courtiers probably took their knightly skills more seriously than we know.

The great popularity of that forgotten genre, the chivalric romance, came partly as a cause and partly as a reinforcement of this almost entirely frivolous chivalric revival. Amadis, Palmerin, Orlando—almost utterly unread now, they were once devoured by young gentlemen and nobles, in all their dozens of volumes and hundreds of cantos.[84] Scores of editions of the multi-volume adventures of Amadis of Gaul and Palmerin of England appeared during the second half of the sixteenth century in French and Italian, the two most common second languages of Elizabethan courtiers; and, from about 1580, many volumes of these and other sagas of knighthood came out in the English of Anthony Munday and his fellow translators.[85] These endless anthologies of chivalric exploits were therefore eminently available to the generation of 1560 during their youth, and apparently had a considerable influence on them. Like "Palladine of England," for instance, these

83. Cf. John Nichols, *The Progresses and Public Processions of Queen Elizabeth* . . . (London, 1823), *passim*; Frances A. Yates, "Elizabeth Chivalry: The Romance of the Accession Day Tilts," *Journ. of the Warburg and Courtauld Institutes*, XX (1957), 9.

84. Some scholars have been of the opinion that the chivalric romances were "coldly received" by the "cultural classes" in England, and that "in general their appeal was to the lower, or at least the ignorant classes" (Rowland Edmund Ernle, Baron Prothero, *The Light Reading of Our Ancestors* [London, n.d.], p. 119; Henry Thomas, *Spanish and Portuguese Romances of Chivalry* [Cambridge, 1920], p. 288). But the evidence for this point of view comes often from the literature of the early seventeenth century, and what may have been true of those gloomy times was not necessarily true of the exuberant 1580's (Thomas, pp. 288-293; Ronald S. Crane, *The Vogue of Medieval Chivalric Romance during the English Renaissance* [Menasha, Wisconsin, 1919], p. 22). Courtly taste was responsible for the initial popularity of the chivalric romance in Italy, in France, and in Germany; it seems likely to have been so in England as well. After the turn of the century the courtiers may well have been disillusioned with war and were probably bored with a dated genre; and by this time the popularity of the romances had probably filtered down to the lower classes. In general, the conclusion of McShane's comprehensive study must be accepted as substantially accurate: "the chivalric romance is popular with every class of sixteenth-century reader and is widely accepted as a worthwhile genre of literature . . ." (Edith McShane, *Tudor Opinions of the Chivalric Romance* [microcards], Washington, D. C., 1950, p. 125).

85. Thomas, pp. 189 n. 1, 207 n. 1, 247-256.

Elizabethan youths received good humanist educations "in the custody of grave and learned tutors, instructed in the languages . . . Greek and Latin . . ." and the rest of it.[86] Like Palladine too, they "practiced knightly chivalry, to manage great horses and all gentlemanlike exercises. . . ." Surely most of these young gentlemen would have preferred, like Palladine, to go on to a life of romantic adventure, rather than, like their fathers, to a life of magistracies and commissions. "Truly I have known men," wrote no less an authority on chivalry than Sir Philip Sidney, "that even with reading *Amadis de Gaule* . . . have found their hearts moved to the exercise of courtesy, liberality, and especially courage."[87] The impact of chivalric literature on the young men of the 1590's was thus described in the introduction to one such book: The youth are "so inflamed with an approbation of good and famous exploits . . . that the hearing hereof, do as it were kindle in their minds an ardent burning desire of imitating, if not matching or over-going the most glorious attempts of the greatest and most excellent."[88] But in the England of Elizabeth, such things did not happen: the duties of the Tudor ruling class were the unromantic chores of the Christian humanist governor —the commissioner, the J. P., and the M. P. Then the war came, and as their military education seemed suddenly relevant, so too did the chivalric idealism they had imbibed from Ariosto and *Amadis*.

Both the old chivalric tradition and the new Italian code of courtly honor gained a new significance in 1585, and for more than a decade continued to guide the actions of the Elizabethan younger generation at war. The Earl of Essex, the military ideal of his generation, was not the only one of them to indulge in daring chivalric exploits or to send challenges to opposing generals. Bands of English horsemen not uncommonly rode over to enemy encampments, gaily bedight in glittering armor and tossing plumes, to dare the Spaniards or the Frenchmen to come out

---

86. [Claude Colet], *The Famous, Pleasant, and variable Historie of Palladine of England* . . . trans. Anthony Munday (London, 1588), p. 7ᵛ.

87. *The Defense of Poesie*, in *Complete Works*, ed. Albert Feuillart (Cambridge, 1922-1926), III, 20; cf. William Vaughan, *The Golden grove, moralized in three Bookes* (London, 1600), pp. 13-15.

88. Thomas Fiston, Preface to William Caxton, *The Auncient Historie of the Destruction of Troy* (London, 1596), pp. A3ʳ-A3ᵛ.

and fight. On one occasion Robert Sidney, Roger Williams, and Sir William Russell led a troop of five hundred knights to the edge of the Duke of Parma's camp, to challenge his host to battle.[89] Lord Thomas Howard, the celebrated Elizabethan admiral, deliberately sailed in close to the North Cape of Spain, "giving the enemy a fair sight of us, that if their hearts served them, they might come out to us. . . ."[90] Dashing young Sir Henry Unton three times challenged the Duke of Guise to meet him on the field of honor to answer for alleged insults to the Queen's Majesty.[91]

Every skirmish was an opportunity for "exploits" by the young gentlemen, carried out according to the approved chivalric-romance or courtesy-book models. The goal of an exploit was the accumulation of honor; and, by honor, the Elizabethan younger generation meant chivalric "renown," with overtones of Italianate "reputation." They saw a battlefield as an outsized tiltyard, and regarded war itself as little more than a magnified duel between gentlemen. Win or lose, honor might be won by graceful, formally correct courage under fire; and that was the real point of it all. In fact, the war itself added new significance to the personal honor and public honors they had long since learned to covet. In the first place, the Spanish War transformed honor from the fetish of gilded youth in search of social distinction into a socially useful virtue. It must have seemed brilliantly simple to these young heroes: they could now seek personal glory in the service of Queen and country—an ideal combination of egotism and social service. In the second place, the war provided many new opportunities for impressive expressions of public honor—from the cheering crowds who hailed returning heroes, to the dignities and honors with which the Queen rewarded good service. The passion for honor was thus intensified in the generation of 1560 by repeated intoxicating experience of it. They came to think of this goal of their most idealistic aspirations as quite within their reach, not years away, but at once, through some bold stroke on land or sea.

89. Earl of Leicester to Sir Francis Walsingham, in *Correspondence of Robert Dudley, Earl of Leicester*, p. 430.
90. *C. S. P., Dom., 1595-1597*, CCLXIV, 64.
91. Thomas Fuller, *The Worthies of England*, ed. John Freeman (London, 1952), p. 31.

In the reign of Elizabeth, then, only a strict Puritan would condemn worldly honors unconditionally, and even the older generations of the ruling class competed for them unashamedly. More importantly, the spread of the Italian code of courtly conduct and the romantic revival of chivalry provided the formal structure of a new secular creed for young Elizabethan courtiers, a creed in which personal honor was the highest virtue. Finally, the coming of the Spanish War seemed to give their passion for public honors and personal honor a real social significance. And yet, important as these things were, they were after all only the forms and rationalizations of the Elizabethan cult of honor. Edward Stanley, battling alone on the walls of a redoubt before Zutphen, was not really under the illusion that he was Amadis of Gaul; and there was nothing in the courtesy books that required the Earl of Essex to leap into the heaving seas to lead the troops ashore at Peniche. For a deeper understanding of the compelling desire for honor which formed such an important part of the Elizabethan aspiring mind, it will therefore be necessary to seek behind the specific formulations of the codes of chivalry and courtesy. The roots of Elizabethan aspiration for honor lay in certain far more fundamental notions of that day—lay at the deepest level, in the very structure of the mind of the Elizabethan younger generation.

iv. The roots of aspiration for honor

The code of honor found support in many areas of Elizabethan life and thought. There were sociological reasons for this unlikely passion; certain intellectual presuppositions of the age made their contribution; and particular aspects of the psychological makeup of the younger courtiers supported them in their eagerness for honor.

The aspiration of the generation of 1560 for honor and for honors was rooted, most obviously, in certain key qualities of Elizabethan society itself. These sociological roots of aspiration for honor are to be found primarily in the society of the court, and in the impact of the courtly culture on young minds growing up under its influence. In particular, the nature of Elizabeth's court helps to account for much of the blindness and folly of these aspiring minds in search of honor.

From the vantage point of several centuries, perhaps the most striking characteristics of the Elizabethan cult of honor are its apparent artificiality and its completely unrealistic attitude. Shakespeare, as he so often did, put his finger on these foibles of his generation. On the artificiality of the courtly Italianate conception of honor, with its emphasis on the formal duel as the supreme test of an honorable man, Touchstone spoke with authority in his celebrated exposition of the techniques of giving —and avoiding—the lie:

> JAQUES. Can you nominate in order now the degrees of the lie?
> TOUCHSTONE. O sir, we quarrel in print, by the book, as you have books for good manners: I will name you the degrees. The first, the Retort Courteous; the second, the Quip Modest; the third, the Reply Churlish; the fourth, the Reproof Valiant; the fifth, the Countercheck Quarrelsome; the sixth, the Lie with Circumstance; the seventh, the Lie Direct. All these you may avoid but the Lie Direct; and you may avoid that too, with an If.[92]

On the utterly unrealistic attitude of the young cavaliers who risked their lives for a chivalric gesture, Sir John Falstaff's remarks more than suffice:

> Can honor set a leg? No. or an arm? No. or take away the grief of a wound? No. Honor hath no skill in surgery, then? No. What is honor? a word. What is in that word, honor? Air. A trim reckoning! Who hath it? he that died o' Wednesday. Doth he feel it? No. Doth he hear it? No. 'Tis insensible, then? Yea, to the dead. But will it not live with the living? No. Why? Detraction will not suffer it. Therefore I'll none of it: honor is a mere scutcheon; and so ends my catechism.[93]

And yet, artificial and unrealistic though their code might seem, young men like Essex and Edward Stanley did commit acts of almost incredible heroism to win this wisp of air, honor. Quite evidently, then, honor was more than a word to the generation of 1560. The explanation for this powerful attraction lies partly

92. *As You Like It*, V, iv, 92-102, in *Complete Works*.
93. *King Henry IV, Part I*, V, i, 132-144.

in certain general aspects of the courtly life of these younger Elizabethans.

The lives of these ambitious young men necessarily centered around the court; and few institutions in history have been more artificial and "unreal" than the court of Elizabeth. At the English court, writes one authority, "extravagant artificiality knew no bounds"; and another declares that in English society as a whole, "the movement during Tudor times was in the direction of elaboration and artificiality."[94] There is no need to particularize: in everything from clothing to conversation, ornateness, over-elaboration, and the most fantastic conventions prevailed. The result, if not the intention, was to make of life itself an exercise in obedience to unnatural conventions. Some of these artificialities, particularly those concerning the relationships between courtiers and Queen, had sound institutional reasons for existing; but even these had grown beyond all bounds and had lost much of their significant content over the years. Some social conventions, like euphuistic conversation, extravagant clothing, and Petrarchan sonneteering, were in part means of social differentiation, of setting the society of the court off from the rest of the country. In part, too, these were no more than the whimsical conspicuous consumption of a new-rich aristocracy. The effect of it all, however, was to make artificiality natural for the Elizabethan courtier. Artificial conventions often completely unrelated to real circumstances became the basis for public action.

Even more striking than the artificiality of life at court was the air of unreality which permeated much of the activity of Elizabeth's courtiers. To the modern scholar, as to the contemporary satirist, these young gentlemen seem to have been pretending about half the time. It is unlikely, for instance, that many of the courtiers of the younger generation felt much real affection for the aging Queen; yet all were required to protest passionate devotion to her person, and that frequently and in the most fulsome terms. Again, masques and tournaments involved a good deal of semi-serious playacting—as when the Queen's champion offered to joust with anyone on the proposition that Elizabeth

94. H. D. Traill, ed., *Social England* (New York and London, 1895), III, 385; L. F. Salzman, *England in Tudor Times: An Account of Its Social Life and Industries* (London, 1926), p. 92.

was the fairest of mistresses. The very magnificence of court and courtiers was far from the hard financial facts which caught up with many a young gallant before the end of the reign; and this magnificent style of living added considerably to the unrealistic atmosphere in which they moved. This atmosphere, elusive though it may be for modern scholarship, was a real and ubiquitous phenomenon at court. Not only did men like Essex and Cumberland love to pretend to be knights errant; but serious, comparatively unromantic men like Robert Cecil and Francis Bacon wrote and even played roles in elaborate allegorical make-believes which sometimes lasted for days. The Earl of Essex in the role of the Knight of the Queen's Day Tourney is no surprise, but there is something intrinsically improbable about little Robert Cecil as the Hermit of Theobalds, welcoming the Queen with an elaborate versified fairy tale about his father's retirement.[95] All these Elizabethans had a remarkable facility for swathing and muffling facts in pink clouds of fiction. They clothed their lives in lovely little Arabian Nights' entertainments which served to soften the rough edge of reality whenever it forced itself upon their consciousness.

Quite naturally, Elizabeth's courtiers carried the artificiality and unreality of their court lives with them to the wars. It was no more artificial to challenge the Governor of Rouen than to fight a serious duel over a silver chessman. The chivalric formulae of the Queen's Day Tilts came naturally to the lips of courtiers at war. The brief, tragic military career of Sir Philip Sidney illustrated perfectly this tendency to carry over the "pantomime extravagance," the "spirit of perpetual dressing up" into the wars of the later 1580's.[96] His life and his writings were permeated with "that element of unreality, or deliberate make-believe" of his time and class.[97] His *Arcadia* was crammed with chivalric episodes, particularly in the revised version of 1590 which became the most popular of Elizabethan books.[98] Of his life, one perhaps extreme interpretation insists that "there is seldom a time when

95. Heffner, "Essex, the Ideal Courtier," 11-12; Algernon Cecil, *A Life of Robert Cecil First Earl of Salisbury* (London, 1915), pp. 46-51.

96. Esmé Wingfield-Stratford, *The Making of a Gentleman* (London, 1938), p. 176.

97. *Ibid.*, pp. 179-180.

98. Mona Wilson, *Sir Philip Sidney* (London, 1950), pp. 139-140, 142; Yates, "Elizabethan Chivalry . . .," 9.

we can be sure that he is appearing in his own proper person, and not in some part of romantic knighthood in which he has chosen to take the stage."[99] And then, almost inevitably, "when he tries to keep up the illusion amid the grim work of war, his life proves to be the forfeit." For Sidney and his fellow young gallants, at least, the unprofitable skirmish at Zutphen was indeed fought "in a pure spirit of knight errantry"; it was "keeping up the masquerade of the Elizabethan court life by playing at soldiers." The generation of 1560 simply carried their romantic daydreams with them to the wars, and went blithely on pretending a siege was just a long tournament, even while the troops were dying of camp fever before their eyes.

The fact that the Elizabethan cult of honor was artificial and unrealistic, even by the standards of these courtiers' own more hard-headed contemporaries, is thus partially explained by the artificial, unrealistic lives they led at home. And much of the artificiality and unreal atmosphere of the court may in turn be explained as the natural product of new affluence, the gingerbread frivolity of pampered youth in an Elizabethan gilded age.

At a deeper level, however, the meaning of honor for young Elizabethans was rooted in some of the fundamental notions of their time. The overwhelming appeal of honor grew partially from two sixteenth-century beliefs about this abstraction—beliefs concerning the ontological status and the broader goal of honor. And these notions were in their turn derived from even more basic ideas about the nature of reality and the desirability of immortality. Let us then examine these philosophical roots of aspiration for honor.

The ontological status which the younger generation assigned to honor was rooted in the commonest of all Elizabethan commonplaces, a fundamental assumption which we may call the doctrine of the invisible world. This universally accepted notion simply asserted the existence of an invisible world of spiritual phenomena, outside, above, yet somehow impinging upon this temporal world of matter. The invisible world was fundamentally the Christian heaven and the Platonic ideal realm; but it was also the world where sacrament and symbol and allegory blended, and the

99. Wingfield-Stratford, p. 180.

misty fourth dimension where ghosts and demons were. The contents of the invisible world varied from imagination to imagination, but for all it was very real. Theoretically, at least, it was "more real" than this earth, since it existed so much higher up the great chain of being, so much closer to the spiritual fountainhead of existence. This invisible world of spiritual phenomena and of platonically absolute values has faded away almost completely in the centuries between those times and our own. But it was real enough for most Elizabethans, and its existence lent a peculiar tone and significance to life on earth.

The ontological status of the notion of honor was determined by this general schema of existence in two worlds: for honor obviously existed primarily in the invisible world of spiritual phenomena and values. The impact of this widespread belief in the invisible world on the Elizabethan concept of honor was twofold. To begin with, the unceasing, centuries-old torrent of propaganda designed to convince dwellers in this material world of the existence of heaven and of platonically real virtues and vices also gave a special reality to other ideal concepts and principles of conduct. If charity or justice "really" existed in some sphere of ideal reality, why not honor? Then too, the endless emphasis on the ineffable superiority of the invisible world over this earth readily carried over to *any* non-material goal of life; thus love, knowledge, or honor became quite acceptable goals for aspiration. Elizabethans might legitimately aspire to salvation and virtue, and even to love and beauty and knowledge—why not to honor?

Honor thus acquired the super-reality of a Platonic Idea, and so gained new emotional appeal and special value for its young worshipers. The ostentatious magnificence which they felt befitted their honorable estates was infused with a higher meaning that was more than aesthetic. The ardor with which they pursued royal favor and public acclaim was redoubled by the consciousness of the highly spiritual nature of their goal, and of its lofty superiority over more worldly concerns. Sir John Harington, the court wit and poet, expressed this reverence for chivalric honor when he wrote "that knighthood doth impress a character of honor into every person, how mean so ever, as baptism doth a mark of

Christianity."[100] And for this glorious ideal, this gleam from another world which touched their souls only at exultant moments when trumpets sounded and crowds roared, for this undying honor, some young zealots were willing to lay down their lives.

Behind this willingness to sacrifice life rather than honor lay the belief that honor could be the means to an even greater end, the belief that eternal honor conferred on its possessor a species of immortality. "For that either late or early the life dissolveth . . . but in true honor and good renown are laid up our monuments of perpetuity and fame so long as we live, and after our death they lift us to immortality."[101] The notion of immortality through fame was an ancient one, and it flourished in Elizabethan England. The Greeks, the Romans, and the Italians, the chief authorities for several generations of Englishmen, generally agreed on the validity of this idea. It is not surprising, then, that the "literati of Renaissance England" themselves gave "prodigious attention . . . to the subject of fame and its allied concepts. . . ."[102] So much attention, indeed, that it is possible to see not only Elizabethan desire for fame, but all kinds of Elizabethan ambition as "outgrowths of the prevailing passion for perpetuity."[103] Certainly the lure of historical or literary immortality made a considerable contribution to the great appeal of the secular religion of high aspiration to the Elizabethan younger generation.

A well-known contemporary French writer explained the attitude of these young men in positive terms, fitting desire for honor into orthodox metaphysics and morality.[104] The world, he said, is composed of things perpetual and things mutable, of things eternal (like the stars) and things transitory (like all life on earth). Human bodies are mortal, but their souls are eternal: therefore, "men, being endowed with a divine and immortal soul, do aspire . . . to . . . perpetuity and immortality."

100. John Harrington, *The Letters and Epigrams of* . . ., ed. Norman Egbert McClure (Philadelphia, 1930), pp. 81-82.

101. Geoffrey Fenton, *Golden Epistles* . . . (London, 1575), pp. 122ᵛ-123ʳ.

102. Louis David Appel, "The Concept of Fame in Tudor and Stuart Literature," Northwestern University, *Summaries of Doctoral Dissertations*, XVII (1949), 10.

103. *Ibid.*, p. 12.

104. Louis Le Roy, *Of the Interchangeable Course or Variety of Things in the Whole World* . . ., trans. Robert Ashley (London, 1594), pp. 129ᵛ-130ʳ.

Most men obey this natural urge toward perpetuity by procreation, perpetuating their name through their children. But "good wits" seek to immortalize themselves through a higher type of creation—through the cult of honor:

There hence ariseth . . . the insatiable desire of honor, stirring them up day and night, not to content themselves with base and casual things, but to seek by virtuous deeds to recompense the shortness of this life by the memory of all posterity. There hence proceedeth the wonderful desire of making themselves known, of leaving a good opinion of them, and getting an immortal renown.

The great soldiers and statesmen of the past—Alexander and Augustus, Cicero and Caesar—had found just such immortality through fame. Of course, Caesar and Cicero were dead, and could not enjoy the "immortality" which an admiring posterity had conferred upon them; and these young seekers after eternal honor would one day be as dead as Caesar, and as insensible of their fame. But the honor accorded to famous men while they were still alive was an exhilirating experience, as young war heroes—and their envious comrades—well knew. The applause of Queen and country for living heroes drowned thoughts of the endless oblivion to all worldly things that lay ahead. Elizabethan aspiring minds enjoyed their immortality vicariously, in the exultation of present honor.

At the deepest level, finally, the fantastic Elizabethan cult of honor was rooted in the very structure of the minds of the young courtiers of the generation of 1560. Among the inner qualities of mind which helped to generate the ardor of their quest for honor, three stood out: a rather surprising other-directedness of character, an inherited authoritarian caste of mind, and a natural, if hyperdeveloped, egotism. Without these inner psychological drives, the cult of honor could never have flourished as it did.

To understand the relevance of the younger generation's tendency toward other-direction for the cult of honor, it will be necessary to glance once more at the multiple meanings of honor as it was understood in those times. The basic sixteenth-century meaning was "high respect, esteem, or reverence accorded to exalted worth or rank. . . ."[105] This could mean public approbation, titles of dignity awarded by authority, or simply personal reputation as a man of justice and valor. If this recognition was accorded to real worth by judicious men, it was "true honor"; if it represented merely the fickle opinion of the mob, it was "false honor." But in either case, honor meant external approbation. By Dr. Johnson's time, on the other hand, the primary meaning of honor had come to be "nobleness of mind, scorn of meanness, magnanimity," or, as the best modern authority puts it, "elevation of character."[106] Over the centuries, in other words, honor has become an intrinsic quality, and the approbation of others has become irrelevant. This internalization of the sense of honor, the shift in emphasis from public reputation to personal integrity, took place largely during the seventeenth century.[107] Since the process had begun before 1600, usages in the last years of the sixteenth century were sometimes ambiguous.[108]

Essentially, however, honor remained a matter of external approval in the last two decades of the reign of Elizabeth. In actual fact, "honor" to these young courtiers was not the fact of their own virtue, but the ego-satisfying recognition of their virtue by others. When a man aspired to high honor, it was generally some mark of favor from his sovereign he had in mind. When a courtier fought to defend his honor, it was his reputation in the world he was protecting. When a soldier undertook extraordinary feats of prowess for the sake of honor, it was popular acclaim and the respect of his fellows he was after. To be dishonored was not necessarily to fall from virtue, but rather to be humiliated or disgraced before the world. In practice too, the distinction between true and false honor evaporated: for who would say that a cheering crowd of London citizens was not composed of good men and true? Who would question the judgment of the Queen when she lavished honors on a favorite? Who would dare to suggest that Lord Mountjoy did not deserve those compliments on his military

---

105. *OED*, V, 367.   106. *Ibid.*
107. C. L. Barber, *The Idea of Honor in the English Drama, 1591-1700* (Gothenburg Studies in English, No. 8; Goteborg, 1957), pp. 96-98.
108. *Ibid.*, pp. 52-55.

campaigns which he found so "extraordinarily pleasing" to hear?[109]

They were, in sum, a very "other-directed" group, these arrogantly individualistic, fiercely competitive young Elizabethans. It is not surprising that this should be so, considering their generational background. They had grown up without acquiring an inner moral gyroscope, a set of internalized precepts to guide their conduct. For their *politique* parents had had few real ideals to pass on to them, and they had rejected most of the platitudinous moralism they had been forced to memorize as irrelevant to the aspiring society in which they lived. The young generation of 1560 had worked out a code of conduct for themselves, true; but it was in essence a ramshackle structure, built on the metaphysical foundations of other ideals. The cult of honor in particular was lacking in positive theoretical development and strong philosophical justification. The "serious" thought of the time was never really mobilized in support of the ideal of personal honor and public honors. Such theoretical support as there was for the cult of honor was by implication or by special application of old dogmas to new ideals. The most powerful sanction available was that of group approval.

It should, however, be stressed that the Elizabethan younger generation was completely unconscious of its own other-directedness. Twentieth-century Americans may publicly pride themselves on "getting along with others," or "fitting in," on being "well liked" and "accepted." But Elizabethans could not admit even to themselves that they were affected by public praise and popularity: this sort of thing was too universally condemned as foolish vanity and even as sin. Instead, they talked vaguely of their "honor," using the term in ways that were frequently ambiguous and even more often completely equivocal. It is doubtful if they themselves always knew whether they meant "true" or "false" honor, inward virtue or external approbation.

But this other-directed Elizabethan cult of honor should not be thought of as a mere matter of shallow dependence on peer-group approval, to be contrasted (unfavorably) with inner strength of character. Honor was one of the key elements of the

109. Fynes Moryson, *An Itinerary Containing His Ten Years Travel . . .* (Glasgow, 1907), II, 262.

secular religion of high aspiration which the generation of 1560 evolved for itself; as such, this new ethical imperative was enveloped in a haze of idealism which generated tremendous internal emotional commitment. Among the elements which help to account for the religious intensity of the Elizabethan's commitment to the cult of honor, two stand out: the authoritarian-mindedness and the extraordinary egotism of these young courtiers.

Authoritarian-mindedness was a quality they shared with Elizabethans of all ages. In the sixteenth century men turned to authorities in many fields which have since been opened to controversy or to personal taste. There were authorities on everything, from religion to politics, from science to morals. Furthermore, sixteenth-century Europeans gave more weight to the words of their authorities than we do; they regularly laced their own expositions and arguments with citations from the relevant authorities.

The standard authorities were of course the Greeks and the Romans, the Bible, the Fathers, and the Schoolmen. But alongside these, the venerable preceptors of many older generations, a new group of authorities had come into being. The majority of these new authorities were Italians, and most of them had lived during the two centuries preceding 1560; yet in outlook they seemed to have much in common with the Elizabethan younger generation. Thus, while the older generation clung still to Seneca and Plato and Aristotle and Aquinas, the young men hung on the words of Petrarch and Castiglione and Machiavelli and John Calvin. There were authorities on honor, too, particularly on chivalric renown and the Italian point of honor. So the younger generation absorbed the forms and the spirit of Castiglione and Della Casa and Annibale Romei, and even of *Amadis of Gaul* and Ariosto's *Orlando.* As for their right to public honors and dignities, their upbringing as future governors had already instilled these convictions in them, in part by references to many classical and Christian authorities. As a result, the Elizabethan younger generation could aspire after honor and honors secure in the belief that they performed daring feats, not for public acclaim or the Order of the Garter, but simply because authorities agreed in recommending such conduct to gentlemen. This aspect of the religion of aspiration had an authoritarian basis, at least on the level of rationalization; the importance of this fact to authority-conscious Elizabethans must not be underestimated. Their psychological need for the approval of their peers and of society was legitimatized by these authoritarian sanctions.

But at the root of the cult of honor, as of the lust for power, lay, in the last analysis, the hugely inflated ego of the young courtier himself. The code of personal honor, the savage competition for place and power, the extravagant dress and hundreds of liveried retainers, even the majestic strut which Elizabethan courtiers and captains affected—these were the external manifestations of tremendous egotism. Such self-conscious egotism, exhibitionism, a desire to stand out and to be admired are characteristic of young people in many ages and societies. These natural qualities were further intensified in this generation of Elizabethans by the lack of more general causes with which they might identify and on which they might focus their zeal. For many of these young men, religion was a collection of platitudes, or at best a set of theological truths only distantly related to daily living. For most of them, the Virgin Queen was an uninspiring old woman, timid, short-sighted, crotchety, and capricious. Their nationalism was still mainly a matter of hating foreigners. And for most of them, there were no other crusades around. They were idealists without a cause; and so they followed their natural instincts—they lavished thought and passion upon themselves.

This tendency was considerably strengthened by the great possibilities which were presented to them as the hereditary ruling class of a rich, expanding nation. From childhood, wealth and the joys of conspicuous consumption were available to these young aristocrats. Then, in the 1580's, the outbreak of the Spanish War opened up opportunities to win fame and honor through personal prowess. Finally, in the 1590's, as these younger men reached an age of relative discretion, great political power came within their reach. It is not surprising that they developed a mountainous self-consciousness, a consuming concern with the possibilities of their own lives and fortunes.

In its most idealistic form, this egotistical self-concern was channeled into an intense passion for honor. And this fundamental egotism helped to transform what might have been a cult of conformity into a religion of personal distinction. These were not timid, characterless men seeking the passive pleasures of peer-group membership and approval. These were hard-driving, ambitious egotists, eager to tower above the group, and to be worshiped by it.

This was the cult of honor of the Elizabethan aspiring mind. It was born of a search for ideals in an artificial, unrealistic court life, formed by borrowed courtly and chivalric traditions, and given substance by certain basic metaphysical assumptions of the age. The coming of the Spanish War gave apparent social relevance to aspiration for personal honor and public honors, and provided an unprecedented opportunity for these young men to secure these idealistic goals. But the compelling force of the notion of honor, the compulsion that drove men to seek the bubble reputation even in the cannon's mouth, lay in the other-directedness, the authoritarian-mindedness, and the tremendous egotism of these young devotees of honor. Like the lust for power which will be examined next, the passion for honor was a vital component of the aspiring mind of the Elizabethan younger generation.

V. *A lust for dominion*

Soon after the outbreak of the Spanish War, a second center of the ambitious activities of the Elizabethan younger generation developed, not on the battlefield, but at court. The war years began in the middle 1580's; what we may call the bottleneck years of political ambition and rivalry at court began in the early 1590's. Both these trends outlasted the reign, though the impact of the war diminished, while political intrigue increased, as the reign drew to a close. The war had focused the idealistic aspirations of young men on the quest for honor. The bitter political competition of the bottleneck years, beginning in the next decade, concentrated the ambitions of a more mature generation in a driving lust for power. The single-minded, often ruthless striving for political dominion which characterized the generation of 1560 in the 1590's is nowhere better exemplified than in the early career of Sir Robert Cecil, Lord Burghley's son and the future Earl of Salisbury, Secretary of State, and Lord Treasurer of England.

i. *An Elizabethan courtier in the political bottleneck years: Sir Robert Cecil*

The education of Robert Cecil, second son of Sir William Cecil, Lord Burghley, was intended to make him both a successful politician and a highly moral man; if anything, the emphasis of his upbringing was on the latter goal. From the point of view of Elizabethan pedagogy, the educational regimen of his childhood was almost ideal. He and his older brother Thomas devoted several hours each day to religious instruction—the catechism, prayers, Bible readings.[1] Under the direction of a private tutor, the boys composed Latin essays on such edifying themes as " '*Omnes ad studium virtutis incitantur spe premii*' (all are incited to the study of virtue by the hope of reward)."[2] Lord Burghley insisted

1. P. M. Handover, *The Second Cecil: The Rise to Power, 1563-1604, of Sir Robert Cecil* . . . (London, 1959), pp. 14-15.
2. *Ibid.*, p. 14.

that in his household "the strictest order" should be maintained always.[3] His ideas on the proper education of his sons were orthodox in the extreme: "Bring thy children up in learning and obedience," was his advice.[4]

And yet, if Robert Cecil's later career is any indication, all this moral indoctrination failed signally to "take," to mold the character of the man. Part of the reason for this failure may be found in Lord Burghley's typical determination not to jeopardize the proper and salutary discipline of his children by showing undue affection for them. Speaking of his first-born, he once declared proudly that "I never showed any fatherly fancy to him, but in teaching and correcting."[5] It is also likely that young Robert Cecil detected a certain apparent disingenuousness in the moralism of the older generation represented most prominently by his father. At St. John's College, Cambridge, for instance, he studied under an old friend of his father's, Dr. Andrew Perne, an "outstanding administrator" whose talent for compromise may have been the salvation of Cambridge under Queen Mary—just the kind of man, in short, who would appeal to Lord Burghley.[6] But there was another side to Dr. Perne: "few men have earned such contempt as Perne for pliancy in religious conviction"; the students called him "Old Andrew Turncoat" and "Judas Perne."[7] The contradictions inherent in receiving moral indoctrination from such a man—or, for that matter, from a strict father whose own career had twisted its way through so many political and religious regimes—can hardly have escaped so shrewd a head as the young Robert Cecil.

But there was another side to the upbringing of Lord Burghley's sons—a side upon which Robert seized with natural avidity. The young Cecils, like the Sidneys and the Bacons and many other sons of the English ruling class, were raised up to be themselves governors of England. Lord Burghley, furthermore, disgusted with the frivolous character of his older son, seems to have intended from the first that Robert should succeed him as the

3. *Ibid.*
4. *Ibid.*, p. 13.
5. *Ibid.*

6. *Ibid.*, p. 24.
7. *Ibid.*

Queen's chief minister.[8] And Robert, a dwarfish hunchback from childhood, apparently took naturally to the pursuit of political power under the tutelage of the old fox himself. He thus became in his youth not only the object of heavy doses of moral indoctrination, but also "a student of political power."[9]

Like other young future governors of England, Robert Cecil grew up close to the court and its secrets, and early came to understand the intricacies of the "courtier system" by means of which the nation was ruled. Cecil's most recent political biographer has admirably summed up the great value of such intimate knowledge of the court to the seeker after political power:

It enabled him to trace the web of human relationships which included not only those tied by blood and marriage, but friends, servants, dependents. He learnt who had quarreled with this one, repulsed that, insulted another, was in debt to him and had been jilted by her: the endless . . . network that governed men's motives. To know these secrets was to know where men were vulnerable and how they could be swayed.[10]

To sway the causes and direct the courses of his fellow men became the dominant goal of the little hunchback's career. The public honors might go to handsome cavaliers like Essex; the reality of power would be Robert Cecil's.

Burghley's protégé learned more than the intricate network of personal relationships that was the court of Elizabeth: he learned also to operate successfully according to the unwritten rules of the courtier system of government. He learned from a master the techniques of patronage, of faction struggles, of securing the all-important royal consent to policies and to promotions. In the early 1580's Burghley wrote out for his son "Ten Precepts" of social and political success, the "outstanding quality" of which was their "realism" of outlook, their understanding and acceptance of the facts of life.[11] The younger Cecil surely took very seriously these maxims on patrons and clients and kindred, on law suits and profitable marriages, on lending and borrowing,

---

8. Joel Hurstfield, "Robert Cecil, Earl of Salisbury: Minister of Elizabeth and James I," *History Today*, VII (1957), 280; J. E. Neale, *The Elizabethan Political Scene* (London, 1948), p. 20; Handover, pp. 31, 34.

9. Handover, p. 17.   *11. Ibid.*, p. 31 and 31 n.

10. Ibid.

and on many other topics of vital concern to an Elizabethan courtier. This side of Cecil's education, then, was eminently practical, pragmatic, even callous.

Meanwhile, in the 1580's, young Cecil's career got under way, under the patronage of his father. The younger Cecil sat in the parliaments of the 1580's, and by 1586 he had begun to take an actual part in the public business of the Commons. Then in 1589, when Robert married and became a landholder of sorts, he was also made sheriff of Hertfordshire, a local dignity commensurate with his new status. During this same decade, furthermore, he twice traveled abroad to develop his knowledge of foreign affairs—to France in 1584 and to the Netherlands with the peace commission in 1588. On both of these journeys he impressed important people with his capacities, increased his knowledge, and developed his own self-confidence.[12] By the beginning of the 1590's, then, Cecil's apprenticeship was ending, his ambitions fully developed and focused on political power. In the political bottleneck years that followed, Cecil enjoyed a degree of success that was almost unique, and certainly unexcelled, at the court of Elizabeth.

Handover suggests that Robert Cecil's ambitions were deliberately directed by his father toward one or the other of the "two posts of supreme power" in Elizabethan England—the offices of Lord Treasurer and of Principal Secretary of State.[13] These posts were held in the 1580's by Burghley himself and by an earlier protégé of his, Sir Francis Walsingham, of the Queen's generation. Whether or not there was so large a degree of calculation in the matter, it is certain that immediately on the death of Walsingham in 1590, Robert Cecil's ambitions turned that way. Supporting his candidacy were his father's immense influence and his own increasingly recognized talents. Against him were his age —he was not yet thirty; the fact that he had never held any important government post; the opposition of the Earl of Essex, the Queen's great favorite; and the aging Queen's growing tendency to procrastinate. For the next six years, then, Cecil aspired to the office of Secretary of State; through those long years, he wheedled, connived, and plotted for it. One by one, the obstacles

12. *Ibid.,* pp. 38-43, 55-62.   13. *Ibid.,* p. 34.

to his appointment were overcome, until at length the place was his. But it is the long campaign leading up to his investiture with the signet seal in 1596 that is of special interest here, for this suit for high office illustrates many of the problems and possibilities of political ambition in the bottleneck years.

The younger Cecil began to share the business of the office long before he held the title. During most of those six years, while the office of Secretary of State was officially vacant, the work of the Secretary was more or less shared by three men: Lord Treasurer Burghley; old John Wolley, the Queen's Latin Secretary; and Robert Cecil.[14] But Burghley's age and gout were telling on him, and he could not add many new duties to his already heavy burden of state business.[15] Wolley apparently concentrated mainly on the bureaucratic routine of the office, as he had during Walsingham's last years.[16] Thus most of the responsibility for the policy decisions of the Secretary of State devolved onto young Cecil. Not much more than a year after Walsingham's death, it could be said with some assurance that "the whole management of the Secretary's place" was in Cecil's competent hands.[17]

Other government business also began to pass through Cecil's hands—and with it, promotion to positions of real responsibility. In 1591 Cecil was summoned to serve on the Privy Council, the one young man among a dozen greybeards. No document was now too important or too confidential to be entrusted to him. About this time, too, he began to sit on government commissions of real significance. In 1592, for example, he was one of the commission to try Sir John Perrot, "his first important trust" of a public nature.[18] That same year he was put in sole charge of the investigation of the illicit looting of the captured Spanish treasure ship, the *Madre de Dios*, a task requiring extraordinary delicacy and diligence. In the Parliament of 1593 Cecil was assigned the vital task of guiding the government supply bill through the House. He thus became "perhaps the only man" ever to become "virtual leader of the House of Commons" with almost no pre-

14. F. M. G. Evans, *The Principal Secretary of State: A Survey of the Office from 1558 to 1680* (Manchester, London, and New York, 1923), pp. 53-55.
15. Handover, pp. 74, 79.   16. Evans, p. 55.
17. *C. S. P., Dom., 1591-1594*, CCXXXIX, 159.
18. Algernon Cecil, *A Life of Robert Cecil First Earl of Salisbury* (London, 1915), p. 52.

vious service of real significance.[19] This exalted role was only in part the result of his father's influence; it was also a recognition of the very real capacity for the business of governing which he had already demonstrated.

Other promotions came to him too, titles and offices of a more honorific nature. Thus his first request for the Secretaryship, in 1591, netted him a knighthood instead. A more chivalric soul would have been greatly honored; a more politically naïve mind might have seen this as a sort of consolation prize, and thus a matter for chagrin. Robert Cecil reacted in neither of these ways. He probably had little use for the knighthood—he was after real power, not honorable trappings; but he was too shrewd a politician to try to push the Queen into moving faster than her cautious nature was willing to go. Cecil saw the knighthood as one step on a long road, at the end of which lay his real political goal.

But even his patience began to wear thin as the years passed and the seal of office still remained beyond his reach. By 1595 it was apparently common knowledge that he was doing the work of the Secretary of State without the title—"in place, but not nominate," as Lady Bacon put it.[20] "As for that," Cecil replied, "I deal nor speak no more of it; but as long as none is placed, I wait still, though I may think myself . . . hardly used."[21] But he knew the facts of political life and was resolved to await her Majesty's pleasure, however long the delay.

Meanwhile, during the early 1590's, the ambitions of Sir Robert Cecil became intertwined with those of other courtiers, particularly with those of the Earl of Essex and the Bacon brothers. Essex was apparently determined that no man's power and honor should overtop his own. He therefore launched a bitter vendetta against the Cecils, a feud that was to divide the court throughout the nineties and that in the end would cost Essex his honor, his power, and his life. Francis and Anthony Bacon, seeking careers in the judiciary and the foreign service respectively, moved from one of these great factions to the other in the course

19. *Ibid.*, p. 61.
20. Lady Bacon to Anthony Bacon, Jan. 23, 1595, in James Spedding, *The Letters and the Life of Francis Bacon* . . . (London, 1890), I, 346.
21. *Ibid.*

of the decade. Francis Bacon felt that the Cecil faction was deliberately ignoring his suits out of fear of any possible competition for Sir Robert, the apple of his father's eye. In any case,
for one reason or another, Francis Bacon's petitions for preferment became crucial points of conflict in the struggle between
Essex, who supported Bacon, and the Cecils, who rejected him.
In this single aspect of the Essex-Cecil feud is epitomized much
of the political intrigue of those intensely competitive years.

Bacon sought first, in 1593, to be named Attorney-General,
one of the highest judgeships in the land. The climax of his long
petitioning came in the celebrated "coach interview" between
Bacon's patron Essex and Sir Robert Cecil, a scrap of recorded
conversation which provides a valuable glimpse of the backstage
bitterness of Elizabethan court rivalry. In this relatively candid
exchange, Essex impetuously announced that he would put all
his influence on the line for Francis Bacon's promotion. He then
went on to hint darkly that "a younger than Francis Bacon, of
less learning, and of no greater experience, was suing and shoving
with all force for an office of far greater importance. . . ."[22] Cecil
passed over the obvious insinuation casually enough; but that
same day he and his father hastened to the Queen and "straitly
urged" her to give the Attorneyship to Bacon's far more experienced rival, Sir Edward Coke, and to appoint Cecil himself
her Principal Secretary of State.[23] In April, 1594, the former
purpose, at least, was accomplished—a blow to Bacon's ambitions
and a defeat for Essex as a patron and faction leader. It was about
the time of this early victory over his dashing rival that Robert
Cecil began to be known to his enemies as *Robertus diabolus*,
Robert the devil.[24]

Next, Francis Bacon sought the lower ranking post of Solicitor-General; and again Essex drew upon all his influence to obtain
the place for Bacon. Once more, too, the Cecils were believed to
be fighting the appointment. Bacon himself wrote to Robert Cecil:
"I was told by asseveration that your Honor was bought . . . for
two thousand angels . . . [and that] you wrought underhand against
me," though of course Bacon could not admit that he believed these

22. Thomas Birch, *Memoirs of the Reign of Queen Elizabeth* . . . (London,
1754), I, 153.
    23. Handover, p. 116.   24. *Ibid.*, p. 119.

rumors.[25] Whoever or whatever was behind the decision, late in 1595, a much more mature student of the law was selected for the Solicitorship. And the decision was certainly another blow to the Earl of Essex, and thus a victory for the Cecil faction. Sir Robert Cecil, however, never crowed over these victories; in fact, he was extremely conciliatory towards the Earl throughout the earlier 1590's. For Cecil was a clever enough politician to know that, though he might win sundry lesser encounters, he would never have the Secretaryship if he broke openly with the Queen's greatest favorite.[26]

The year 1596 was a crucial one for the Cecil-Essex feud, and for the political ambitions of Robert Cecil. That year brought great glory to Essex; and it saw the accomplishment of Cecil's first major bid for political power. But before the year was over, it was evident to wiser heads that Cecil alone had truly triumphed.

In the summer of 1596, Essex sailed away to Spain, to conquer Cadiz and win undying fame. By leaving the court, however, he abandoned the political battlefield to his rival—always a cardinal error in courtly intrigue. Cecil was not slow to take advantage of the opportunity for unimpeded political maneuver thus afforded him. Between him and the Secretary of State's office there now stood only the Earl's much less forceful candidate, the learned Sir Thomas Bodley. With his usual shrewdness, Cecil deliberately avoided a confrontation with Bodley: in fact, he conciliated and even cultivated the man Essex sought to pit against him. Thus, with Essex gone and Bodley won over, the road was open at last; and Robert Cecil reached once more for the political prize he had coveted for six long years. Again he petitioned the aging Queen to grant him the Secretary's post, a position for which his noble father recommended him, and for which he had long since demonstrated his capacity. And this time, with Essex's voice no longer whispering at her ear, Elizabeth granted the Cecils' request. Early in July, 1596, her Majesty conferred upon Sir Robert Cecil the great signet, the seal of the Principal Secretary of State. While Essex was reaping his greatest harvest of honor, Cecil had taken the first giant step on his road to unchallenged power.

For with the seal of office, real power came to Sir Robert Cecil.

25. Francis Bacon to Robert Cecil, March? 1595, in Spedding, I, 355-356.
26. Handover, p. 128.

As the bearer of the signet, for one thing, Cecil became the Queen's official voice to her ministers in the Privy Council. Even more important, with the seal he received the privilege of readiest access to her Majesty, to that royal personage who was the ultimate source of all favor and preferment, the fountainhead of all political power in England. Those who considered Cecil their enemy winced at this sharp increase in his already considerable power: "Sir Robert," Laby Bacon warned her son Francis, "hath now great advantage and strength. . . ."[27] The "power and policy" of the Cecils loomed up more impressively than ever before.[28] Sir Robert Cecil himself, not surprisingly, saw his new place in terms of the great power it brought to him. In a brief tract on the powers of his office, he described the unique authority of the bearer of the signet seal:

All Officers and Councillors of Princes have a prescribed authority by Patent, by Custom, or by oath, the Secretary only excepted, but to the Secretary . . . there is liberty to negotiate at discretion at home and abroad with friends and enemies in all matters of speech and intelligence.[29]

The Principal Secretary of State, he wrote, with perhaps a trace of exultation, "hath no warrant or commission . . . but the virtue and word of his Sovereign."[30] The real business of government, he indicated, the key decisions, might even be worked out by the Sovereign and her Secretary in private consultation, and the results simply rubber-stamped by the rest of the Council.[31] Here was power enough to intoxicate any aspiring mind.

That same autumn, as a postscript to Cecil's victory and a demonstration of his new power, came a series of stinging rebuffs to the Earl of Essex. The gallant Earl returned from Cadiz crowned with laurel and decked with honors—only to be baffled at every turn by the hunchbacked little politician. Essex, for instance, planned to have a eulogistic account of his glorious deeds in Spain printed up for popular consumption; but the new Secretary of State circumvented this move by personally com-

27. Lady Bacon to Anthony Bacon, July 10, 1596, in Birch, II, 61.
28. *Ibid.*
29. Robert Cecil, Earl of Salisbury, *The State and Dignitie of a Secretarie of Estate's Place* . . . (London, 1642), p. 1.
30. *Ibid.*, p. 2.   31. *Ibid.*, pp. 2-3.

posing an official, government-approved version. The Earl expected nothing but praise for his valor and chivalry; the Secretary saw to it that Essex was pressed hard for an explanation of the mundane but essential fact that the expedition had failed even to pay for itself, let alone show a profit. Cecil went further; he made it his business to pry as much of the Queen's own investment as he could out of the swashbuckling heroes of Cadiz. In all these ways the fame of Cadiz was tarnished and rendered useless for political purposes. After a particularly galling session on the expenses of the expedition, Essex wrote in a rueful humor to a kinsman of Cecil's: "This day I was more braved by your little cousin than ever I was by any man in my life."[32] The Earl's frustrated followers fumed at Cecil's victory over their patron, cursed him—among themselves—for a dog and viper, jeered at his deformed body and scuttling walk, and swore to be damned before they would trust Robert the devil again.[33]

From this first major success in his struggle for political power, the road wound steadily upward for Sir Robert Cecil. Three years after his appointment, with Lord Burghley only months in his grave, an observer wrote that the aged Queen was "wholly directed by Mr. Secretary, who now rules all as his father did."[34] Two years thereafter Cecil saw his dashing arch-rival die on the scaffold, the greatest casualty of the political wars of the bottle-neck years. By this time James VI of Scotland could write of Cecil, "He is King there, in effect"; and a popular ballad put the universal opinion into jog-trot verse:

> Little Cecil trips up and down,
> He rules both Court and Crown. . . .[35]

Modern scholarship agrees that under Elizabeth, Sir Robert Cecil became, next to the Queen herself, "the dominant force in the country."[36] Nor is there any doubt that Cecil successfully made the dangerous transition from one reign to the next, and even in-

32. Earl of Essex to Anthony Bacon, Sept. 8, 1596, in Birch, II, 131.

33. Handover, p. 145; cf. Sir William Knollys to the Earl of Essex, June, 1597, and same to same, n. d., in Birch, II, 350-352.

34. *C. S. P., Dom. 1598-1601*, CCLXXI, 106.

35. Ballad, 1601, P. R. O. State Papers, Domestic, 12/278/23, quoted in Handover, p. 230.

36. Evans, p. 57.

creased his greatness under James I. During the first decade of King James, Cecil continued to be "alpha and omega in council," became in addition Lord Treasurer and Earl of Salisbury, and acquired landed estates in twenty counties.[37]

In his steady rise to power Sir Robert Cecil, like his less successful fellows, was driven by high political aspirations. His friendliest biographers agree that the little Secretary was ambitious. Even his Victorian descendant admits that, at this early stage of his career, Robert Cecil was gripped by a compulsion to succeed in the politics of the courtier system. The Victorian Salisbury understands some of the psychological mechanism at work, but he surely understates the case when he writes that Robert Cecil "was as anxious as most young men of ability to attract notice" and that he "preferred his own promotion before that of other people."[38] Biographers of those other outstanding personalities of his generation with whom Cecil's ambitions brought him into conflict have often condemned him outright as a scheming, unprincipled climber, an understandably exaggerated position. Nevertheless Hurstfield, whose brief treatment of Cecil is probably the most objective available evaluation, describes his career in the 1590's as "that of a cunning and greedy politician."[39]

There seems to be no doubt, then, that the primary goal of his political ambitions was power. He sought sovereignty, dominion. He sought the power to sway causes, to dispense patronage, to impose his will upon the policy of the English nation, to be the real King of the English court. He was, says one biographer, "not hungry for titles that carried no access of political power."[40] "What he looked for," another student of this complex man declares, "was the reality, not the semblance of power."[41] Sir Robert Cecil aspired to political power with the same tenacity of will that the Earl of Essex dedicated to his quest for honor. And Robert the devil was at least as successful in his realm as the chivalric Earl was in his.

37. Roger Wilbraham, *The Journal of Sir Roger Wilbraham . . . 1593-1616* (Camden Soc. Pub., 3rd ser., Vol. IV; London, 1902), p. 106; Hurstfield, "Robert Cecil . . . Minister of Elizabeth . . .," 284; Algernon Cecil, p. 314.

38. Algernon Cecil, p. 356.

39. Hurstfield, "Robert Cecil . . . Minister of Elizabeth . . .," 279.

40. Handover, p. 66.   41. Algernon Cecil, p. 254.

Robert Cecil's career was a model of political success under the courtier system of government. One biographer has described him, without much exaggeration, as "the only one of Elizabeth's courtiers whose career suffered no reverse."[42] Cecil's skill, good fortune, and success comprised the ideal to which politically ambitious members of the generation of 1560 aspired. He was born with ideal family connections and complete access to the court; he possessed real talent for governing—diligence, a head for detail, and skill at administration and negotiation. Thus equipped, Cecil went from promotion to promotion and from victory to victory in the faction-ridden 1590's. To trace even a portion of his career is to delineate the archetypal political success of the time, to see what his contemporaries all desired to have, if not to be.

ii. The two generations in the bottleneck years

The coming of the war in the 1580's had clearly revealed the generational fissures which divided the Elizabethan ruling class; in the 1590's the developing political ambitions of the younger men brought the two generations into direct conflict. The Elizabethan political scene in the nineties is usually interpreted in terms of the long feud between the Cecils and the Earl of Essex, or of the triangular rivalry and brief, ill-starred triumvirate of Robert Cecil, Essex, and Raleigh. From a broader point of view, however, this turbulent decade of seething ambitions and Machiavellian intrigue may be better understood as a generational revolution. The younger generation, too long denied place and power by their elders, revolted against the leaders of the older generation, against the determination of the old men to retain control of court and country. The young men bickered among themselves—they could hardly avoid it in those years of too many ambitious courtiers and too few available places—but they were always conscious of the common enemy, the capricious old Queen and her domineering ministers. On the difficulties and frustrations of this common struggle, even the bitterest enemies could agree.

The courtier system of government, in which the aspiring

42. G. Ravenscroft Dennis, *The Cecil Family* (Boston and New York, 1914), p. 149.

minds of the generation of 1560 sought to participate, was a deceptively simple, if rather unstable way of running a country. The basic structure of the system, within which these young men had grown up, was always before their eyes. At its center stood the majestic figure of the monarch, the aging but still formidable Queen Elizabeth, the soul of the older generation. About the foot of the throne were grouped the inner circle of royal favorites— the greatest ministers, the most renowned peers, all those upon whom Majesty smiled most freely and most frequently. By 1590 most of these were also old men, the aging leaders of Elizabeth's own generation, the few survivors of Burghley's. Beyond this inner circle of great favorites, however, there was a much larger ring of aspirants to the power and public honors only the Queen could bestow. And a great many of these were younger men, men of the generation of 1560.

The courtier system operated through patronage and personal favoritism, often effectively by-passing established institutions, from Parliament to Privy Council. Through the great royal favorites, services and petitions were channeled from the base of the power pyramid to its apex, and authority and rewards from the top down. In theory at least, all rewards were conferred as just remuneration for good service to the crown. Actually, the system operated to a large extent on the basis of extra-legal gratuities and bribes, and of a delicate balance of factions carefully maintained by the shrewd old Queen.

Elements of old and new practices and institutions blended in the courtier system of government and ruling-class careerism. MacCaffrey, referring apparently to the older Elizabethans, describes them as "virtually the first generation of that compact yet flexible 'aristocracy' which in another hundred years would elbow aside the monarchy and in the eighteenth century would enjoy a golden age of uncontested power and privilege."[43] The Elizabethan courtier class, he says, "shared a new conception of politics as a career," a conception that envisioned tremendous rewards through service and skill at the politics of the court. But the younger Elizabethans were the heirs of the past as well as the

43. Wallace T. MacCaffrey, "Place and Patronage in Elizabethan Politics," *Elizabethan Government and Society*, ed. S. T. Bindoff, J. Hurstfield, and C. H. Williams (London, 1961), pp. 98-99.

heralds of the future of English politics. Historically, the Elizabethan aristocracy stood midway between the fighting barons of the Wars of the Roses and the parliamentary politicians of Walpole's day. Their courtier system of government included many recognizable features of the politics of later times, certainly. But it also permitted rivals for honor and power to settle their differences directly, with sword and dagger. And in the sixteenth century, as in earlier times, the fallen favorite quite often lost not only his political power, but his property, his freedom, and even his life. The primitive brutality of an earlier day thus mingled with the subtlest political manipulation in the career of the typical ambitious courtier of the Elizabethan younger generation.

For the young aspiring mind, there were many roads to success through the courtier system. Obviously, continuous good service could bring considerable success to a hard-working courtier, as it did to both Lord Burghley and his son Robert Cecil, each in his turn. But the feeling that valuable services were not always adequately rewarded was too widespread to be entirely without foundation. The Dean of Durham once preached a sermon on the subject before the Queen herself, "complaining that rewards were not bestowed by those in authority upon such as deserved them . . . often and covertly inveighing at the nice point of niggardness at court."[44] The ambitious Elizabethan courtier, therefore, seldom depended on good service alone to win him the rewards of the courtier system.

At the opposite extreme, ingratiating court manners, if practiced indefatigably enough, might carry a man far. Robert Carey, for example, was a courtier's courtier: he cultivated the best people, attended every ball, masque, and tilt, dressed with as much attention to the latest fashion as any man—and ended his long life as a leading officer of the royal household and first Earl of Monmouth to boot.[45] Flattery was also a basic ingredient of success at the court of Elizabeth; and the most fulsome compliments and most passionate protestations of devotion were of course reserved for the Queen herself. Lord Mountjoy was a past master of this minor art, and an extract from one of his letters to Queen

44. Mr. Faunt to Mr. A. Bacon, March 12, 1584, in Birch, I, 48.
45. C. H. Firth, "Robert Carey," *DNB*, III, 984-985.

Elizabeth will serve to re-create much of the atmosphere of this side of the courtier system in action:

Sacred Majesty,

If darkness be the mother of fearful apprehensions, excuse me that so long have wanted those beams of yours, that only give light and lightness to my heart, which cannot but be troubled in so tempestuous a sea, having lost the sight of my only star. But since by your divine letters I feel the influence, though I cannot see the heavenly substance, my mind shall sing in the midst of all dangers: for I cannot be so weary, but your voice will make me go cheerfully forwards; nor so sick but I shall be sound if you bid me be whole. Yet shall I never bid farewell to all bitterness, till I kiss your sweet hands, who have only power to lift up or depress my mind. . . .[46]

For the ambitious Elizabethan courtier, such elegant epistles were little more than business letters, and their composition was a necessary skill.

Even more essential to the success of Elizabethan ambitions, however, was coin of the realm, and plenty of it: money for the fees, gratuities, and bribes which lubricated the machinery of the court and the government; money to buy the highest offices within the gift of the Queen's ministers. Even such models of public rectitude as Lord Burghley and the great jurist Sir Edward Coke were not above such dealings.[47] As the Earl of Essex wrote to a client, aspiring young Sir Henry Unton: "Mr. Vice Chamberlain gave me his word to do his best [for you], and the more for my sake. But I think your best friend unto him will be your £1,000."[48] When his wife was caught selling places in the garrison at Berwick, another rising courtier replied tartly but accurately that "it is not the use in any place . . . to do good turns *gratis*."[49] At the court of Elizabeth, where getting ahead depended in large measure upon good turns, this was a fact of great significance to the ambitious courtier.

One of the great pitfalls of the courtier system, as the older

46. Godfrey Goodman, *The Court of King James the First* . . . (London, 1839), II, 28-29.

47. J. E. Neale, *The Elizabethan Political Scene* (London, 1948), pp. 6-7.

48. Great Britain, Hist. MSS Comm., *Calendar of the Manuscripts of . . . the Marquis of Salisbury* . . . (London, 1883), IV, iv, 276.

49. Calendar of Border Papers, ii, 787, quoted in Neale, p. 8.

generations had discovered, was its liability to factionalism. Feuds between rival factions for the Queen's favor were often bitter struggles in which the careers of even the greatest hung in the balance. "I have beaten Mountjoy and Knollys in the Council," exulted Essex after winning the Lord Lieutenancy of Ireland from his rivals, "and by God I will beat Tyrone in the field!"[50] But when he set out to reconquer Ireland, he was already environed with enemies, and in the end rival factions pulled even the great Essex down. Elizabeth has been given much credit for her skill in manipulating court factions to her own advantage; but for the courtiers themselves, the feuding factions were more often than not an unadulterated curse.

This was the courtier system of government, the system through which the Queen and her chief ministers governed the country, and through which her courtiers sought to rise to honors, to power, and to the wealth necessary to attain these ends. In the best of times, it was a difficult method of ruling, and an even more difficult arena in which to make a successful career. The young gentlemen of the generation of 1560 simply did their best with it, as their fathers had done.

Toward the end of the reign, moreover, this already unstable system was put under a tremendous additional strain by the swelling demands of the younger generation for their share of the high places and the power. The "soaring bribes and the feverish competition for place and favor," says Neale, "have the appearance of an inflationary movement: too many suitors pursuing too few privileges."[51] Such an inflationary movement did in fact take place toward the end of the sixteenth century. By the 1590's it was becoming increasingly difficult to make "the mass of the gentry pay for the benefits which were confined to a limited number of peers and courtiers."[52] This recalcitrance, combined with the tremendous expense of the Spanish War and with Elizabeth's increasing parsimoniousness, cut the flow of royal rewards and gifts to a trickle, and left her servants discontented and impoverished. At the same time, the rise of many families to new

50. Essex to John Harrington, n. d., in Thomas Park, ed., *Nugae Antiquae* . . . (London, 1804), I, 246.
51. Neale, p. 19.
52. Lawrence Stone, "The Inflation of Honors, 1558-1641," *Past and Present*, No. 14 (Nov., 1958), p. 46.

riches in the second half of the sixteenth century created an unprecedented demand for titles of honor as recognition of their new
status—a demand which was further intensified by the war.[53]
Inevitably, the more talented and ambitious of these climbers,
men like Francis Bacon and Sir Walter Raleigh and Charles
Blount, Lord Mountjoy, also demanded a share in the ruling of
Elizabethan England. They sought seats on the Privy Council,
high legal or administrative posts, supreme military commands.
They wanted not only dignities, but real authority; not only
honor, but power.

Seen in a generational context, the situation was even more
disturbing for the youth of those bitterly competitive years. The
dying off of the great names of the Queen's generation—Leicester,
Walsingham, Drake, Hawkins, and finally Burghley himself—
in the late 1580's and the 1590's has often been commented upon
by historians of the period. More important from a generational
point of view, however, was the fact that the regime itself, in the
person of the shrewd, crotchety old Queen, lived on too long. As
long as Elizabeth lived, her old favorites and advisers retained a
deathgrip on high offices and dignities. And even when her
venerable ministers passed away, the Queen procrastinated for
years about appointing new men to the posts their deaths left
vacant. During those last years of her forty-five-year reign, she
often lamented that there seemed to be no young men capable of
filling the thinning ranks of her "elder statesmen."[54] Whether
or not she was correct, her views on the matter were final. And
the resulting abnormal generational situation made a decisive
contribution to the increasing frustration of the political ambitions of the generation of 1560.

This is not to say that there was a great deal of direct competition for particular offices or honors between the generations.
Bacon's rivalry with a much older lawyer for the office of Solicitor-General, Essex's dispute with the old Lord Admiral over
administrative precedence—these were more the exception than
the rule. But the failure of the reign to end, bringing the inevitable shakeup of the highly personal power structure of the
court, gave the older generation of the Elizabethan ruling class a

53. Ibid., pp. 46-47.
54. G. B. Harrison, ed., *The Letters of Queen Elizabeth* (London, 1935), p. 284.

unique opportunity. During these last years of the reign, the inner circle of the older generation quietly arranged the transfer of their places to selected members of the rising generation—most commonly sons, nephews, or other young relatives of their followers, their allies, and themselves. In a time when so many "new men" and second- or third-generation aristocracy were clamoring for places, for their share of royal favor, and for employment in which they might earn promotion, this rigging of the competition was intolerable.

Furthermore, as they moved into the 1590's, the generation of 1560 made a shocking discovery. They realized suddenly that they were no longer young; and the realization fanned into a fierce flame the growing lust for dominion, for self-assertion and power smouldering within them. Youths became men much earlier in those times than they do today, and men died much sooner. In Elizabethan England youths were expected to shoulder the responsibilities and to share the aspirations of adults from their late teens. Many of these young courtiers had thus been seeking advancement, and experiencing the frustrations of failure, for ten or fifteen years before the bottleneck years even began in earnest. In the late 1570's Francis Bacon was already attached to the embassy in France, and Walter Raleigh was fighting in the continental wars: no wonder their patience was wearing thin by the early 1590's. Then too, the expected life-span of these Elizabethans was perhaps half what it would be today: sickness was more common and more painful, and in the 1590's a number of the comrades of their early years were already dead.[55] Their youth was spent: Shakespeare was in his thirties when he wrote of himself:

> In me thou seest the glowing of such fire,
> That on the ashes of his youth doth lie. . . .

It was the autumn of his life, and only winter lay ahead:

> When forty winters shall besiege thy brow,
> And dig deep trenches in thy beauty's field,
> Thy youth's proud livery, so gazed on now,
> Will be a tattered weed, of small worth held. . . .[56]

55. L. I. Dublin, *et al., Length of Life* (rev. ed.; New York, 1949), p. 32.
56. Sonnets lxxiii and ii.

In their thirties, then, these men began to see themselves as men whose lives and careers lay more behind them than before. And with the realization of oncoming age, a new note of desperation entered into their ambitions and their rivalries. Courtiers who had spent their youths to no purpose grew increasingly nervous and still more intense in their pursuit of the main chance. They fought in deadly earnest now, and every failure was a nail driven into the coffin of their high aspirations.

The very atmosphere of the court in the 1590's reeked of ambition, of political intrigue and of frustrated aspirations. "For matters of Court," wrote Sir Henry Lee to a friend in 1591, "all is as I last writ . . . nor men better pleased," for there were only a few places in the court and commonwealth exalted enough to satisfy the lust for dominion of a Raleigh or an Essex or a Bacon.[57] Lord Thomas Howard, the successful Elizabethan admiral, was one of the few to attain the zenith of his political ambitions. A decade after Elizabeth's death, Lord Howard was Earl of Suffolk and Lord Treasurer of England. His sons were all married to incomes of £1,000 or more per annum, and his oldest son and his three sons-in-law were all leading royal favorites, peers of the realm, and holders of high offices. Power in full measure was his then—power to raise mansions and palaces, to make or break the King's chief councillors, to bear all before him at the Council.[58] It was to such power as this that the Elizabethan younger generation aspired in the 1590's; but few in fact achieved it.

These young courtiers had grown up in the courtier system and knew its ways; and as their ambitions grew fiercer and more desperate with the passing years, they played the game with a new grimness that obeyed no rules and gave no quarter. The result was that "the standard of public morality was declining sharply during the last decade or so of the reign."[59] Lord Burghley noted and deplored the trend: "I will forbear," he wrote, "to mention the great and unusual fees exacted lately by reason of buying and selling offices, both judicial and ministerial. . . ."[60] The bitterness

57. Sir Henry Lee to the Earl of Shrewsbury, June 21, 1591, in Edmund Lodge, *Illustrations of British History in the Reigns of Henry VIII, Edward VI, Mary, Elizabeth, and James I* . . . (London, 1791), III, 30.

58. Wilbraham, p. 115.   60. Quoted in *ibid.*, p. 19.

59. Neale, p. 15.

and venality of the competition increased: the Essex-Raleigh-Cecil feud did not end till one of the rivals was dead and another in the Tower. But as the fratricidal strife within the generation of 1560 grew more intense, so did the resentment of the younger generation as a whole against the leaders of the older generation. However fiercely they competed with each other, both young Cecil and young Essex were among the many courtiers of their generation who awaited eagerly the new regime which would follow the death of the Queen. Essex, Cecil, and others among the Elizabethan younger generation risked their lives and fortunes in the later 1590's to correspond secretly with King James of Scotland, Elizabeth's most likely successor. They had all but abandoned hope for profit under the Elizabethan older generation; increasingly, their hopes were directed toward the time when the death of the Queen would clear the board and give them a fresh start. The accession of King James would be the accession of the Elizabethan younger generation to power.

In 1603, then, the death of Queen Elizabeth released the pent-up frustration of the now middle-aged generation of 1560. A contemporary analyzed the situation lucidly:

It is the manner, after the death of a long-reigning prince, that by discontented minds or wits long starved for want of employment, many new projects, suits, inventions, and infinite complaints are brought to the successor . . . so it happened at this time.[61]

Those who had not dared to run the risk while Elizabeth lived now "sent each secretly their friends and agents into Scotland to prepare their way with his Majesty. . . ."[62] The new King, in need of all the support he could get, deemed it expedient to try to satisfy the ravenous demands of these courtiers who had been too long excluded from the Elizabethan closed corporation of power. The result was the notorious auctioning of places and dignities, and the deliberate multiplication of titles and offices to supply the demand which the preceding regime had repressed for so long. Elizabeth's peerage of fifty-nine titled individuals, representing little increase over that of the preceding three centuries, was more

61. Wilbraham, p. 57.
62. *Ibid.*, p. 55; Francis Bacon to Mr. Kenney, 1603, in Henry Ellis, *Original Letters, Illustrative of English History* . . . [1st ser.] (London, 1825), III, 60.

than doubled by James I, and that in a reign only half as long.[63] Not only were titles of honor multiplied, so too were the great offices of state: the number of Privy Councillors, for instance, was also doubled. Twenty-five years after Elizabeth's death, a diplomat could report from England that "the number of councillors and titled persons [is] so constantly multiplied that they are no longer distinguishable from common people."[64] And yet, as will become evident presently, even this unparalleled distribution failed to satisfy the aspirations of the generation of 1560.

Other generations of course contributed to the welter of ambition and faction of the 1590's, and to the Jacobean trade in honors and places. Nevertheless, the leading personalities behind the mounting demand for a wider distribution of power in late Elizabethan England were members of the generation of 1560. Older men were already more or less satisfied, or were reconciled to their lot after too many years of failure. Younger men, with rare exceptions, were simply too young to be considered eligible for most positions of authority; most of them seem to have devoted their time to the pleasanter aspects of court life, or to the wars. In the political world of the 1590's, it was the generation of courtiers born about the year 1560 that surged to the fore.

The greatest authority on Elizabethan politics has noted the importance of the advent of the younger generation on the political scene of the 1590's. A "fundamental harmony in age and outlook between sovereign and statesmen," says Neale, had kept the realm on an even keel despite the factions and feuds of the earlier years of the reign.[65] But when Elizabeth's great contemporaries died one after another in the late 1580's and earlier 1590's, power had to be transferred too soon to younger men— slow though the transfer seemed to them. And "a new generation does not respond so readily to the restraints of a moral code which it inherits and does not create. The generation coming into power in the 1590's was out of tune with the old Queen and her ways."[66] The new generation and the old had drifted apart during the early years of the Spanish War; in the political bottle-

63. Charles R. Mayes, "The Sale of Peerages in Early Stuart England," *Journ. Mod. Hist.*, XXIX (1957), 21.

64. *C. S. P., Ven.*, XX, 763.   66. *Ibid.*, p. 19.

65. Neale, pp. 19-20.

neck years, the two generations were sundered completely the one from the other.

iii. The forms of aspiration for power

For a clear understanding of the forms of power as the Elizabethan younger generation conceived of them, the most useful sources of data are not to be found in the lives of this generation, but in their artistic creations. Source material on the real attitudes of Elizabethans toward political power is extremely limited; for unlike the semi-legitimate ideal of honor, power was not something one generally discussed even in private. If we are to comprehend the forms which the lust for dominion assumed in the minds of these ambitious young Elizabethans, it will therefore be advisable to focus our attention, not on men, but on literary stereotypes. Above all, a great deal of the truth about Elizabethan aspiration for power will be found in the archetypal figure of Tamburlaine the Great, and in the Tamburlaine-like heroes who stalked across Elizabethan stages in the plays of Marlowe and his fellows.

The heroes of the drama of the late eighties and the early nineties were often big men—"brave Ned Alleyn" big. They aspired high, and they succeeded tremendously: they dominated Fortune, defied the gods, changed the world. They were giants of courage and resolution: cities and nations bowed to their iron wills. They stormed through the world as conquerors, striving mightily and achieving greatly, destroying and creating kingdoms, laying empires at the feet of their ladies. They were incarnations of human power and achievement, fantastic projections of the passion for dominion that burned in Cecil and Essex and all their generation.[67]

Christopher Marlowe, the most famous dramatist of the years before Shakespeare's rise to pre-eminence in serious drama, was also the authentic voice of the aspiring mind of his genera-

67. A good playwright was one who " 'had a strife with Nature to outdo the life' . . . This 'outdoing the life' is, to put it roughly, achieved by heightening the figure of the hero beyond life-size, mostly through an extraordinary intensification of emotional stress" (Levin Ludwig Schucking, *The Baroque Character of the Elizabethan Tragic Hero* [London, 1938], p. 8).

tion. In his most famous plays, the two parts of *Tamburlaine the Great*, the lust for power which was such an important element of the aspiration of his contemporaries found its truest expression.[68] "There is throughout," writes a recent critic of *Tamburlaine*, "an emphasis upon human power. . . ."[69] Marlowe cast Providence out of history and viewed events as purely the consequences of human will in conflict with a capricious Fortune.[70] In such a harshly realistic world, pious moralism became essentially irrelevant to human conduct: it was success that counted.

Tamburlaine is a hero not because of any Christian virtues, but because of a Machiavellian *virtu* which enables him to master Fortune and win success in his enterprises. The theme of the play is a glorification of *virtu*. . . . which does not study the path to virtue, but rather the path to success.[71]

Will, resolution, *virtu*—these were key concepts in the younger generation's ethics of aspiration; and "success" to them as to Tamburlaine meant power, manifested in terms of achievement or conquest, mastery or dominion.

Tamburlaine was the highest aspiring mind of them all, and the most famous spokesman for the aspiring minds of his creator's generation. Bradbrook sees "the most direct statement of his nature" in the following description of him:

> . . . he was never sprung of human race,
> Since with the spirit of his fearful pride
> He dares so doubtlessly resolve of rule
> And by profession be ambitious.[72]

It was an awesome spectacle that Kit Marlowe put upon the stage, this godlike man who dared "so doubtlessly resolve of rule, and by profession be ambitious"—an embodiment of the inward drives of so many young courtiers of that generation. Tamburlaine was

68. C. F. Tucker Brooke, *The Reputation of Christopher Marlowe* (New Haven, Conn., 1922), p. 365.
69. Irving Ribner, "The Idea of History in Marlowe's *Tamburlaine*," *ELH*, XX (1953), 259.
70. *Ibid.*, pp. 252-260; Leo Lowenthal, *Literature and the Image of Man: Sociological Studies . . .* (Boston, 1957), p. 57.
71. Ribner, "The Idea of History . . .," 257-258.
72. *Tamburlaine the Great, Part I*, II, vii, quoted in M. C. Bradbrook, *Themes and Conventions of Elizabethan Tragedy* (Cambridge, 1960), pp. 137-138.

the incarnation of the ambition for power which comprised such an important part of the religion of high aspiration.

It was Marlowe's Tamburlaine who gave this side of the high aspiring mind its classic poetic expression:

> Nature, that fram'd us of four elements
> Warring within our breasts for regiment,
> Doth teach us all to have aspiring minds;
> Our souls, whose faculties can comprehend
> The wondrous architecture of the world,
> And measure every wandering planet's course,
> Still climbing after knowledge infinite,
> And always moving as the restless spheres,
> Wills us to wear ourselves and never rest,
> Until we reach the ripest fruit of all,
> That perfect bliss and sole felicity,
> The sweet fruition of an earthly crown.[73]

This famous passage is generally read as a praise of the "aspiring mind" in the modern sense of the term—a mind eager for self-improvement, for knowledge of a higher spiritual, philosophical, or even artistic sort. According to this common interpretation, lines 4-7 of the passage contain the central meaning, and the last three lines are dismissed as "bathos."[74] But the fact is that the basic Elizabethan meaning of the term "aspiring mind" was simply "ambitious man," and that Marlowe built upon this meaning. It would therefore appear more logical to reverse the emphases given above, to read the passage as a simple statement of Tamburlaine's high opinion of an earthly crown. That the passage combines this eulogy of worldly power with praise for the intellectual capacities of the soul seems to indicate that these Elizabethans possessed an interesting capacity for combining material and spiritual goals, a baroque talent which will be discussed in some detail presently. At any rate, Battenhouse is surely correct in seeing the lines in question as an expression of the "frank worldliness of Tamburlaine's ambition."[75]

73. *Tamburlaine the Great, Part I*, II, vii, 18-29.
74. Cf. Una M. Ellis-Fermor, *Christopher Marlowe* (London, 1927), p. 29; John H. Ingram, *Christopher Marlowe and His Associates* (London, 1904), p. 106.
75. Roy W. Battenhouse, *Marlowe's Tamburlaine: A Study in Renaissance Moral Philosophy* (Nashville, Tenn., 1941), p. 3. Battenhouse, however, gives the impression that Marlowe's purpose in writing these lines was that of the moralist, to present Tamburlaine as a horrible example of the Elizabethan vice of am-

But beyond the direct statement of his high aspirations, the vaulting ambitions of Tamburlaine are depicted concretely and symbolically throughout both parts of the play. The plot, such as it is, chronicles the unbroken success of Tamburlaine's effort to conquer the world; and the world-conqueror's character, particularly in the second part, is that of a monster of ambition. Power is the goal of Tamburlaine's highest aspirations: he dreams of being master of all nations, all empires. Marlowe employed every device available to the Elizabethan stage to present this abstraction, human power, in ways that his audience would understand and appreciate. From these various concrete representations of human power as a goal of aspiration, then, we can get a clearer idea of the forms of power as they were conceived by the aspiring minds of Marlowe's generation. In the late sixteenth century, these forms or particular meanings of power included the power to defeat one's enemies, the power to rule, and power over one's own destiny. All three were clearly depicted in *Tamburlaine,* and in its many imitations.

To begin with, Marlowe, like many other Elizabethan playwrights, made liberal use of spectacular processions across the stage, with drums, trumpets, and as many "extras" as could be collected. These processions, here as elsewhere, were quite often intended as Roman triumphs, "a conventional method for depicting a glorious hero at the height of his fortune."[76] Such triumphs were in fact still staged in sixteenth-century Europe: Elizabeth celebrated the Armada victory with such a spectacle. On the stage the triumphal procession presented the conqueror, his army, his prisoners, and often his rich booty, for the admiration of the spectators. The symbolism was simple, and was not lost on symbol- and allegory-conscious Elizabethans, for whom analogical reasoning was almost as natural as causal thinking has become for us. Here, marching in splendor to a crescendo of mar-

bition. Any other interpretation, he feels, would wrongly "identify Marlowe with doctrines which were anathema to every Elizabethan moralist" (p. 7). The attitude taken in the present study is that, whatever his own views on the matter, Marlowe was a professional dramatist who gave his audiences what they wanted to hear; and that this play, with its emphasis on worldly ambitions, was slanted toward the young men of his own generation who shared the attitude toward ambition expressed in word and deed by Tamburlaine the Great.

76. Alice S. Venezky, *Pageantry on the Elizabethan Stage* (New York, 1951), pp. 29-30.

tial music, was a mighty man; and about him, as overwhelming evidence of his power, were both the instrument of his will (his army) and the proof of his achievement (his prisoners and his booty). Tamburlaine the Great was above all such a man of invincible power. His very first entrance upon the stage was made with soldiers, prisoners, and treasure.[77] The "most remembered" lines in the play were Tamburlaine's jeering injunctions to the "pampered jades of Asia," the conquered kings who pull his chariot in a later triumph.[78] This was a form of power that men of the generation of 1560 could readily grasp, a form that some had already experienced, that many hoped to enjoy.

A second symbol of power in *Tamburlaine* and in many other romances and history plays was the crown, the emblem of royalty. Kingship of course had many significances in the royalty-conscious sixteenth century, but one of the most commonly emphasized characteristics of the king in the Elizabethan theater was his immense, awe-inspiring power. On the Elizabethan stage the crown was above all "the symbol of power and rule."[79] For Tamburlaine, "that fiery thirster after sovereignty," the power of the royal seat is its greatest attraction:

> To wear a crown enchas'd with pearl and gold,
> Whose virtues carry with it life and death;
> To ask and have, command and be obeyed. . . .[80]

The awesome power of kingship was presented in cosmic terms by the anonymous author of *Edward the Third*:

> Now, boy, thou hearest what thundering terror 'tis
> To buckle for a kingdom's sovereignty:
> The earth, with giddy trembling when it shakes,
> Or when the exhalations of the air
> Breaks in extremity of lightning flash,
> Affright not more than Kings, when they dispose
> To show the rancor of their high-swollen hearts.[81]

The power of kings was supernatural, for kings were God's vice-regents here on earth: "It is not certainly any power of man,

---

77. *Tamburlaine the Great, Part I*, I, ii.
78. Tucker Brooke, 370-371.   79. Bradbrook, p. 143.
80. *Tamburlaine the Great, Part I*, II, vi, 31; II, v, 60-62.
81. *The Reign of King Edward the Third*, III, i, 125-131, in Karl Warnke and Ludwig Proescholdt, eds., *Pseudo-Shakespearean Plays* (Halle, 1883), Vol. III.

but a more supernatural thing, to keep the nations of the earth in such awe and order as we see them in," affirmed Lancelot Andrews.[82] And Tamburlaine of course agreed: to a lieutenant's orthodox assertion that "to be a king, is half to be a god," the world-conqueror replied, ". . . a god is not so glorious as a king. . . ."[83] The golden crown of the sovereign was the ultimate symbol of earthly authority and power for sixteenth-century Englishmen; and though they might only aspire so high in stage plays, yet sovereignty itself, to "command and be obeyed," was as great a goal of aspiring minds as was triumphant conquest.

A third symbolic representation of power as a goal of aspiration was the new relationship between the aspiring mind and the fickle goddess Fortune. In the plays of the late 1580's and the early 1590's, the discouraging traditional image of futile ambition rising on the wheel of Fortune, only to fall at the next turn, was replaced by a new, startling myth of Fortune and the aspiring mind. In his first appearance on the stage, Tamburlaine the aspiring Scythian shepherd announces the new dispensation:

> I hold the Fates bound fast in iron chains,
> And with my hand turn Fortune's wheel about,
> And sooner shall the sun fall from his sphere
> Than Tamburlaine be slain or overcome.[84]

This mightiest of aspiring minds

> . . . hath Fortune so at his command,
> That she shall stay and turn her wheel no more,
> As long as life maintains his mighty arm. . . .[85]

The idea reappeared again and again in the plays of these years.[86] Humber, King of the Huns, "leads Fortune tied in a chain of gold"; Alphonsus of Aragon locks Fortune "in a cage of gold, to make her turn her wheel as I think best"; Pompey the Great "fettered Fortune in a chain of power."[87]

82. Lancelot Andrewes, "A Sermon Preached before Queen Elizabeth . . . A.D. MDXC," in *Ninety-Six Sermons* (Oxford, 1899), II, 21.

83. *Tamburlaine the Great, Part I*, II, v, 56-57.

84. *Ibid.*, I, ii, 173-176.   85. *Ibid.*, V, ii, 311-313.

86. Bradbrook, p. 95.

87. *The Lamentable Tragedy of Locrine* . . ., ed. R. B. McKerrow (London, 1908), l. 473; Robert Greene, *The Comical History of Alphonsus King of Aragon*, IV, iii, 1481-1482, in *The Plays and Poems of Robert Greene*, ed. J. Churton Collins (Oxford, 1905), Vol. I; *The Wounds of Civil War*, quoted in Bradbrook, p. 95.

Fortune was the commonplace symbol used by moralists and preachers for all the mishaps and miseries that are the lot of poor sinners here below. In this context, the significance of the rash of superman-heroes that followed Tamburlaine across the stage in the 1590's becomes apparent. Fortune was the capricious mistress of this world, as contrasted with the certainty and immutability of the celestial realms above. Thus in mastering Fortune, Tamburlaine and his emulators affirmed that it was in their power to accomplish what all good Christians knew to be impossible—not only to conquer and rule men, but to be masters of their own destinies as well—to make their own fortunes by imposing their wills upon the forces of circumstance. In real life, there were no such supermen; but there were many who strove heroically against whispering enemies at court, against mounting debts and impending bankruptcy, against a courtier system that had become hopelessly rigged. They were the same men who faced casual violence, camp fever and scurvy, private expense in public service, and a tight-fisted, timid government that would rather send an army to lose than to win if it would save on the charges. They were resolute men, men who sought in themselves an iron will, not the infected will which inevitably seemed to undermine the grand schemes of the erected wit. Their chief goal in the 1590's was power—power to overcome adversaries, sovereignty that commanded and was obeyed, dominion over an unfriendly world. For in each burned a secret conviction—sometimes guttering but never extinguished—that he like Tamburlaine was "made his fortune's master and the king of men."[88]

The triumph, the crown, and Fortune mastered—all these symbols were well chosen to impress upon Elizabethans the forms of power for which Tamburlaine stood, and which many young men sought for themselves. Pomp and pageantry—extravagant royal progresses, gorgeous chivalric displays, elaborate church services, splendid masques and sumptuous, formal feasts—thrilled Elizabethans. A contemporary described a stately banquet at which Lord Mountjoy was so "majestical" that he changed the hearts of the awed Irish chieftains there assembled: "No doubt," the writer theorized, "there is a secret mystery of state in these

88. *Tamburlaine the Great, Part I*, II, i, 35-36.

solemn pomps."[89] It was even possible for Elizabethans to conceive of actual human ambition reaching so high as the crown. Essex's indictment accused him of "conspiring . . . to raise himself to the Crown of England"; and his own chaplain told him to his face, in the privacy of his prison cell, that his "end was an ambitious seeking of the Crown. . . ."[90] Essex himself admitted that he had intended to seize the person of the Queen and to use her as a figurehead—to control the source rather than the symbol of power.[91]

These, then, were the forms of power toward which the generation of 1560 directed their aspirations. For such a man as Essex, power was likely to mean conquest in foreign wars and, more important, victory in the endless feuds of the court. For little Cecil, power apparently meant pre-eminently sovereignty, domination over others, to control policies and sway men's causes. For an imaginative introvert like Sir Walter Raleigh, power was perhaps to a considerable extent simply to be the master of his fate, to transcend the limitations which flesh is heir to and prove himself the master of his own fortunes. In any event, these were the primary forms of power—power as victory, power as sovereignty, power as the mastery of Fortune.

iv. The roots of aspiration for power

The ambition for political power which was thrown into such bold relief during the bottleneck years had in part been bred into these Elizabethan aristocrats from birth. In fact, the constitutional trend of the last half of the century had been in the direction of a broadening of the power franchise. The wider distribution of the new wealth, the need for more efficient administrators in the new Tudor polity, and the presence of women and children on the throne for half a century had all contributed to this trend. The result was a much less steeply pyramidal power structure than in the days when the great earls towered in lofty splendor over a countryside of serfs and franklins. The powers of the highest

89. Fynes Moryson, II, 263, 376.
90. G. B. Harrison, *The Life and Death of Robert Devereux Earl of Essex* (New York, 1937), p. 316.
91. *Ibid.*, p. 319.

state offices—including those of the Lord Treasurer, the Lord Keeper, and the Secretary of State—had been vastly enhanced by the ambitious, hard-driving men who held them.[92] The House of Commons had expanded as the wealthy, property-owning classes had grown—though not by any means proportionately—from 297 members at Henry VIII's accession to 458 at the death of his daughter Elizabeth.[93] The Privy Councillors wielded a tremendous amount of power during the last half of the century in particular; and, as the century turned, the House of Commons began the offensive which would in fifty years more seize power, first from the Council and then from the King himself.[94] The power pyramid was leveling off, opening up opportunities for many more than before.

Furthermore, these Elizabethan gentlemen and nobles had been educated specifically to become the governors of England. "Every office and aspect of life was ordered for the gentleman by the fundamental assumption that he was . . . the leader, the governor of the common people. . . ."[95] His home, his clothing, his manners were all designed to make sure that he would "never forget his essential superiority to the rabble."[96] It was, after all, only this "essential superiority" which justified the great houses and gorgeous clothes. The same hierarchic principle of society and of the cosmos which forbade him to rise higher also assured the young aristocrat or gentleman that his natural place was quite high on the scale.

In addition, the humanist education had been deliberately designed, as Elyot intended his *Governor*, for "forming the gentle wits of noblemen's children, who, from the wombs of their mother, shall be made . . . apt to the governance of the public weal."[97] Gentlemen of lesser rank were urged to perfect themselves in humanistic learning because "it is learning and knowl-

92. See Frederick C. Dietz, *English Public Finance, 1558-1641* (New York and London, 1932), pp. 6 ff; Evans, pp. 23-61; Birch, I, 10.

93. A. F. Pollard, *The Evolution of Parliament* (2nd ed.; London, New York, and Toronto, 1934), pp. 323-324.

94. Evans, pp. 41-42.

95. Ruth Kelso, *The Doctrine of the English Gentleman in the Sixteenth Century* (Urbana, Ill., 1920), p. 13.

96. *Ibid.*, p. 14.

97. Thomas Elyot, *The Boke Named the Governour*, ed. Henry Herbert and Stephen Croft (London, 1883), I, 28.

edge which . . . maketh the children of the needy poor to become noble peers. . . ."[98] Whether the humanistic education really either fitted a man for governance or guaranteed him a place among the governors of England did not much matter: the important point is that students were led to believe that they were destined for positions of authority. Their chief responsibility was to prepare themselves to help rule the state: they naturally assumed that political power awaited them at the end of the road.

But probably the most important social factor in focusing the aspiration of the Elizabethan younger generation on political power was the fact of vaulting political ambition in the real world about them. So many of the great men of the recent past and of their own time were veritable incarnations of high political aspirations: Wolsey and Cromwell, the great Lord Burghley himself, Tom Stukeley, the would-be Marquis of Ireland, the Guises father and son, Don John of Austria, Antonio Perez, the fallen favorite of Philip II—there was no end to them. To the older generation, such men were too often dangers to the state and to the established order. These older men, who still remembered the troubled decade of Edward and Mary, readily distinguished between the overreaching ambition which could destroy a commonwealth, and their own prudent aspirations. The younger generation were not emotionally atuned to such sophistical distinctions. Their sympathies lay wholly with the Tom Stukeley of Peele's play:

> King of a mole-hill had I rather be,
> Than the richest subject of a monarchy.
> Huff it, brave mind, and never cease t'aspire,
> Before thou reign sole King of thy desire.[99]

There was encouragement for this ambitious outlook to be found in the intellectual trends of the sixteenth century also. According to orthodox humanists, and to Christian moral and political writers generally, princes and magistrates had the divinely ordained right to rule. But as God's selected agents, they were expected to rule according to moral principles, with the

98. Thomas Nashe, *The Anatomy of Absurdity* . . ., in *The Works of* . . ., ed. Ronald B. McKerrow, revised by F. P. Wilson (Oxford, 1958), I, 34.

99. George Peele, *The Battle of Alcazar* . . ., II, ii, 81-84, in *The Works of* . . ., ed. A. H. Bullen (London, 1888), Vol. I.

welfare of the commonwealth as their sole objective. This was not, of course, the way even the best-intentioned governors actually behaved, as the younger generation of the ruling class soon realized. Not unnaturally, then, the aspiring minds of the generation of 1560 were attracted to the more realistic approach to history and political theory characteristic of a handful of recent writers—chief among whom was, of course, Machiavelli.[100] Here was a man who knew what diplomacy and war, politics and the courtier system were all about, and who gave practical advice on how to succeed at the business of ruling in a real world. Perhaps even more important than specific advice, however, was the new goal of governorship that was implicit in the tone and general attitude of Machiavelli's writing, and that was made explicit in his most famous work, *The Prince.* For Machiavelli was one of the first theorists to accept the fact that the goal of most governors was power.

In the real world of politics and war, moral principles were often of little use as guides to realistic action; and the welfare of the commonwealth was, at best, only one of the ends toward which real governors labored. Machiavelli was the first European writer of significance to admit this obvious fact of political life. Furthermore, by judging conquerors and governors on the basis of their own intentions, he tacitly recognized the validity of the standard of power.[101] Or so it surely seemed to young men raised on the sententious moralism of the orthodox mirror-of-princes and education-of-governors literature. To these young Elizabethans, the mere absence of the customary moral strictures, coupled with evident admiration for political success, must have constituted a real, and welcome, endorsement of this real goal of their own careers. To get some idea of the actual context in which Bacon, Raleigh, Sidney, Greville, and many other young Elizabethans read Machiavelli, one has only to imagine the Florentine's famous commentary on the career of Caesar Borgia as

100. The influence of Machiavelli on leading Elizabethan courtiers and writers has been made clear in a number of articles and books. Mario Praz provides some bibliography and discusses a number of these writings in a useful essay ("The Politic Brain: Machiavelli and the Elizabethans," *The Flaming Heart* [New York, 1958], pp. 90-145).

101. E.g., Nicolo Machiavelli, *The Prince and the Discourses,* ed. Max Lerner (New York, 1940), pp. 13, 24-30, 35, 56-57, 65-66.

it would have been written by, say, Erasmus, or William Baldwin of the *Mirror for Magistrates*. The discovery of Machiavelli was undoubtedly as exciting an intellectual event as any in the life of the generation of 1560.[102] Against the prevailing theological and moralistic world-view, "Machiavelli had raised the ancient ideal of power acquired and enjoyed on earth. . . . To this aim he had made all the rest, even religion, subservient. . . . Domination was the chief aim."[103] For young Elizabethans, Machiavelli had written not only a "grammar of power," but a praise of power as well.[104]

The original orientation toward political ambition thus came from upbringing, education, growth to maturity in the environment of the courtier system, a number of outstanding contemporary models, and probably some reading in realistic political analysts like Machiavelli. In addition, some of the psychological causes which helped to intensify the passion for honor had a similar effect on the lust for power. In particular, the pampered egotism of many naturally demanded with vehemence its right to rule. The driving force of such egotism, reacting to the strains and pressures of the bottleneck years, accounted for much of the bitterness of younger-generation ambition for power.

But all these factors still do not account for all we know about the nature of the lust for dominion which formed such a vital part of the Elizabethan aspiring mind. Most notably, these factors do not really explain the extravagant aims and the religious fervor with which some of these ambitious courtiers sought for power. To understand more fully these aspects of the desire for power which animated this generation, it will be necessary to look at some of the associations and connotations of the Elizabethan concept of power.[105] For the meaning of a word, or of an idea, is always modified and even to a large extent determined by the associations it calls to mind. An idea is not merely a set of clear propositions and definitions: it is a complex amalgam of basic statements, corollaries, associations, and emotional reactions of all kinds. In trying to understand the minds of real people,

102. Cf. Praz, pp. 97-98, 100-102, 122-123.
103. *Ibid.*, pp. 131-132.
104. Cf. Lerner, Introduction to Machiavelli, p. xxxiv.
105. Cf. *O. E. D.*, VII, 1213-1214.

then, we must think in their own terms, including as much as we can of this congeries of related concepts, images, and attitudes.

Besides the personal forms of power already discussed, Elizabethans were familiar with two other types: divine power and legal power. These two impersonal types of power colored significantly the Elizabethan reaction to the forms of personal power toward which they aspired. The power of God, to begin with, was wonderful and mysterious; his hand could be seen everywhere, molding individual lives and directing the course of history. Legal power too had much of its ancient religious sanction about it still; theoretically, at least, all law was but divine law particularized to fit specific human circumstances. Then too, in addition to these non-personal types of power, a third sort of power, involving elements of both the personal and the impersonal, was familiar to Elizabethans. This was the conglomeration of natural and supernatural powers, of planetary influences, devil's tricks, and personal magnetism connected in the public mind with astrologers, alchemists, witches, and other dabblers in occult mysteries. Some of the supernatural and awesome qualities of these familiar types of power inevitably colored Elizabethan reactions to great conquerors, powerful rulers, men who were masters of their stars.

We should also glance briefly at some sorts of power with which Elizabethans were *not* familiar, and at the impact this very lack of familiarity may have had on their reactions to personal power. It should be remembered that the ubiquitous power of modern bureaucratic institutions and of science and industry, everyday facts of life in the twentieth century, were almost totally unknown to Elizabethans. Over the four centuries between their time and ours, technological and institutional power, man's ability to control his physcial environment and his fellow men, has increased beyond the wildest dreams of earlier ages. The instruments of technological and institutional power, the machines and the mechanical cities, the corporations and the governmental bureaucracies, are all about us: but the sixteenth century was much less familiar with these types of power. In Elizabethan England, power machinery was generally unimpressive, unfamiliar to aristocrats, and devalued for them by the very fact that it was mechanical, and thus beneath the notice of the master of the liberal arts. Formal institutions, with the single great exception of the crown, were almost equally unimpressive: bureaucracies were totally inadequate and generally ineffectual in their efforts at even such simple social regimentation as military conscription or tax collection. Precisely because they were so unfamiliar with real power in the physical and social realms, sixteenth-century Englishmen were probably more awed by it than we can well imagine. In those days personal power was not a daily commonplace, but an infrequent miracle. The incredible power of a king, able to set whole armies in motion with a word from his royal lips, was for them sure proof that the monarchy was a divinely ordained institution. And the private man who possessed this magical quality, this thing called *power*, was surely regarded by many with a species of veneration generally reserved for great natural wonders or supernatural phenomena.

When he aspired for political power, then, the ambitious courtier saw his goal as a rare and marvelous thing, and associated it with the providential or miraculous power of divinity, the revered authority of the law, and even the occult influences of the stars. Personal power, however underhandedly achieved, however sordidly materialistic its rewards, still possessed an aura of spiritual potency, a faint affinity with the supernatural. The mighty Tamburlaine-like heroes of the Elizabethan drama stalked across the stage wrapped in a haughty majesty second only to the divinity that hedged great kings. Typically, too, they moved in a haze of cosmic imagery, wide as the universe—an imagery of suns, stars, mountains, seas, continents, and worlds. Shakespeare's king-maker Warwick was "he that moves both wind and tide."[106] Tamburlaine himself overwhelmed the world, turned his cannon upon the firmament, mounted the Milky Way to meet Jove face to face, all in high rhetorical terms that would surely please the hyperbolic aspiring minds of Marlowe's generation. For they themselves, these egotistic, aesthetically oriented courtiers, probably felt sometimes a surge of exultant power as they progressed majestically through the streets, with a train of liveried followers behind and trumpeters before them. They too moved in glitter

106. *Henry VI, Part III*, III, iii, 48.

and color and pungent perfume, surrounded by troops of brilliant retainers and preceded by a blare of trumpets.

Finally, beneath the level of associated meanings and awesome unfamiliarity, beneath even the primal forces of egotism and aesthetics, there seems to lie a psychological explanation which would help greatly to understand Elizabethan aspiration for power. This psychological fact seems to have been very seldom formulated intellectually, and to have found its most characteristic expression only in emotion and poetry. Essentially, it seems to have consisted in a merging of the ideal and the material realms of experience. The result of this psychological merging was that these young men were able to lavish their highest idealism on objects which to more orthodox minds seemed sordidly materialistic—objects which included political power.

In generational terms, the development of this unique talent was a matter of adapting the valued goals of an older generation to fit the sensibilities of youth. To young minds who had not learned to think and feel expediently, the theoretical conservatism and actual opportunistic self-seeking of the older generation appeared to be in direct conflict with each other. As they grew up, however, there was constant psychic pressure on the young to accept this self-contradictory outlook: for they were continually urged to accept highly idealistic spiritual values which were clearly opposed to their practical apprenticeship in winning material success through the courtier system. In the end, they partially solved their problem by accepting the material goals of their fathers, and by discovering a new set of ideal values of their own. But the younger generation could not easily hold in suspension such contradictory elements: they lacked the special talent of the burned-out older generation for this kind of psychological self-deception. And so they effected a merging of their emotional and normative reactions to the "idealistic" and the "materialistic" sides of their lives. They had been taught to react very differently to these contraries: but now, since both the contraries had become real, emotionally felt goals, they learned to react with equal enthusiasm toward both. They could pour equal amounts of self-righteous passion into the desire for infinite knowledge and for lucrative public office. At the wars, they could mingle lofty acts of chivalric courtesy with orgies of looting. This was not hypocrisy: they simply wanted both the honor and the loot, the esoteric knowledge and the high office, and were able somehow to take them all with enthusiastic ardor and even a positive sense of moral righteousness. As far as their emotions and their sense of values were concerned, the material and the ideal were one.

These are of course only speculations, but they seem to fit many of the facts. These Elizabethans reveled in material things and in high ideals, in the supremely beautiful and the utterly garish. From year to year through the 1590's, public admiration for the work of the new playwright, William Shakespeare, grew apace; and every year, too, ruffs and padding grew, by inches, and there was more lace, more gold stitching, bigger plumes in the hats and longer retinues of servants. From our vantage point, the contrast is grotesque between the beplumed and perfumed dandies whose approval made Shakespeare's reputation, and the formal excellence of the writing itself. How could the same human beings have combined such materialistic vulgarity with such sensitivity to artistic excellence? For them, evidently, the two characteristics were not incompatible.

Marlowe's classic statement of the creed of the aspiring mind, climaxing in the praise of earthly power, illustrates perfectly the emotional and normative equivalence of the material and the ideal realms in the minds of his generation.[107] Into a justification of ruthless, overweening worldly ambition, he cheerfully introduced a eulogy of intellectual aspiration for infinite knowledge. Modern minds may see "bathos" in the speech's primary message; it was not so for Marlowe's generation. For them, the two disparate elements actually reinforced each other. The same was apparently true in the lives of the courtiers of this generation. The merging of the idealistic and materialistic goals of their aspirations multiplied the intensity of their drive for power; and the court became a seething cauldron of ambition and rivalry.

This peculiar capacity for merging the physical and the spiritual in a single direct apprehension of and reaction to reality has not gone entirely unnoticed. It has been alleged that the society of the late sixteenth and early seventeenth centuries in

107. See page 148.

England possessed special "abilities to include everything and to concentrate many orders of experience on a single point."[108] These men had "a view of life which does not specialize and does not exclude . . . . sets of emotions and ideas which for us are non-transferable from one context to another, were in that age, for the kind of mentality that Donne and Shakespeare represent, fully transferable." For this age, then, "it was always possible—and they were always attempting it—to build bridges from subject to subject, emotion to emotion. . . ." These men were able to build such bridges to link even "the spiritual and the political," to establish in their own minds "an absolute identity, between the spiritual, the political, and the personal." This was the psychological merging of apparent contradictories which enabled these younger Elizabethans to direct their highest idealism toward the most materialistic of goals.

How this interpenetration of the ideal and the real could come about is not very hard to understand if we remember how close the two realms were, even in orthodox thinking. This world and the invisible world were, after all, bound together in many ways —by Platonic "participation" of this-worldly particulars in other-worldly forms; by neoplatonic "emanations" of reality and value flowing down the great chain of being; by Christian sacramental and symbolic interpretations of the physical world in terms of moral or spiritual truths; by the elaborate system of correspondences between the various hierarchies of the universe, and between the macrocosmic universe itself and man the microcosm. All of these ideas were more or less familiar to educated Elizabethans, and all of them stressed the close relationship of the physical and the spiritual worlds, between the realm of matter and the realm of ideas and ideals.

Early in the following century, Galileo dared to announce the autonomy of the material realm for purposes of investigation, and Descartes drew the hard line between mind and matter which science is only today beginning to dissolve. The seventeenth-century Puritans probably carried this view of the universe to large numbers of people, with their rigid separation of the City of God from the City of Satan, the spiritual from the

108. Patrick Cruttwell, *The Shakespearean Moment* . . . (New York, 1964), p. 107.

worldly. But in the late sixteenth century, Elizabethans believed equally in both worlds, and more important, saw them as closely related. This they made clear in emblem book and bestiary, in scriptural exegesis and in the aura of spiritual significance which enveloped the very worldly heroes of their drama.

It was only a step from this belief in the close relationship between the two worlds to the discovery of equal emotional appeal in both, and to the assignment of equal ethical and aesthetic value to both worlds. Such an equivalence would have been impossible for the spiritually oriented medieval mind, as it is impossible for the materialistic modern mind. It was, however, apparently possible at the pivotal place in European history in which the English ruling-class generation of 1560 grew up. The vital catalyst was probably the rush of economic prosperity which created the Elizabethan gilded age. With luxury goods available in unparalleled profusion, with the whole upper level of society scrambling for jewelry and coaches and country estates and mansions along the Strand, it became increasingly difficult to go on giving lip-service to the ascetic ideals of the poverty-stricken past, especially for young men with a sincere desire for glorious ideals. The ideals they did fix upon—those of the Italian code of courtesy, the revival of Burgundian chivalry, and what we might call a Faustian fascination with knowledge of this world—were secular and materialistic enough to allow and even to justify luxuriously this-worldly living. For this generation true honor seen as a spiritual quality and ego-satisfying worldly honors merged and mingled; for them, personal power partook of the divine even while it stabbed its enemies.

The high aspiration of the Elizabethan younger generation, we have said, was a secular religion—or, more precisely, a secular expression of religious feeling. But the religious feelings which these young men channeled into worship of their own power and adherence to their own code of honor were the prevailing religious feelings of their own time, place, and group. Their religiosity was that of ruling-class Englishmen in the dawn of the age of the baroque. It was therefore a baroque religiosity which they poured into their high aspiration, with all the baroque extravagance and sensuousness and love of splendor.

This complex and controversial term, "baroque," seems to have an almost unlimited number of possible meanings. From a political point of view, however, "baroque" has particularly been defined in terms of "a restless search for power."[109] It was, says Carl J. Friedrich, "an age which was intoxicated with the power of man," an epoch possessed with a "sense of power in all its forms, spiritual and secular, scientific and political, psychological and technical." A fascination with power was the "common denominator" beneath all these "varied expressions of a common view of man and the world," a view in which the passion for power became "all-engulfing." In particular, the politicians of this age of courts and the courtier system "made a cult of power and of its adornments. . . . The meteoric rise and cataclysmic fall of favorites, conquering heroes, royal concubines, were highly symbolic of the baroque." The giants of this period were so many Tamburlaines, "storming heaven, plunging into damnation, crying out, 'I shall yet force my fate.' "[110] The last years of Elizabeth apparently saw the beginning of the development of the baroque outlook in England; it is therefore not surprising to see this fascination with human power existing already in the generation of Francis Bacon and Christopher Marlowe.[111]

The infusion of baroque religiosity into the aspiring mind of the generation of 1560 was natural enough. On the Continent, huge, ornately gorgeous cathedrals were built to draw the eyes of the faithful back to God. In the England of the Elizabethan older generations, the Queen decked herself and her court in Asiatic splendor to awe a shaken and rebellious nation into reverent submission. And the younger generation, whom neither the God nor the Queen of their fathers could move to passion, arrayed themselves in worldly magnificence to convince themselves that they were indeed men set apart, very gods of this earth.

109. Carl J. Friedrich, *The Age of the Baroque* (New York, 1952), p. 43.
110. Ibid., pp. 44-45, 47, 65.
111. "The commencement of the English Baroque is not as hard to fix as at first appears. 1590 is a spot where one might well drive in a tentative peg. By 1600, certainly there is a well-defined Baroque sensibility" (Roy Daniells, "English Baroque and Deliberate Obscurity," *Journ. of Aesthetics and Art Criticism*, V [1946], 17).

VI. *Grand schemes, impossible to accomplish*

The extravagant ambitions of the Elizabethan younger generation apparently knew no bounds. This is not surprising, considering their own ardent natures, and the nature of the world they lived in. The life of a country squire, with its local power and county-wide prestige, was not enough for such men as these, living in such an age of opportunity. They bustled off to the wars to seek undying honor and glory; they thronged to the court to vie with their peers for ultimate power. For the leaders of the generation of 1560, nothing less than immortal glory or absolute sovereignty would do. They were, in short, extremists. For a real understanding of the mind of this generation, some special attention must be paid to the nature of this extremism, to the ultimate heights to which these men dared to aspire.

i. Elizabethan aspiration writ large

In the 1580's and '90's a number of the greatest of the Elizabethan younger generation embarked upon ambitious projects of breath-taking scope and grandeur. Some of these dazzling schemes got no further than extravagant prospectuses; others, through great effort and at considerable risk to their promoters, were translated into equally extravagant reality. So distinctive were these great adventures in their sheer magnificence that they seem to deserve a particular descriptive appellation. Let us call them "grand schemes." And let us make use of them to improve our understanding and broaden our feeling for the Elizabethan aspiring mind. For in these grand schemes Elizabethan aspiration was inscribed in characters large enough to be clearly read even at this distance in time. Through these grandiose ventures, we may study the aspiring mind, not only in action, but strained to the utmost, its effects many times magnified.

The Elizabethan grand scheme took many forms. Some of these ambitious young men, for instance, poured their family fortunes into vast military expeditions. They sold their lands and borrowed tremendous sums to hire armies of mercenary soldiers and equip armadas of warships and privateers. Often they set out themselves as captains-general of their own regiments and fleets, to hunt the Spanish treasure galleons or loot the cities of the Spanish Main. Other leaders of this ardent younger generation dedicated their careers to political supremacy. They strutted about the court, wearing the revenues and mortgages of ancient estates upon their backs, straining every nerve to impress England's Majesty and her entourage of portly, glittering greatness. They sacrificed their days to difficult, costly administrative or diplomatic services, and their nights to endless political intrigue. Such ambitious men would bankrupt themselves for an important judgeship and risk their political futures for a seat on the Privy Council. In the course of their scheming for place and favor, these young courtiers worked out devices and projects that sometimes verged on the impossible—and seriously presented them for consideration, or even attempted to carry them out themselves. A few of these grand schemes had significant consequences for the history of England. Others have faded with the passage of time; but many were as celebrated at the time as the great projects which have won themselves a place in history.

Sir Walter Raleigh's daring colonial ventures were certainly among the most famous and grandiose enterprises of the period. Both the Virginia and the Guiana projects required the outfitting and directing of a whole series of large-scale expeditions. Raleigh in fact repeatedly hazarded his political and financial future in his determination to build almost single-handed an English empire in the New World. The cost was immense, and the risk even greater; but the potential gains, as Raleigh saw them, were incalculable.

Less well-known to posterity, but equally typical in its combination of concrete propositions with extravagant aims, was a strategic military scheme worked out by the dashing Earl of Essex.[1] The project, which survives in the form of a manuscript by the Earl himself, was an aggressive plan to crush the power of Spain, the universal octopus of Europe. This glorious consummation might actually be achieved, the Earl insisted, through

[1]. L. W. Henry, "The Earl of Essex as Strategist and Military Organizer," *EHR*, LXVIII (1953), 363-393.

a single co-ordinated military and economic assault on the Spanish homeland. To begin with, he urged, a mighty expeditionary force should be dispatched to seize and hold key points on the Iberian coast, particularly the vital ports of Cadiz and Lisbon. A British army and a British navy might then be permanently established on the southwest coast of Spain itself. Such a force could thereafter proceed methodically to ravage the coastal cities and annihilate the shipping of Spain—and, most important, to cut off the flow of trade which was the economic lifeblood of Philip II's huge empire. English fleets based at Lisbon could range as far north as the Bay of Biscay, effectively blocking the rich commerce of the Spanish Netherlands and the German States. English ships sailing out of Cadiz could reach as far into the rich Mediterranean as Marseilles. And the combined fleets could easily cut off the flow of gold and silver and spices from the Spanish New World and the Portuguese East Indies. Such a multiple blockade would soon bring King Philip to his knees: "We shall not only impeach and interrupt his traffic with all other countries of Christendom," exulted young Essex, "but stop and divert his golden Indian streams . . . and [thus] let out the vital spirits of his estate. . . ."[2] Surely a vast and daring undertaking, though Essex himself referred to the scheme almost casually: "I speak of plain and easy ways. . . ."[3] Both his enterprise and his nonchalant confidence in it were worthy of one of the paramount leaders of this aspiring generation.

Less sensational, but similar in daring and sweep, was a grand political scheme worked out by Sir Robert Cecil in his later years. Superficially, the devious Cecil had little in common with such gaudy figures as Raleigh and Essex; but he shared with them the breadth of mind and grandiose vision of their generation. In 1610 Robert Cecil, by then Earl of Salisbury and the King's right hand, proposed his celebrated "Great Contract" between King James and his increasingly hostile Parliament. By the terms of this revolutionary Contract, the King would have given up his ancient feudal dues in exchange for a parliamentary grant of £200,000 a year in permanent revenues. Had it gone through, the Great Contract would also have to a considerable extent dis-

2. Fulton MS. fol. 10ᵛ, quoted in *ibid.*, p. 364.
3. Fulton MS. fol. 10ᵛ, quoted in *ibid.*, p. 369.

armed the Parliament at the very beginning of its historic struggle with the Stuart monarchy. After due consideration, Parliament found the suggested arrangement unacceptable, and the Great Contract was tossed onto the trash heap of historic failures. But Cecil's plan for a vital readjustment of the financial relations between King and Parliament was surely a grand scheme in the best Elizabethan tradition, and one that might have significantly modified the course of English constitutional history.[4]

The whole career of George Clifford, the "buccaneer Earl" of Cumberland, illustrates this predilection of the younger Elizabethans for extravagant ventures. Cumberland launched a dozen privateering expeditions against Spain in the 1580's and '90's, eternally hopeful of huge profits which never materialized. Certainly his greatest raid, the Puerto Rico expedition of 1598, reveals the boldness of the typical Elizabethan grand scheme. Cumberland swooped down on Puerto Rico with more than a score of ships; he seized the port, overwhelmed the fortress, and looted the city. The Spanish authorities in the New World were horrified; they went so far as to stay the treasure fleet in Havana for fear of the English raiders. And there was consternation in Spain: "If Cumberland can stay at Puerto Rico," wrote the Venetian ambassador at Madrid, "the danger will be immense."[5] But Cumberland did not hold Puerto Rico; and, like many of these grand schemers, he returned without even enough profit to pay the charges he had incurred. Some blamed the Earl himself for the failure: it was said that "he neglected present profit in hope of greater matters, and so forsook the substance for the shadow."[6] If it were so, it was a weakness altogether typical of the aspiring mind of the Elizabethan younger generation.

No Elizabethan was more adept at constructing magnificent projects than the famous adventurer and sometime charlatan, Sir Anthony Sherley. Perhaps his most notorious effort was his grand tour of Europe in the guise of ambassador of the king of Persia, leading an exotic caravan from capital to capital across Europe, living magnificently, and piling up huge debts along the

---

4. Joel Hurstfield, "Robert Cecil, Earl of Salisbury: Minister of Elizabeth and James I," *History Today*, VII (1957), 288.

5. *C. S. P., Ven., 1592-1603*, IX, 741, 744.

6. John Chamberlain to Dudley Carleton, Oct. 3, 1598, in *The Letters of John Chamberlain*, ed. Norman Egbert McClure (Philadelphia, 1939), I, 47.

way. But Sherley's most daring project was probably his ingenious plan to shift arbitrarily one of the oldest trade routes connecting Europe and Asia. In essence, he intended to re-route some hundreds of miles to the northward, through Russia, the commerce which had for centuries flowed through Egypt. A hard-headed Venetian diplomat had nothing but scorn for such an extravagant notion:

I find that the Englishman has proposed [to the Spanish ambassador] to take over the captaincy of the mouth of the Red Sea, where all the India traffic passes on its way to Suez. . . . His object is to divert the India trade altogether from Egypt, and to send it through Muscovy. Grand schemes, impossible to accomplish.[7]

Cooler heads would surely have passed a similiar judgment on many of the extravagant adventures of this generation.

These grand schemes are of great value for the study of Elizabethan aspiration, for they provide ideal case histories of the Marlovian aspiring mind at work. Precisely because of their broad scope, they reveal much more under close examination than do the lesser efforts of these young men. The reason for this is essentially that so little remains in the way of evidence of less spectacular striving for high place and honors—usually no more than a handful of letters, perhaps only an allusion or two. With such limited source material, it is especially difficult to understand the fundamental motivation of these men—which is unfortunate, since it is precisely these basic motives with which we are most concerned here. But the gigantic scale of the grand scheme reveals motives and goals much more clearly. Whole books were written about these large-scale projects, sometimes by the men who planned them. These undertakings often unfolded before the awed eyes of the Elizabethan public, and many men commented on them from many different points of view. Then too, the originators of such schemes were usually the leaders of their generation, and as such they have had the benefit of many succeeding generations of scholarly investigations. These projects represent Elizabethan ambition writ large; they thus provide ideal case studies of the Elizabethan younger generation.

7. *C. S. P., Ven., 1592-1603*, IX, 940.

For a closer look at the Elizabethan religion of high aspiration, let us then turn to two outstanding examples of the Elizabethan grand scheme. Sir Walter Raleigh's quest for El Dorado in the steaming jungles of Guiana shows the aspiring mind operating in the real world, struggling against almost insuperable physical obstacles. Despite its unique objective, Raleigh's Guiana venture is essentially typical of the grand scheme carried from the realm of theory and rhetoric into the real world of action. Francis Bacon's project for the advancement of practical science, on the other hand, never got beyond the planning stage: the New Atlantis never existed outside the pages of Bacon's books. This very fact, however, makes Bacon's grand scheme particularly useful, since it reveals the aspiring mind in its purest form, uncontaminated by reality. Simply because he never found the opportunity to realize his scheme, Francis Bacon, unlike Sir Walter Raleigh, did not have to compromise with the facts of life. From Raleigh's aspiring mind in conflict with brute reality, and from Bacon's soaring free, we may learn a great deal about the mind of their generation.

ii. In search of El Dorado: Sir Walter Raleigh

Sir Walter Raleigh was the Marlovian mind *par excellence.* Striking similarities between the temperaments of Raleigh and of Marlowe have more than once been pointed out.[8] Scholars have also seen vital resemblances between Raleigh and Marlowe's most famous creation, Tamburlaine the Great: there seems to be about them the same "Elizabethan spirit of self-assertion," the same "vaulting ambition."[9] It has even been suggested that the mighty figure of Tamburlaine was modeled on "the aspiring mind of Raleigh."[10] In any event, it is no exaggeration to say, with Tucker Brooke, that "The imagination that executed and described the Discovery of Guiana was of the same gorgeous pat-

8. E.g., V. M. Ellis-Fermor, *Christopher Marlowe* (London, 1927), p. 166.

9. Philip Edwards, *Sir Walter Raleigh* (London, New York, Toronto, 1953), p. 54; Eleanor Grace Clark, *Ralegh and Marlowe: A Study in Elizabethan Fustian* (New York, 1941), p. 407.

10. Clark, p. 398.

tern as that which traced the march of Tamburlaine and followed the argosies of Barabas."[11]

The very fact of Sir Walter Raleigh's ambition has, however, often troubled his biographers. Their feeling seems to have been that personal ambition was a rather unfortunate trait in a national hero, a characteristic which must somehow be explained away. Writers on Raleigh have dealt with this problem in a number of ways. Some have ignored the obvious fact of his ambition; they have represented his rapid advancement in Elizabeth's favor as nothing more than a well-earned reward for his noteworthy services to his country.[12] Others have assigned Raleigh more laudable, "higher" motives for his actions than crass personal ambition. In particular, his privateering and colonial ventures have often been viewed as primarily motivated by patriotism, by love of Queen and country and by eagerness to advance their cause.[13] Still others admit that Raleigh was ambitious, but consider this failing as a function of some more noble or more spiritual faculty—of a too-vivid imagination, for instance, or of a naturally ardent and impassioned nature.[14] Some few have ruefully admitted that Raleigh's complex and paradoxical character did include such flaws as self-seeking ambition. But such admissions are often coupled with the hasty explanation that ambition was a fault common to many in his time, a vice of the age rather than the man.[15]

All of these approaches seem essentially irrelevant. No useful purpose can be served by denying the fact that Raleigh was ambitious—all the evidence indicates that he was. Nor is there any point in attempting, in various ways, to soften the blunt fact that Raleigh was a self-seeking man, a man in the grip of an almost neurotic thirst for self-advancement. The problem is

11. C. F. Tucker Brooke, "Sir Walter Raleigh as Poet and Philosopher," *ELH*, V (1938), 110.

12. Arthur Cayley, *The Life of Sir Walter Raleigh* (2d ed.; London, 1806), I, 104; II, 210; Walter Raleigh, *The Works of Sir Walter Raleigh, Kt. . . .* (London, 1751), I, x, xx.

13. Edward Edwards, *The Life of Sir Walter Raleigh . . . Together with His Letters . . .* (London, 1868), I, 62, 190, 722; Milton Waldman, *Sir Walter Raleigh* (New York, 1928), pp. 97-98.

14. Patrick Fraser Tytler, *Life of Sir Walter Raleigh* (Edinburgh, 1833), p. 428.

15. William Stebbing, *Sir Walter Raleigh: A Biography* (Oxford, 1891), pp. 40-41, 400.

rather to understand just what it means, after all, to say that Raleigh was ambitious. What exactly was he after? What was he ambitions *for*? What did he aspire to *be*? The nature of Raleigh's ambition is perhaps most clearly revealed in the grand scheme for the conquest of El Dorado—though even here some biographers have confused the issue in their efforts to convert an unconventional Elizabethan into a respectable Victorian.

The Guiana venture was just the sort of thing one might have expected from Sir Walter Raleigh. As will be explained shortly, he first heard stories of El Dorado, the gilded man of Guiana, in the 1580's. According to rumors which had taken in many a Spanish conquistador before they reached Raleigh's ears, there still existed an undiscovered Indian empire, richer than those of the Incas and the Aztecs, somewhere in the interior of the Spanish province of Guiana, in the northern part of South America. So rich was this wonderful country that its king celebrated special holidays by coating his whole body with gold dust and appearing in public as a veritable man of gold. During the 1590's Raleigh dispatched several expeditions to Guiana in pursuit of this mythical monarch. In 1595 Raleigh himself sailed to Guiana, ignoring the long-standing Spanish claim to the area, and explored far up the Orinoco in search of El Dorado. On his return he wrote a best-selling book on the golden promise of Guiana; but he never aroused enough public interest to finance the large-scale expeditions necessary to conquer the empire of the gilded man. Throughout his long years in the Tower, his interest in Guiana remained strong, and his last expedition, in 1618, took him once more to the mouth of the muddy Orinoco.

What then was the nature of the motivation that drove Raleigh into the Guiana scheme? What did he really hope to gain in his strange, quixotic quest for a golden kingdom in the jungles of South America?

Three likely aims for the Guiana project are commonly suggested. In the first place, it is often said that Raleigh intended to channel the resources of Guiana into the struggle with the national enemy, Catholic Spain. It is also urged that he hoped to utilize the gold of Guiana in his campaign to recover from Essex the coveted place of reigning court favorite. Finally, there is a growing tendency to admit that the gold itself was an important motivating factor. All of these desires almost certainly played some part in Raleigh's complex motivation.

There seems to be no reason to question the sincerity of Raleigh's West Country hatred of the King of Spain, whom he had been fighting ever since he first volunteered to serve the Protestant cause in the 1570's. The greatest of contemporary historians, William Camden, believed that Raleigh intended the Guiana venture as a strategic master stroke in the Spanish War.[16] Raleigh certainly agreed with the commonly held theory that the awesome power of Spain was based on the wealth she drew from her American empire. The gold and silver mines of Mexico and Peru, so knowledgeable Englishmen believed, paid the wages of the *tercios* and laid the keels of the mighty galleons of the Armada. As Raleigh himself put it, it was "by their gold from thence" that the Spaniards were able to "vex and endanger all the estates of kings."[17] But Raleigh's vision was broader than that of most patriotic privateers and raiders. He apparently believed that, if they were to defeat the Spaniards, the English must first carve out a rich American empire for themselves.[18] He warned that "We must not look to maintain war upon the sinews of England" alone, but must seek comparable sources of wealth abroad.[19] His answer to Potosí was Guiana. Through the conquest of Guiana, Queen Elizabeth would become "Lord of more gold . . . than . . . the king of Spain. . . ."[20] George Chapman, writing as one of Raleigh's publicists, described Guiana as possessing gold in plenty, gold

> Enough to seat the Monarchy of earth,
> Like to Jove's Eagle, on Eliza's hand.
> Guiana, whose rich feet are mines of gold. . . .[21]

16. William Camden, *The History of the Most Renowned and Victorious Princess Elizabeth* . . . (4th ed.; London, 1688), pp. 499-500.

17. Sir Walter Raleigh to Sir Robert Cecil, Nov. 13, 1595, and same to same, November 30, 1595, in Edwards, II, 111, 112.

18. Waldman, p. 98; David B. Quinn, *Raleigh and the British Empire* (London, 1947), pp. 162-163.

19. Walter Raleigh, *The Discoveries of the large rich and beautiful Empire of Guiana*, ed. V. T. Harlow (London, 1928), p. 10.

20. *Ibid.*, p. 16.

21. George Chapman, "De Guiana, Carmen Epicum," in Lawrence Keymys, *A Relation of the Second Voyage to Guiana* (London, 1596), sig. Aᵛ.

The search for El Dorado was thus in part a military expedition against Spain. It was a soldier's grand scheme, in the same vein as Essex's plan for a base on the Spanish coast, or Cumberland's great raid on Puerto Rico. As such, the Guiana expedition may be considered a typical Elizabethan younger-generation quest for honor and glory. "What work of honor and eternal fame," exulted Chapman of the coming conquest of Guiana, "for all the world to envy and us to achieve. . . ."[22] Of Raleigh's return from his preliminary journey up the Orinoco, an interested party wrote: "Sir Walter is safely landed . . . with as great honor as ever man can. . . ."[23] Alas, it was not so: he returned to the sneers and jeers of lesser men, slanders which stung him to the quick.[24] But honor was surely one of his goals in Guiana—the public honor so dear to the souls of his generation. And what honors, what glory would have been heaped upon the knight who brought final victory to the Queen's arms in her long struggle with the military might of Philip II?

But the Guiana expedition was more—it was a daring political move in the intricate chess game of court intrigue in which Raleigh was so deeply involved. The curve of Raleigh's political fortunes had risen steadily during the 1580's; but from about the year of the Armada, competition for the Queen's favor had become much stiffer. To maintain his high place, he turned to military service, particularly naval service: "Action at sea was Raleigh's response to increased competition at Court."[25] Year after year—in 1588, 1589, 1591, 1592—he financed or served on naval expeditions in the Queen's employ. Then, late in 1592, came Raleigh's great disgrace in the scandal over his marriage to Bess Throckmorton. From the Queen's antechamber, the royal favorite passed with sickening suddenness to the Tower of London. He described his own woeful state, the awful situation of the courtier out of favor, in a colorful if somewhat confused metaphor: "like a fish cast on dry land, gasping for breath, with lame legs and lamer lungs"—that is, unable to serve or to plead with her Majesty.[26] Under these desperate circumstances, he turned once more to

22. *Ibid.*

23. Salisbury MSS, V, 396, in A. L. Rowse, *Sir Walter Raleigh: His Family and Private Life* (New York, 1962), p. 184.

24. Raleigh, *Guiana*, pp. 3-4.   25. Quinn, p. 173.

26. Sir Walter Raleigh to Sir Robert Cecil, July, 1592, in Edwards, II, 50.

foreign service and to the sea in his effort to recover his place in the Queen's good graces.

One of the earliest commentators on Raleigh's career, Robert Naunton, saw the desire to win back royal favor as the primary motive behind the Guiana scheme.[27] Many biographers since have stressed the importance of this political motive behind Raleigh's quest for El Dorado.[28] And Raleigh himself realized how necessary success in South America was to success at the court of Elizabeth. He seems sometimes to have seen his whole future bound up in the Guiana adventure: "If it be now forslowed, farewell Guiana for ever. Then must I determine to beg or run away. Honor, and gold, and all good, forever hopeless."[29] It seems evident, then, that one of Raleigh's motives was political. He hoped that, by providing the Queen with an inexhaustible source of revenue in the New World, he might recover his former high place in royal favor. In this, he was driven by a thirst for the political power he had once tasted. He wanted to defeat his rivals, to reign again as the Queen's principal favorite, with all the favorite's powers to dispense and dispose.

As for the third motive commonly attributed to Raleigh, the gold of El Dorado itself, little more need be said. Considerable evidence of his belief in the richness of the Guiana mines has already been presented. This ardent conviction, formed during the 1580's and '90's, remained with him throughout his years of eclipse. His last expedition to Guiana, after his release from the Tower, set out with the avowed purpose of discovering a workable gold mine somewhere up the Orinoco.[30] In short, there is no question that Raleigh expected to find fabulous wealth in the kingdom of the gilded man.[31]

27. Robert Naunton, *Fragmenta Regalia*, ed. Edward Arber (London, 1870), p. 49; Cayley, p. 156.
28. Donald Barr Chidsey, *Sir Walter Raleigh, That Damned Upstart* (New York, 1931), pp. 143-144; Waldman, p. 98; Walter Oakeshott, *The Queen and the Poet* (London, 1960), pp. 60-61, 64-65; Irvin Anthony, *Raleigh and His World* (New York and London, 1934), pp. 153-155.
29. Sir Walter Raleigh to Sir Robert Cecil, in Edwards, II, 117.
30. Sir Walter Raleigh to Robert Cecil, Earl of Salisbury, 1607? in Edwards, II, 391; same to same, 1611, quoted in Agnes Latham, "Sir Walter Raleigh's Gold Mine: New Light on the Last Guiana Voyage," in Geoffrey Tillotson, ed., *Essays and Studies, 1951* . . . *Collected for the English Association* (London, 1951), IV, 97; Sir Walter Raleigh to the Lords of the Council, 1616?, in Edwards, II, 338.
31. Raleigh, Guiana, p. 8.

What he intended to do with his Indian gold has also been in large part answered. The riches of El Dorado could buy victory for England in the war with Spain—and all the honors due the victor for Sir Walter Raleigh. This inexhaustible new source of national revenue could also buy the gracious favor of the Queen, whose concern for finances was well known, and whose smile could mean the most exalted powers for Raleigh. More simply and directly, of course, the gold of Guiana could purchase the influence and respect that every courtier coveted, the more modest power and honor that were his stock in trade.

But there was a fourth, and still more typical ambition behind Raleigh's Guiana venture—quite simply, the desire to conquer and to rule the land of El Dorado. Raleigh lusted after the powers and the honors which could accrue to the conqueror and governor of an English New World empire. More precisely, he wanted to be an English conquistador, after the admired Spanish model.

Undoubtedly Raleigh was a considerable student and an ardent admirer of the Spanish conquistadors, and had been such long before he first conceived of the Guiana voyage. "No Elizabethan," says one authority, "studied Spanish-American experience with greater zeal" than did Walter Raleigh.[32] The same source suggests that Raleigh first heard the adventures of Cortez and Pizarro in his boyhood. As a young man, he is known to have purchased expensive Spanish manuscripts to help Richard Hakluyt in his early researches.[33] In the 1580's the successful courtier gave much time and effort to study the history of the Spanish Empire, both in books and in conversation with such eyewitnesses as came his way, from Spanish prisoners to French and English privateers.[34] By the mid-1590's Raleigh was himself something of an authority on the Spanish conquest, and the author of a (lost) treatise on the Spanish West Indies.[35] He had for almost a decade been reading and hearing about "the great and golden city of El Dorado."[36] And, if we are to judge by the documents appended to his *Discovery of Guiana*, he already possessed con-

32. Sidney Lee, "The Call of the West: America and Elizabethan England—The Example of Spain," *Elizabethan and Other Essays*, ed. F. S. Boas (Oxford, 1929), p. 227.

33. *Ibid.*, pp. 227-228.

34. Quinn, pp. 162-166.

35. Raleigh, *Guiana*, p. 6.

36. Quinn, p. 164; Cayley, p. 155.

siderable specialized knowledge of the Orinoco region, where that fabled city was supposedly located.*37*

But Sir Walter Raleigh had accumulated more than detailed knowledge of the Spanish conquest of the New World: he had developed a great admiration for and desire to emulate the Spanish conquistadors. He came by his attitude toward the great Spanish captains naturally in Elizabethan England. A number of writers during the later Tudor period, from Richard Eden to the younger Hakluyt, had expressed their enthusiasm for the Spanish achievement in the New World.*38* Growing up with this point of view, Raleigh came to admire "intensely . . . the Spaniards' constancy, courage, and enterprise."*39* He wrote of the conquistadors:

I cannot forbear to commend the patient virtue of the Spaniards. We seldom or never find that any nation hath endured so many misadventures and miseries as that people have done in their Indian discoveries; yet, persisting in their enterprises with an invincible constancy, they have annexed to their kingdom so many goodly provinces as to bury the remembrance of all past dangers.*40*

The accounts of the Spanish conquest which Raleigh studied and which so aroused his admiration were in fact success stories of the most inspiring sort. As described by Spanish writers, the puissant deeds of Cortez and Pizarro and their followers, and the honors heaped upon them by an admiring world, must have stirred the soul of many a young Elizabethan. In the pages of Zarate's *History of the Discovery and Conquest of Peru,* for instance, an ambitious young Elizabethan could learn how a Spanish country squire had sallied forth to win a golden throne in the high Andes.*41* Zarate recounted in detail Pizarro's troubles with skeptical officials, unfriendly Indians, and financial difficulties—problems Raleigh would face with unshaken confidence in his search for El Dorado, remembering the recompense which had come to the conqueror of the Incas. For the persistence of Pizarro had been rewarded by success beyond even Elizabethan dreams of power and glory. Again, in Gomara's authoritative *History of the Conquest of New*

37. Raleigh, *Guiana,* pp. 77-85.   38. Lee, pp. 220-224.

39. Edward Thompson, *Sir Walter Raleigh, Last of the Elizabethans* (New Haven, 1936), p. 104.

40. Quoted in Tytler, pp. 145-146.

41. Augustin de Zarate, *The Strange and Delectable Historie of the Discovery and Conquest of the Provinces of Peru . . .,* trans. T. Nicholas (London, 1581).

Spain, Hernando Cortez was depicted conquering great cities and invincible empires with the chivalry of a Roland and the might of an Alexander. "There was never Captain that did with like army overcome so infinite a people," wrote Gomara in tribute to the military power of his hero.[42] And the celebrated poet of chivalry Ariosto accorded particular honor to the conqueror of Mexico by listing him prominently among Charles V's "Captains invincible."[43]

Raleigh's Guiana expedition has been described as "an exact counterpart of Spanish experience."[44] He believed the Emperor of Guiana to be a direct descendant of the last Inca of Peru, and expected the realm of El Dorado to be at least as wealthy.[45] That Raleigh considered himself to be following in the footsteps of Cortez and Pizarro is witnessed by the numerous references to the Mexican and Peruvian conquests which he sprinkled through his own account of the Guiana expedition. The man who conquers Guiana, he declared, "shall perform more than ever was done in Mexico by Cortez, or in Peru by Pacaro [Pizarro]. . . ."[46] When Raleigh set out for Guiana, therefore, he was to a large extent deliberately imitating the Spaniards whose conquests he so admired, whose glory he so envied.

At first glance, this seems to be a common enough interpretation. The belief that Sir Walter Raleigh was a pioneer of English empire is to a large extent responsible for his high place among England's national heroes. Victorian scholars in particular tended to see Raleigh as the first British empire builder, an illustrious ancestor of Cecil Rhodes and Lord Lugard.[47] But in the case of Raleigh's Guiana expedition, at least, the image of Raleigh as Britain's first apostle of empire must be reshaped to fit the image of Raleigh as a disciple of Cortez. And there are considerable differences between the idea of empire entertained by nineteenth-century scholars and that held by sixteenth-century filibusters.

For the nineteenth century empire building was ideally moti-

42. Francisco Lopez de Gomara, *The Pleasant Historie of the Conquest of the West India, Now Called New Spayne* . . . (London, 1578), p. 23.

43. Ludovico Ariosto, *Orlando Furioso*, trans. W. S. Rose (London, 1823), XV, xxvii.

44. Lee, p. 229.

45. Raleigh, *Guiana*, pp. 17-18.

46. Ibid., p. 16; cf. also pp. 29, 71.

47. Waldman, pp. 97-98; Stebbing, p. 122.

vated by a selfless patriotism, with overtones of the white man's burden; and it was only too easy for scholars to imagine such ideal motivation in the imperial pioneers of the distant past. In fact, however, sixteenth-century conquistadors carved colonies out of the wilderness primarily from motives of personal ambition. Both the Spanish and their English imitators risked their lives and fortunes for their own personal power, wealth, honor, and fame. Raleigh's own attitude was typical of his time and generation. He did of course hope that Guiana might be conquered under the aegis of the English government, and with the material support of Queen Elizabeth. But this is not to say that a deep affection for either his country or his Queen was a basic driving force behind the expedition. Material help and protection he was eager to have; but his main object was the better fortunes of Sir Walter Raleigh.

There is plenty of circumstantial evidence that Raleigh was in fact thinking primarily of his own interests in Guiana, where he hoped to conquer and reign as English viceroy. To begin with, he was desperately afraid that some other adventurer—even if he were an Englishman—might beat him to the conquest of Guiana.[48] He insisted, of course, that he was thinking only of the Queen's best interests: no rival was so likely to succeed as he, so that if others were allowed to meddle, "the Queen's purpose will be frustrate." But the Queen, as it became increasingly evident, had no purpose in Guiana—she was too shrewd a businesswoman to invest in El Dorado. Raleigh, on the other hand, had a very real purpose there: "Guiana," as one eminent scholar puts it, "had gone to his head. . . ."[49] Raleigh himself admitted his anguished concern for his personal ambitions on the Orinoco when he wrote that, if his rivals, English or foreign, "attempt the chiefest places of *my* enterprise, *I* shall be undone."[50] Again, we know that Raleigh made a great point of showing the natives pictures of Queen Elizabeth, and of impressing them with her greatness. But such efforts would yield obvious tactical benefits, both in Guiana

48. Sir Walter Raleigh to Sir Robert Cecil, Dec., 1594, and same to same, Nov. 13, 1595, in Edwards, II, 104-105, 109.
49. Rowse, p. 185.
50. Sir Walter Raleigh to Sir Robert Cecil, Dec., 1594, in Edwards, II, 105. Italics supplied.

and at the English court. And however much he may have propa-
gandized for his Queen, it was apparently *his* name the Indians
remembered some twenty years later. As he wrote his wife in 1617:

To tell you that I might be here King of the Indies were a vanity;
but my name hath still lived among them. Here they feed me
with . . . all that the country yields; all offer to obey me.[51]

Raleigh was an empire builder, true—but the empire he hoped to
hack out of the jungles of the New World was one like that Cortez
had conquered and ruled. He summed up his real ambitions in a
letter to the younger Cecil:

I hope I shall be thought worthy to direct those actions that I
have at mine own charges labored in; and to govern that country
which I have discovered and hope to conquer for the Queen, without her cost.[52]

The essential elements of Sir Walter Raleigh's ambition may
be reduced to the two key elements of the aspiring mind of his
generation. Of his "thirst for power," a friend declared: "He
desired to seem to be able to sway all men's fancies—all men's
courses."[53] His passion for honor appears clearly enough in his
own writings. He might have been referring to his own Guiana
venture when he wrote: "All enterprises attempted by Arms are
honorable; but those that are done in Countries remote are more
praisable: for the less they be in knowledge, the greater is the
glory to achieve them."[54]

To Raleigh, El Dorado meant just such power and glory—the
great dominion and the high honor that had come to his illustrious predecessors through equally unlikely adventures more
than half a century earlier. Cortez had won immortal fame by
conquering the Empire of the Aztecs, and as Marquess of the
Valley of Huaxacac had held absolute sway over vast lands and
peoples. Raleigh wanted the same rewards for himself for his
conquest of the Empire of Guiana. He believed passionately that

51. Sir Walter Raleigh to Lady Elizabeth Raleigh, Nov. 14, 1617, in Edwards,
II, 349.
52. Sir Walter Raleigh to Sir Robert Cecil, Nov. 13, 1595, in Edwards, II, 109.
53. Harlow in Raleigh, *Guiana*, p. xx; Lucy Aikin, *Memoirs of the Court of
King James I* (London, 1822), I, 58.
54. Walter Raleigh, *The Cabinet-Council: Containing the Chief Arts of Empire,
and Mysteries of State . . .*, ed. John Milton (London, 1858), p. 142.

"the shining glory of this conquest will eclipse all those so far extended beams of the Spanish nation."[55] He sought the same sort of military honor in the upper reaches of the Orinoco that Essex sought at Rouen and Cadiz, but on a truly epic scale: he would conquer, not a city, but an empire. He wanted also the power that would come to the conqueror of the kingdom of El Dorado. He hoped to be viceroy of Guiana, as Cortez had been of Mexico —the governor of "so great riches, and so mighty an Empire," as to constitute "a better Indies for her majesty than the King of Spain hath. . . ."[56]

Raleigh's search for El Dorado was thus typical of his generation. He sought honor—through victory over the King of Spain, through the conquest of the empire of El Dorado, and through the establishment of himself as viceroy of a fabulous British Empire in South America. He sought power—the restoration of his supremacy at court, the unlimited personal power that the gold of Guiana would bring him, and the sense of power that must surge through the veins of the conqueror and master of El Dorado.

iii. The Tamburlaine of the mind:
Francis Bacon

There seems to be no doubt that Francis Bacon was ambitious, and no good reason why he should not have been. Like most of this generation of courtiers, he was born and raised to a life of high political aspiration. His father, Sir Nicholas Bacon, was Lord Keeper of the Great Seal; his uncle was the great Lord Burghley, the Queen's chief minister. Queen Elizabeth herself dandled young Francis on her knee, and "would often term him, *the young Lord-Keeper.*"[57] It has been suggested that, growing up under these circumstances, Francis Bacon early developed an "inner drive to emulate his father, to go from the same law school to the same position as Lord Keeper. . . ."[58] Certainly it is not surprising that such a brilliant boy, born into the inner circle of

55. Raleigh, *Guiana*, p. 71.   56. *Ibid.*, p. 6.
57. In Paul H. Kocher, "Francis Bacon and His Father," *HLQ*, XXI (1958), 148.
58. *Ibid.*, p. 149.

Elizabethan government and politics, should come to "aspire after civil dignities."[59]

The record of Bacon's career is itself sufficient evidence that he was one of the highest aspiring minds of his generation. Under Elizabeth, he deluged his powerful relatives and patrons with petitions for high office: while still in his thirties, he aspired to be Attorney-General, Solicitor-General, Master of the Rolls. All to no avail; his ambitions were frustrated by court factions and a prudent old Queen. But under James, he began at last to rise. He became successively Solicitor-General, Attorney-General, Privy Councillor, Lord Keeper, and Lord Chancellor. He was knighted by his King, and named Baron Verulam and Viscount St. Albans. Such success does not come to unambitious men, then or now. And certainly his contemporaries regarded Francis Bacon as an ambitious climber. A diarist recorded that at the climax of Bacon's career, when he was created Viscount St. Albans in 1621, "all men wonder at the exceeding vanity of his pride and ambition."[60] It is not likely, in short, that the celebrated philosopher was ever wholly carried away by the contemplative planet.

The fact of Francis Bacon's social and political ambition has presented his biographers with a serious problem—a problem of particular significance for a proper understanding of Bacon's grand scheme. Most writers on Bacon have naturally been concerned with him as a thinker, with the Bacon of the *Essays*, of the *Great Instauration* and the *New Atlantis*. Modern scholars have focused particularly on Bacon the prophet of science in the service of man. Unfortunately, personal ambition is no part of our modern image of the ideal scientist or philosopher. We expect such men to possess much of the sanctity of the priests of earlier times —to be high-minded, thoroughly disinterested seekers after truth. The problem of the Bacon biographer, then, is how to reconcile the essayist and philosopher with the ambitious courtier. Students of Bacon have developed two solutions to this problem: some worship at the shrine of Bacon the prophet of the scientific revo-

59. James Spedding, *The Letters and the Life of Francis Bacon* . . . (London, 1890), I, 3.

60. D'Ewes, MS Journal, p. 54, quoted in Godfrey Goodman, *The Court of King James the First* . . ., ed. John S. Brewer (London, 1839), I, 283 n.

lution; others agonize over the moral failings of Bacon the politician.

William Harris, the eighteenth-century antiquary and writer on the reign of James I, drew Bacon in harsh colors as "a flatterer, a time-server, a court tool, a cringer to, and a low suppliant to a very Scoundrel."[61] But the most famous and scathing attack on Bacon's ambition was that of Lord Macaulay, in the nineteenth century.[62] Macaulay condemned Bacon bitterly for his "narrowness and selfishness," his "disingenuousness," his "servility," and his "unworthy ambition." He felt that Bacon was not sufficiently "high-minded," and proved it by pointing to what he considered the low level of Bacon's ambitions. "His desires," Macaulay pointed out, "were set on things below. Wealth, precedence, titles, patronage—the mace, the seals, the coronet—large houses, fair gardens, rich manors, massy services of plate. . . ." No "man of lofty character," sniffed the nineteenth-century critic, would have been so afraid as Bacon was of "the loss of court-favor," of "being left behind by others in the career of ambition." It is a slashing condemnation of Bacon the politician, and not inaccurate in its facts.

But most biographers of Bacon put the major emphasis on his undeniably great philosophical accomplishments. Such students consider his philosophical enterprise as not only the most significant endeavor of his life, but as almost the sole serious one. His political ambitions they casually subordinate to his philosophical goals, following an ingenious formula which Bacon himself suggested. Early in his career, Francis Bacon explained why he was offering his services to the state, when his real interest lay solely in "the study of Truth."[63] He did so, he said, "because I hope that, if I rose to any place of honor in the state, I should have a larger command of industry and ability to help me in my work. . . ." This logical explanation has been eagerly seized upon

61. Dr. William Harris to Dr. Birch, Jan. 26, 1763, in Henry Ellis, ed., *Original Letters of Eminent Literary Men* . . . (Camden Soc. Pub. No. 23; London, 1843), p. 400.

62. [Thomas Babington Macaulay], Review of Basil Montagu, ed., *Works of Francis Bacon,* in *The Edinburgh Review,* Vol. LXV, No. 132 (1837), 104, 39, 24, 30.

63. "Proem" to *Of the Interpretation of Nature,* in Spedding, III, 85.

by a number of Bacon experts.[64] Court politics, as these interpreters see it, was merely a means to the higher end of philosophical inquiry. Political power would put at his disposal the funds and the manpower for a large-scale reconstruction of knowledge. The use of such an unworthy tool for such lofty ends can surely be forgiven the prophet of modern science.

Unfortunately, neither of these interpretations seems properly to reconcile the Bacon of the Great Instauration with the arrogant Lord Chancellor. Simply to state that Bacon, despite his learning and love of mankind, was personally a despicable, conniving politician is really no explanation at all: it begs the question. There do seem to be real differences between the servant of all mankind and the self-serving politician: the question is how to reconcile them. Nor does the attempt to explain away his ambition as the ignoble means to a noble end really fit the facts. Bacon spent too much of his energies in pursuing worldly ambitions for the latter to be dismissed as merely means to an end.

But if Francis Bacon is considered as a typical aspiring mind of the generation of 1560, the contradictions between his political ambitions and his intellectual aspirations are readily enough reconciled. In fact, all such conflicts simply evaporate. It has already been argued that this generation of Elizabethans possessed a unique capacity for merging the crudest of material goals with the loftiest idealistic aims. The most gallant Elizabethan cavaliers looted Spanish churches; the most unscrupulous Elizabethan political schemers were capable of poetry. In the mind of Francis Bacon, then, there simply was no real "clash between his public and private ambitions."[65] The worldly magnificence of Lord Bacon, Baron Verulam, Viscount St. Albans, Lord Keeper of the Great Seal, Lord Chancellor of the Realm, and the magnificent vision of Francis Bacon the philosopher, who would lead mankind to the mastery of the universe—the two were one and the same. They were not merely two sides of the same coin—they were inextricably intermingled, each reinforcing and modifying the other.

A number of Bacon's biographers have caught this mutual dependence of the material and the ideal, so characteristic of his

64. E.g., Spedding, I, 107; Edwin A. Abbott, *Francis Bacon: An Account of His Life and Works* (London, 1885), pp. 321-326.
65. Farrington, p. 71.

generation as a whole.[66] Bacon, as one authority points out, was no Descartes, "brooding and puzzling in front of a stove," no Hobbes, "content to be a dependent of a noble family. . . ."[67] Francis Bacon was not that kind of a man. For him, the Great Instauration would have been disgraced if it had been the work of a menial—of any, in fact, but a mighty potentate. "Bacon," as D. G. James continues, "must move between the Court, York House, and his splendid manor of Gorhambury. . . . He needed the stimulus of great scenes, great affairs, of wide vistas and splendid prospects to release the peculiar power of his ample mind." Thus the splendor of his Gorhambury estate was so dazzling that "it seemed as if the court had been there, so nobly did he live."[68] His sumptuous table was strewn with "sweet herbs and flowers, which he said did refresh his spirits and memory." And he "would many times have music in the next room where he meditated." Thus only, meditating to music, could the great Lord Bacon create his magnificent grand scheme for the conquest of truth and the mastery of the material universe. This was the nature of Bacon's life, as of his thought—and both were in the grand style.

Only our post-Puritan, post-Cartesian minds would see a problem in this merging of the "materialistic" and "idealistic." We see too sharply still Descartes's dichotomy between the realms of matter and mind, the hard Puritan line between the flesh and the spirit. For Elizabethans like Bacon, the two worlds mingled and merged, melted together in a gorgeous vision of magnificence that ravished at once the senses and the spirit. Bacon thus naturally aspired to both political and philosophical triumphs. Far from contradicting each other, the two went easily together in his mind, merged into a single splendid image—the image of himself as the Great Lord Bacon.

But it is Bacon's philosophical aspirations which are of particular interest here—his grand scheme for laying the foundations of a new knowledge, upon which a new society might be built.

66. E.g., J. G. Crowther, *Francis Bacon, The First Statesman of Science* (London, 1960), p. 1; F. H. Anderson, *The Philosophy of Francis Bacon* (Chicago, 1948), pp. 6-7.

67. D. G. James, *The Dream of Learning: An Essay on "The Advancement of Learning," "Hamlet," and "King Lear"* (Oxford, 1951), p. 24.

68. John Aubrey, "Aubrey's Gossip," in Francis Bacon, *A Harmony of the Essays*, ed. Edward Arber (London, 1871), p. xix.

For his extravagant proposal to take all knowledge for his province had all the scope and concreteness of a typical Elizabethan grand scheme. It has in fact a real claim to be considered a grand scheme in the intellectual sphere comparable to those of Raleigh in the colonial, Essex in the military, and Cecil in the constitutional realms. It will be worthwhile to glance briefly at the broad outlines of Bacon's Great Instauration, before examining the quality of his mind in the light of this, its most awesome creation.

Bacon's scheme was tripartite, consisting of a master plan, a new method, and an original institution. The basic plan was to be provided by his master work, the *Great Instauration*, of which he published a first part in 1620. The over-all conceptual framework which his generation had inherited had, he believed, proved inadequate to the real progress of knowledge. "There was but one course left, therefore," he wrote "—to try the whole thing anew upon a better plan . . . . to commence a total reconstruction of sciences, arts, and all human knowledge. . . ."[69] This "better plan" Bacon himself intended to bequeath to posterity. Bacon hoped also to develop a new method of inquiry, particularly suited to the investigation of the natural world with which he was concerned. The secret, he declared, lay in the substitution of a modified form of inductive reasoning for the deductive logic which was basic to Aristotelian and Scholastic thought. Bacon had great faith in his inductive method, which was, he expansively declared, "copied from a very ancient model; even the world itself and the nature of things."[70] Finally, Bacon's grand scheme required the establishment of a radically new institution for research and study of the true nature of the physical world. This was the famous "Solomon's House" of the *New Atlantis*, with its libraries, museums, laboratories, agricultural stations, and other research facilities. Bacon expected great things from the new institution, which he described as "the noblest foundation, as we think, that ever was upon the earth."[71]

69. "Proemium" to *Instauratio Magna*, Francis Bacon, in *The Works of . . .*, ed. James Spedding, *et al.* (London, 1864), VIII, 18.

70. "The Plan of the Work," and "Epistle dedicatory to King James," *Instauratio Magna*, Bacon, *Works*, VIII, 46, 23.

71. *New Atlantis*, in *Selected Writings of . . .*, ed. Hugh G. Dick (New York, 1955), pp. 562-563.

Here, apparently, was a typical Elizabethan grand scheme, combining unbelievably broad scope with concrete, practical detail. The scheme encompassed nothing less than the transformation of the human environment through the renovation of knowledge. But Bacon himself could begin the practical steps leading to this incredible consummation; he could write the master plan, explain the new inductive method, even perhaps secure the buildings of some existing college or school in which to establish "Solomon's House."[72] There remains, however, one more question to be answered before Bacon's Great Instauration can be accepted as a real Elizabethan grand scheme: Just how "serious" was Bacon in these proposals? Was the Great Instauration a serious enterprise which its creator really hoped to see brought to fruition? Or was it merely the elegant incidental philosophizing of a careerist politician in days when belles lettres were a necessary adjunct to the complete courtier?

It would seem that Bacon's scheme was in some sense seriously intended. In the first place, the Great Instauration was a lifelong project, probably begun as early as his Cambridge years, and developed decade by decade, in letters and notes as well as in full-dress literary productions. Bacon's secretary, furthermore, wrote after his master's death:

His book of *Instauratio Magna* (which, in his own account, was the chiefest of his works) was no slight imagination or fancy of his brain; but a settled and concocted notion: the production of many years' labor and travail. I myself have seen at the least twelve copies of the *Instauration* revised, year by year, one after another: and every year altered and amended. . . .[73]

Bacon himself insisted that the project was possible of accomplishment, urging his followers to "be of good hope, nor . . . imagine that this Instauration of mine is a thing infinite and beyond the power of man. . . ."[74] For this ambitious generation, nothing was beyond the power of man. In general, then, the testimony seems to support Spedding's view that Bacon "never doubted that the thing might be done if men would but think

72. Anderson, p. 23.

73. William Rawley, "The Life of the Honorable Author," in Bacon, *Works*, I, 47.

74. "Preface," *Instauratio Magna*, in Bacon, *Works*, VIII, 37.

so, and that it was his mission to make them think so and point out the way."[75]

Let us now turn, therefore, to the quality of Bacon's mind as it is revealed in this intellectual grand scheme. In the first place, it is evident that the supreme arrogance that could take all knowledge for its province was truly Marlovian in quality. Bacon considered himself no dusty, logic-chopping theoretician, but a prophet, a light-bringer, whose ideas might transform the world. He saw himself as the discoverer of new realms of truth, the conqueror who would bring the physical world under the dominion of mankind. A single piece of Baconian rhetoric should make clear this Marlovian quality:

But above all, if a man could succeed, not in striking out some particular invention, however useful, but in kindling a light in nature—a light which should in its very rising touch and illuminate all the border-regions that confine upon the circle of our present knowledge; and so spreading further and further should presently disclose and bring into sight all that is most hidden and secret in the world,—that man (I thought) would be the benefactor indeed of the human race,—the propagator of man's empire over the universe, the champion of liberty, the conqueror and subduer of necessities.[76]

That man was, of course, to be Francis Bacon. His egotistic self-confidence was as towering as that of any of Marlowe's heroes. "I have made a beginning," he wrote loftily, "a beginning, as I hope, not unimportant: the fortune of the human race will give the issue. . . ."[77]

The metaphor that most accurately summed up Bacon's image of himself is that of the conquering general—"the propagator of man's empire over the universe, the champion of liberty, the conqueror and subduer of necessities." The Marlovian hero whom he most resembled was not Faust, who made this world his playground, but Tamburlaine, who conquered it. Bacon himself more than once used military metaphors to describe his great philosophic enterprise. He rallied his cohorts of thinkers, "to overcome, not an adversary in argument, but nature in action. . . ."[78]

75. Spedding, III, 83-84.
76. "Proem," to *Of the Interpretation of Nature*, in Spedding, III, 84-85.
77. "Plan of the Work," *Instauratio Magna*, in Bacon, *Works*, VIII, 53.
78. "Preface," *Novum Organum*, in Bacon, *Works*, VIII, 63-64.

To his mind, he too was Cortez, drawing his line in the sand to separate faint hearts from high adventurers. He proposed a breakthrough unparalleled in the history of human thought, and a victory for mankind greater than that of any military conqueror. As he saw himself, Francis Bacon was indeed the Tamburlaine of the Elizabethan mind.

The motives behind Bacon's grand scheme for the advancement of learning in the service of man therefore deserve more detailed analysis. One such motive he himself stressed as fundamental: "Believing that I was born for the service of mankind," he wrote, "I set myself to consider . . . what service I was myself best fitted by nature to perform."[79] According to Bacon himself, then, "the service of mankind" was the primary motive behind the Great Instauration. The concept of service to one's fellow men was, of course, not new: in fact, the idea of serving mankind may well represent a typically grandiloquent expansion of the old cliché of service to the commonwealth, a notion popular among the older Elizabethan generations.[80] In any case, it is hard to believe that Bacon—self-serving courtier, arrogant politician, and corrupt judge—was driven to years of intellectual labor exclusively or even primarily by love of his fellow man. This is not to deny to Bacon all altruistic motives: strange combinations of the selfish and the selfless were possible to the baroque minds of these Elizabethans. But other motives were there as well, two of which stood out with exceptional clarity. The first of these was honor, in the Elizabethan sense of public approbation; the second was a surging sense of unlimited power.

Francis Bacon's notion of honor and honors contained little of the medieval contempt for this world and its rewards. "For honor," he wrote, speaking of public positions of honor, "is, or should be, the place of virtue. . . ."[81] Virtue might thus cheerfully accept public honors as its just reward: certainly Bacon never hesitated to do so. It was also Bacon's view that the acceptance of public honors might be legitimatized by the intention to utilize places

79. "Proem" to *Of the Interpretation of Nature* in Spedding, III, 84.

80. In the paragraph quoted above, Bacon himself makes clear the connection between his idea of service to mankind and the older conception of service to the commonwealth.

81. "Of Great Place," Harl. MS. 5106, 1607-1612, in *A Harmony of the Essays*, p. 290.

of honor and credit for the public good. Honors could in this way provide "the vantage ground to do good."[82] And since the betterment of man's lot was the object of his grand scheme, Bacon probably considered public honor in due measure to be a perfectly proper additional goal of his aspirations.

For Bacon did see his role as leader of the advance of human knowledge to be one highly deserving of honorable recognition, by the public and by posterity. To begin with, he considered the development of sciences, arts, and crafts to be extremely important. A useful invention, he thought, was far more worthy of praise than a political coup or a military victory.[83] We know, too, that Bacon considered his own grand scheme a far greater contribution than the specific researches of the scientists of his own time, mere tinkerers at "petty tasks," puffing themselves up mightily over some single discovery.[84] He did not invent the concept of the dignity of science, but he probably did more than any other single human being to win widespread acceptance of the notion.[85] And since he proposed, through his Great Instauration, to make a gigantic contribution to the advancement of science, he quite likely felt that he deserved great honor for his effort.

Finally, Bacon actually urged that honor and renown were due to such Columbuses of human civilization as he conceived himself to be. He reminded the public that those who contributed to "the discovery of new arts, endowments, and commodities for the bettering of man's life" were in ancient times most highly honored—were sometimes even accorded divine honors and worshipped as gods by a grateful people.[86] In the Solomon's House of his *New Atlantis*, Bacon imagined statues of all the great inventors and discoverers, from the inventor of writing to Christopher Columbus.[87] These effigies were to be intricately carved of marble or cedar, silver or gold, depending on the value society set upon

82. "Of Ambition," in *Harmony of the Essays*, p. 228.

83. Farrington, pp. 6-7; "Proem" to *Of the Interpretation of Nature*, in Spedding, III, 84; *Novum Organum*, Bk. I, Aphor. cxxix, in Bacon, *Works*, VIII, 162.

84. "Preface," *Instauratio Magna*, in Bacon, *Works*, VIII, 31-32.

85. Elizabeth Rosemary Ryman, "The Scientific Attitude of Francis Bacon," University of Cambridge, *Abstracts of Dissertations . . . 1952-1953* (Cambridge, 1955), p. 112.

86. "Proem," *Of the Interpretation of Nature*, in Spedding, III, 84; *Novum Organum*, Bk. I, Aphor. cxxix, in Bacon, *Works*, VIII, 161.

87. *New Atlantis*, in Bacon, *Works*, VIII, 305-306.

the discoverer's contribution to civilization. How glorious a statue of himself Bacon must have expected posterity to raise in the great hall of some future Solomon's House!

The concept of power was also vital to the Great Instauration. In his willingness to discuss and speak with frank enthusiasm of power, Bacon provides a rare insight into the minds of his contemporaries. For the notion of power was not a respectable one in Elizabethan England. Many a courtier would confess to an immoderate passion for honor; but no politician would admit that he lusted after power, after dominion over his fellows. Bacon, however, justified power of a sort, on the same grounds he had used to legitimatize a thirst for honors: "Power to do good," he wrote, "is the true and lawful end of aspiring."[88] An ambitious statesman's climb to political power could thus be justified when that power was to be used for the good of man. Bacon avowedly saw himself in this role, and no doubt did justify some of his own political ambition on just these grounds.

Much more important, however, was his profound belief that knowledge is power: "human Knowledge and human Power," he said, "do really meet in one."[89] Bacon insisted that "the sovereignty of man lieth hid in knowledge; wherein many things are reserved, which kings with their treasure cannot buy, nor with their force command. . . ."[90] The awe-inspiring power of scientific knowledge was revealed, for instance, in the amazing differences between European civilization and the primitive existence of the American Indians—differences due solely to the comparative sophistication of the practical arts and sciences of Europe.[91] Such power, such "dominion over natural things," was the primary object of that natural philosophy of which Bacon proposed to make himself the master.[92] He sought through the advancement of learning to "extend more widely the limits of the power . . . of man"—and in so doing, wielded enormous power himself, power over the "spirits of men."[93]

88. "Of Great Place," in *Harmony of the Essays*, p. 282.

89. "The Plan of the Work," *Instauratio Magna*, in Bacon, *Works*, VIII, 53; *Novum Organum*, Bk. I, Aphor. iii., *ibid.*, VIII, 67.

90. "Mr. Bacon in Praise of Knowledge," in Spedding, I, 125.

91. *Novum Organum*, Bk. I, Aphor. cxxix, in Bacon, *Works*, VIII, 161-162.

92. *New Atlantis*, in Bacon, *Works*, VIII, 260.

93. *Novum Organum*, Bk. I, Aphor. cxvi, in Bacon, *Works*, VIII, 147; *Ad-*

Such power as Bacon sought was, he believed, not only greater, but more noble than lesser forms of power. Political power, for its own sake, he wrote, was a "vulgar and degenerate" goal; military conquest "has more dignity, though not less covetousness. But if a man endeavor to establish and extend the power and dominion of the human race itself over the universe, his ambition (if ambition it can be called) is without doubt both a more wholesome thing and a more noble than the other two."[94] This was in fact the goal of his own ambitious grand scheme—power to mold society, to build a brave new world. It was no mere political or military power that he sought, but—in his own Marlovian phrase—"the enlarging of the bounds of human empire, to the effecting of all things possible."[95]

Thus Francis Bacon, despite his intellectual preoccupations, conceived perhaps the grandest of all the extravagant schemes concocted by his aspiring generation. He formulated, and hoped to see implemented, a magnificent project for the advancement of knowledge in the service of man. In so doing, he was motivated to a large extent by the two ruling passions of his generation— honor and power. He was impelled to his theorizing partly by a thirst for public honors and for posthumous glory as the prophet of a new age. At the same time, he labored to give to mankind a new dominion over this world—a dominion which, he believed, it was within his own mortal power to bestow.

iv. The feeling of progress

One further aspect of the Elizabethan grand scheme remains to be considered, and that is its possible relationship to the rise of the idea of progress. A number of social groups have already been pinpointed by scholars as causal factors in the rise of this radical new view of human society. The question raised here is: Can a case be made for the notion that the Elizabethan aristocrats of the younger generation also contributed to the spread of this

---

vancement of Learning, in *Moral and Historical Works*, ed. Joseph Devey (London, 1909), p. 68.

94. *Novum Organum*, Bk. I, Aphor. cxxix, in Bacon, *Works*, VIII, 162.
95. *New Atlantis*, in Bacon, *Works*, VIII, 297.

idea? Specifically, did the Elizabethan aspiring mind in general, and its grand schemes in particular, help to bring about the spread of the idea of progress in England?

The basic attitude of the courtly culture of late Elizabethan times toward human society and human life is generally considered to have been much too pessimistic to be compatible with the idea of progress. The fact of change in society was of course recognized—but, at least in formal literary productions, change was generally viewed with regret and dismay. Mutability, as it was commonly labeled, meant decline, degeneration, decay. Passages may be found in the writings of many of the younger generation, as well as of their elders, indicating that the governors and literati of late Elizabethan England saw change as, of necessity, change for the worse.

There were at least two basic reasons for this common expression of the view that mutability and decay were synonymous. First, it has been pointed out that the literary productions which expressed this view were generally written "in the classical tradition."[96] Sophisticated, serious Elizabethan literature was generally based on the Latin classics, or on the fourteenth-, fifteenth-, and sixteenth-century vernacular literatures which were themselves saturated with classical influences. It was in this tradition that the Elizabethan aristocracy, and the writers who catered to their taste, were educated. And the classical attitude, from Plato onwards, repeatedly expressed the "idea of the senility of the world," and of "the degeneration of man."[97] The conventional wisdom, in other words, dictated the view that social change meant social degeneration. How could men indoctrinated with this pessimistic outlook make any serious contribution to the spread of the idea of progress?

The answer to this fundamental objection involves the whole question of the extent to which opinions expressed in Elizabethan belles lettres can be taken as representative of the real views of their authors. Of course, popular literature like the stage play often reflected—incidentally and even unconsciously—the

96. Rebecca Arnell Dewey, "The Idea of Progress in Elizabethan Literature," Stanford University, *Abstracts of Dissertations . . . 1946-47* (Stanford, California, 1947), p. 31.
97. *Ibid.*

opinions of the age. But the insistence on deliberate "sincerity" and "honesty" which the twentieth century prizes in its serious literature appears in fact to be an innovation introduced mainly by the Romantic writers of the later eighteenth and earlier nineteenth centuries. In Elizabethan times, a serious literary production seems to have been more nearly akin to an exercise in style than a confession of faith. The ideas and opinions expressed were often culled straight from commonplace books: the university wit's contribution lay in the realm of form, in rhetorical embellishment, in structure and versification. It thus seems a rather debatable procedure to base conclusions as to the real beliefs of the Elizabethan upper classes on their more formal literary productions alone. This is especially true when the opinions in question are so obviously part of the inherited classical tradition which filled the commonplace books. It would seem, in short, that the fact that Elizabethan literature overwhelmingly supported the thesis that change and decay were identical proves little or nothing about the real opinions of the Elizabethan younger generation.

There was, however, a second reason for the common impression that the Elizabethan ruling class was too pessimistic about social change to have supported the idea of progress. It seems to be a fact—as the following chapter will attempt to demonstrate —that in their later years, many of the Elizabethan younger generation did come to accept this melancholy view of life and the world. It was after the turn of the century that Shakespeare wrote his "dark" plays, that John Donne began to preach to his fellow sinners, and that Sir Walter Raleigh composed his sober and melancholy *History of the World*. In these declining years, the schoolbook clichés of mutability and decay do seem to have taken on real meaning for the generation of 1560. How, then, could men who had actually come to accept their educational indoctrination on the subject of change and degeneration be at the same time ardent apostles of the idea of progress?

The answer to this objection is simply that they probably did not entertain both notions at the same time, but rather at quite different stages of their development. In generational terms, at least, it is not logical to deduce the opinions of the young men of the 1580's and 1590's from the views of the old men they became after the turn of the century. It took years of disillusioning experience to transform the aspiring minds of the last years of Elizabeth into the melancholy men of the reign of James I. But as young men, they lacked this experience; enthusiasm and self-confidence ruled their ardent natures. It is therefore intrinsically unlikely that the gloomy maxim that change means inevitable decay impressed the generation of 1560 in their youth and middle age as strongly as it did in the twilight of their lives.

The evidence for the common assumption that the attitude of the Elizabethan ruling class was generally pessimistic on the subject of change and mutability seems to be somewhat questionable. What, then, can be said for the theory that the generation of 1560, at least, shared in some sense the progressive outlook which was just beginning to gain currency in their time? Certainly a number of other individuals and groups seem to have begun, by the end of the sixteenth century, to think in ways conducive to the development of the idea of progress. J. B. Bury has traced the development of the idea by European thinkers from the sixteenth century onwards.[98] Ernst Troeltsch has presented the case for Protestant influences on the concept; and it has been urged that the millennial sects of the early seventeenth century also helped to implant the idea of progress in the Western mind.[99] Edgar Zilsel has pointed out the important contribution of technicians of various sorts to the genesis of the idea.[100] And the notion of progress has, not surprisingly, been found at work in the minds of the extremely mobile, energetic, and ambitious Elizabethan middle classes.[101] Without questioning the contributions of any of these groups, I should simply like to suggest the addition of yet another group of Elizabethans to those who were beginning to think of society in terms of some sort of progress. For it does seem somehow unlikely that such

98. J. B. Bury, *The Idea of Progress* (London, 1924).

99. Ernst Troeltsch, *Protestantism and Progress* (New York, 1912); Ernest Lee Tuveson, *Millennium and Utopia: A Study in the Background of the Idea of Progress* (Berkeley and Los Angeles, 1949).

100. Edgar Zilsel, "The Genesis of the Concept of Scientific Progress," *JHI*, VI (1945), 325-349.

101. Dewey, "Idea of Progress in Elizabethan Literature."

alert, energetic, and imaginative young men as the courtiers and writers of the younger generation should have failed utterly to sense this exciting new view stirring in the back of so many contemporary minds.

To understand the specific contribution of the generation of 1560 to the spread of this new concept, however, it will be necessary to analyze this early faith in progress more closely. The notion of social progress, which became a veritable cult in later centuries, may be considered to have two fundamental components —one intellectual in nature, the other emotional or psychological. We are dealing, not only with an *idea* of progress, but also with a *feeling* of progress. From the point of view of intellectual history, the latter is almost as important as the former. And it is to the rise of this *feeling* of progress that the younger generation of the Elizabethan ruling class probably made an important contribution.

An idea does not gain currency, does not appeal to relatively large numbers of people, merely because it is logical or can be clearly demonstrated empirically. In fact, an *idea* as such, a bare concept, has almost no appeal at all to anybody except a handful of thinkers. An idea must have relevance and urgency to catch the attention of most people. It must, in other words, make an appeal to the emotions as well as to the intellect: it must be felt as well as understood. In fact, if it can be felt intensely enough, it often hardly matters whether the concept is clearly understood or not. As far as causes and origins are concerned, the feeling of progress is certainly as important as the idea of progress. And the origins of this feeling may be found, at least in part, in the optimistic, positive outlook of the Marlovian aspiring mind.

The feeling of progress consisted basically of the emotionally held conviction that man could master his environment, could change his world for the better. This conviction was strong enough to impel men to take action, to run risks, to pick themselves up after each disaster and renew the assault. This feeling of the possibility of progress need not have been verbalized or even formulated intellectually: its existence was demonstrated pragmatically, by the actions of its adherents. And such a conviction, such a conscious or unconscious faith in progress, grew naturally from the self-confidence characteristic of driving personal ambition.

A theoretical reconstruction of the rise of the feeling of progress among the Elizabethan ruling class must begin with the obvious fact of change. Change was a part of the lives of Elizabethans: change in the economic, political, and social spheres, in the realms of intellect and art, and increasingly in the area of political power. But ideas catch up with events very slowly. When confronted with the fact of change, men had for centuries been frightened and bewildered by the incomprehensible transformation of their social world. Medieval theorists had found solid philosophical justification for this opposition to changes in society. Human institutions, after all, existed by God's will and *fiat*; human laws reflected the immutable truths of God's natural law; the fixed classes of society fitted into the eternal hierarchic structure of God's universe. Well into early modern times, apologists for the social and political status quo continued to proclaim the permanence of the institutions they defended, asserting that any changes in the structure of society were unnatural, and therefore evil. Those whose interests were above mere temporal things admitted that change was the normal lot of man here on earth—which only proved the ineffable superiority of the next world to this mortal coil of mutability. It required a generation rendered optimistic about social change by a lifetime of increasing opportunity, and concerned primarily with this changing temporal world, even to begin to accept the idea of progressive change.

But the idea of progress, as formulated by Francis Bacon and passed on to the modern world, did not consist solely in the assertion that social change might be for the better. It included also the insistence that change might be deliberately initiated and controlled by men for the continuous increase of their own well-being. On the personal level, at least, this belief was certainly common among the aspiring minds of the Elizabethan younger generation. They saw themselves as masters of their fates, quite capable of changing their personal status for the better. The personal ambitions of many of these young men, furthermore, were large enough to bring them into conflict with the very structure of their world. They were driven by vaulting aspiration into repeated collision with the limitations imposed upon the men of their time by their social and physical environments. A medieval system of taxation and a hopelessly rigged courtier system, contrary winds and camp fever and many other facts of life as it was lived in the late sixteenth century, all conspired against them. But the sheer intensity of their aspiration impelled them again and again to try to break through these barriers wherever their ambitions were blocked by social or physical realities.

This was particularly true of the grand schemes, which, in the grandeur of their objectives and the scope of their operations, transcended almost qualitatively the petty ambitions of the average cavalier or courtier. Robert Cecil's plan for a Great Contract with Parliament required of him a real confidence that venerable political institutions might, through his efforts, be transformed for the better. Essex's strategic conception of an English expeditionary force permanently maintained upon the coast of Spain revealed an amazing assurance that he could successfully overcome the immense physical limitations which an age of primitive logistics imposed upon much less extravagant operations. These aspiring minds evidently felt strongly that fundamental aspects of the world they lived in might be controlled by men—at least in particular instances and for the benefit of certain fortunate individuals.

This same belief in the possibility of advancement for the individual, generalized into a broadly optimistic view of the world, was also characteristic of another important segment of the population—the flourishing and highly mobile Elizabethan middle classes. The comparison is illuminating, and tends to lend weight to the present view of the progressive instincts of the younger generation of the Elizabethan ruling class. For it has been suggested that, in the case of the Elizabethan middle class also, soaring, self-confident ambition created a feeling of progress within which the idea of progress could grow and flourish.[102] The basic formulation is essentially the same, beginning reasonably enough:

Our survey of the literature of the middle class in Elizabethan England impresses upon us their faith in their ability to better

102. *Ibid.*, pp. 33-34.

their earthly lot. This group made great strides in the individual's appreciation of himself, a prerequisite for an idea of progress.

The author considers the "spirit of enterprise" shown by this class —and certainly essential to the aspiring mind of the aristocratic ruling class—to be "one of the basic principles relating to an idea of material progress." For the middle class, the transition from personal ambition to the broader idea of social progress was accomplished as follows:

Elizabethan writers of the middle class reveal that for them the development of enterprise for private profit was very closely associated with a nationalistic patriotism for a greater England and with a religious fervor for the extension of God's earthly kingdom. Their mission was before them; the whole world was the prize.

The same process of generalization, from the personal to the universal, of course went on in the minds of the upper classes. Raleigh, Cumberland, and Essex worked out their grand schemes at least partly from a determination to topple the Spanish empire; real altruism, and certainly a desire to transform the human condition in general, were part of Francis Bacon's motivation. Nor is this similarity surprising. The middle classes on the one hand, the gentry and new nobility on the other, were the two most aggressively mobile segments of Elizabethan society. It was only natural that these two groups should come to see the world itself as a place in which progressive change was at least possible.

Finally, further evidence of the existence of a feeling of progress among the Elizabethan younger generation is provided by their new version of the myth of Fortune's wheel. The new myth, like the extravagant ventures themselves, not only bears witness to the feeling of the possibility of a sort of personal progress; it also hints at the extension of this feeling beyond personal advancement, into the realm of man's relationship with the world at large.

The symbolic presentation of Fortune mastered and the Baconian plan for mastery of the world sprang apparently from a common feeling of man's ability to mold his environment, to bend circumstance to his will. The theatrical supermen of the late 1580's and the 1590's boasted that they would turn Fortune's wheel with their own hands—that is, they would seize upon and control for their own benefit the "natural" course of human events. Fortune was no less than this: a popular symbol for the uncertain course of human life, and for the certainty that into each life a good deal of rain must fall. To master Fortune, then, was to master the very nature of things in the interest of personal welfare.

From this egocentric ambition, how large a step was it to Bacon's aspiration to master the natural processes for the welfare of mankind as a whole? In Bacon himself, the personal and the altruistic, private political ambitions and broad philosophic aspirations, were inextricably mingled. Surely Bacon's scheme of progress and the popular new myth of Fortune mastered represented at least a common impulse in the generation of 1560. Where Bacon's genius constructed a monumental philosophical system, his contemporaries wrote only a new version of an old fairy tale. But the philosophy and the myth were built upon the same foundation—the new feeling of confidence in the success of human efforts to alter the human condition in the interests of man's own well-being.

The role of the aspiring mind of the Elizabethan younger generation in the growth of the idea of progress was thus a diffuse but important one: it helped to create a progressive mood, in which such an idea might flourish. It might even be said that this feeling of progress provided the motive power which propelled this novel idea from the minds of a few scholars and technicians into the public domain. For it was the feeling of the real possibility of great personal success which gave the idea of universal progress its relevance and its emotional appeal.

The ruling-class generation of 1560 did not accomplish this feat alone, of course. The contributions of other contemporary social groups have been mentioned already. It is also likely that succeeding generations of the ruling class, as of the middle class, felt the same surge of confidence in the possibility of worldly achievement. For in the last decade of the sixteenth century, upper-class generations who had forgotten the mid-Tudor revolutions began to seize the initiative in government through their parliamentary assembly. This process would continue for a hundred years, and would make these men of landed property the masters of England for yet another century and a half after the victory of 1688. In the first decade of the seventeenth century, furthermore, the development of eastern trade and American colonies began, with the organizing of the East India and Virginia companies. For the next three centuries this mercantile and imperialistic expansion would pour profits into the coffers of the landed and commercial classes who had the foresight to invest. Political and economic aspiration and achievement on an unprecedented scale thus continued among these groups of Englishmen; and among these groups, the idea of progress spread till it became an article of faith. Through three hundred years and more after the Elizabethan younger generation passed from the stage, the rapid and broadening stream of actual progress flowed on, the feeling of progress grew, and the idea flourished.

VII. *The melancholy malcontents*

By 1603 the generation of 1560 had ceased to be a younger generation in any sense of the word. Sir Walter Raleigh, whose birth marked the beginning of their generational span, had passed his fiftieth year; Essex, had he lived, would have been in his late thirties. By and large, even the younger members of this generation were in their forties, an age which, in those times, was generally considered at best the autumn of one's life.

More important, by 1603 the generation of 1560 had shot its bolt. The successful among them had already begun to bask in the warmth of the new regime and to anticipate further advancement. The failures were firmly settled on the downward slope, or had already been cast aside. As individuals, their paths were determined, their characters fixed. And as a generation, they were losing their identity, beginning to merge with the generation of the 1540's, as the generations of Elizabeth and Burghley had merged in their later years. We need follow this generation no further. We should, however, take one last look at these men, no longer young, to see how their ambitious lifetimes of striving ended.

i. A generation of failures

The Queen was dead. For the generation of 1560, the long agony of the bottleneck years was over, and the dragging, futile Spanish War was ending. The king was now James Stuart, a man of their own generation, whose special needs for loyalty and money would make him particularly willing to satisfy their demands for honors and power. After twenty years in limbo, the ruling-class generation of 1560 came into its birthright: its members were now the governors of England.

But the cost of their long struggle had been high. Many of their leaders had fallen—Sir Philip Sidney in the war, Essex in the political infighting of the bottleneck years. Many other aspiring minds had also perished in the wars, or had been cast into the political dust bin. Indeed, of all the eager young men who had come to court in the early 1580's, only a few had built successful careers for themselves. Bustling little Robert Cecil rose steadily to the pinnacle of political power; Sir Robert Sidney attained the rank and prestige of Viscount Lisle and Earl of Leicester; but these were among the small minority who achieved what we may assume to have been their highest ambitions. Whether they sought promotion through a military career or labored for political preferment, the rule for the generation of 1560 was not success, but failure.

The ardent quest for military honor on which this generation embarked in the mid-eighties quite often led only to misery and an untimely death. John Donne, veteran of two of the great military expeditions of the 1590's, wrote that England could but lament

> . . . that her sons did seek a foreign grave
> (For, Fate's or Fortune's drift none can soothsay,
> Honor and misery have one face and way.)[1]

And many an aspiring mind did find the end to all his ambitions in a shallow battlefield grave. They brought the brilliant Sir Philip Sidney home to bury him, but lesser men were buried where they fell, or dropped into the sea. Five sons of Sir Allen Apsley, wrote a granddaughter, "went into the wars in Ireland and the Low Countries, and there remained none of them, nor their issues, when I was born. . . ."[2] In 1595, after a decade of hostilities, a list of seventy captains who had served in France or the Netherlands was drawn up, and it was discovered that thirty-two of them had been killed—a casualty rate among commanding officers of close to 50 per cent.[3] Dangers and discomforts abounded too on the great sea raids: the fever that struck down Sir Francis Drake did not spare younger men. Even the heroes of 'eighty-eight, who scarcely sailed out of sight of the home island, suffered abominably from lack of supplies in their tiny ships. They reported that they "left off the pursuit of the Spanish fleet for want

---

1. "The Storme," in *The Complete Poetry and Selected Prose of John Donne*, ed. Charles M. Coffin (New York, 1952), p. 126.
2. Lucy Hutchison, *Memoirs of the Life of Colonel Hutchinson* . . . ed. C. H. Firth (rev. ed.; London, 1885), I, 13.
3. *C. S. P., Dom., 1595-1597*, CCLII, 83.

of powder and victuals; and [were] driven to such extremity, that the Lord Admiral had been obliged to eat beans, and many of the men to drink their own water."[4]

The wars could mean not only physical dangers, but terrible financial burdens for the young seekers after honor. The debts and losses of Sir John Burgh, with which we shall deal in a moment, were typical of the economic strain that the war imposed upon his generation. Sir Robert Sidney was not the only young commander who had to borrow money at humiliating terms just to pay his troops.[5] And even worse mishaps could befall the young gentlemen who volunteered for the sea raids of the 1580's and '90's, placing themselves at the mercy of wind and storm, seasickness and scurvy. A young man thus described the wait for a favorable wind to sail on the islands voyage of 1597:

. . . . daily our fleet grows less and less, our victuals spending, and our soldiers sick and weak . . . many of the gentlemen adventurers already gone, some for seasickness discouraged by the last storm, some . . . hopeless now to make profit of the voyage, for which end only they undertook the journey, and some for want, long since spent to the uttermost of their credits and abilities . . . to such fortunes are men subject that seek foreign adventures. . . .[6]

The ambitious young nobleman or knight who, like the "buccaneer Earl" of Cumberland, undertook to outfit such privateering expeditions himself, at a cost of thousands of pounds, of course suffered proportionately when a contrary wind frustrated his intentions.[7]

Disappointment was also the rule rather than the exception during the political bottleneck years, when the court was accurately described by an aged and unrewarded courtier poet as

> A joy to youth, a pain to age,
> Where many lose and few do win. . . .[8]

Thomas Nashe's biting characterization was much less exaggerated than one might expect:

4. *C. S. P., Dom., 1581-1590*, CCXIV, 53.
5. *A. P. C., 1596-1597*, XXVI, 563-564.
6. Henry Slingsby, *The Diary of* . . . (London, 1836), pp. 250-252.
7. *C. S. P., Span., 1587-1603*, IV, 472, 487, 495, 501; *C. S. P., Dom., 1591-1594*, CCXXXVIII, 17, 82.
8. Thomas Churchyard, *A pleasant Discourse of Court and Wars* . . . (London, 1596), p. A3ᵛ.

With less suit (I assure you) is the Kingdom of Heaven obtained,
than a suit for a pension or office to an earthly King; which though
a man hath twenty years followed, and hath better than three parts
and a half of a promise to have confirmed, yet if he have but a
quarter of an enemy in the Court, it is cashiered and non-suited.[9]

The twenty-year suit was no rhetorical exaggeration. Francis Bacon
made his first humble petition for office as early as 1580, when
he was not yet twenty; by 1603 he had gotten no further with all
his petitioning and intriguing than a reversion of the Clerkship
of the Star Chamber—and that office did not actually become
vacant for nineteen years after he secured the reversion.[10]

Nor did the coming of the new reign prove the millennium
many had hoped for, despite all James I could do to satisfy the
ambitions of his new subjects. At Whitehall in the spring of 1603,
there was much dissatisfaction among the promenading lords
and ladies, "every man expecting mountains and finding molehills."[11] The sad fact was that "shortly after his Majesty came to
London . . . discontents began to discover themselves, as none
could tell whom to trust . . . it were too tedious . . . to recite
all that I have heard of discontented minds since his Majesty's
coming. . . ."[12] The prodigious aspiration which Elizabeth would
not satisfy, James could not. The pair of conspiracies which sent
Essex to the block and Raleigh to the Tower involved only a
small number of frustrated courtiers; but they expressed the
desperation of a frustrated generation.

Nor were hard-won honors and powers sure once lives and
fortunes had been risked for them. A capricious Queen could
withdraw favor and cancel honors for any reason or no reason, as
all her captains and ministers of state knew too well. The dashing
Earl of Essex was prodigal with honors on his campaigns; but the
Queen could make his young knights tremble in their shoes if she
thought the honor unwarranted. Lamented Sir John Harington

9. Thomas Nashe, *Christ's Tears Over Jerusalem*, in *The Works of . . .*, ed.
R. B. McKerrow (London, 1910), I, 102.

10. Francis Bacon to Lady Burghley, Sept. 16, 1580, and same to Lord Burghley,
Sept. 16, 1580, in James Spedding, *The Letters and Life of Francis Bacon . . .*
(London, 1890), I, 12-14.

11. Anne Clifford, *The Diary of . . .*, ed. V. Sackville-West (New York, 1923),
p. 5.

12. Quoted in Godfrey Goodman, *The Court of King James the First*, ed.
John S. Brewer (London, 1839), II, 69.

after the disastrous Irish expedition: "In good sooth I feared her Majesty more than the rebel Tyrone, and wished I had never received my Lord of Essex's honor of knighthood."[13] As for the public adulation which these young cavaliers so adored, the fickle public proved quite as likely as the Queen to laugh at the pretensions of the spade-bearded heroes of Rouen or Cadiz. It is perhaps illuminating to remember that Falstaff was Shakespeare's most popular character.[14]

The greatest political success, too, could come in the end to disaster. Francis Bacon rose higher than his father, held the greatest judicial offices in England—but died a disgraced man, the victim of his enemies' vindictiveness and his own ambition. Charles Blount became Lord Mountjoy and then Earl of Devonshire and a Privy Councillor, but he died in his early forties, disgraced and unlamented. Politicians with Sir Robert Cecil's talents for survival and aggrandizement were rare; and even he, who inherited his place as chief minister of the Crown and earned a peerage for himself, had his moments of misery and doubt. Political power was as hard to keep as military reputation—and sometimes even more dangerous.

Finally, whether they succeeded or failed in the end, all these aspiring minds knew their share of failure along the way. Elizabeth's soldiers and statesmen, almost without exception, spent money they did not have and strength that could not last for rewards that were, at the very best, far from sure. To Robert Cecil and Anthony Bacon, to Sir Robert Sidney and Sir John Burgh—to all these men, ultimate failures and successes alike, a large share of frustration and wretchedness was allotted. When and if success finally came, it was only after a long lifetime of bitter experience with disappointment, indebtedness, disgrace, and failure.

This was a generation of Phoenixes: their careers began as romantic quests for unique honor and absolute supremacy—and ended all too often as a taste of ashes in the mouth. The audacity of their aspiration was stupendous; and they littered the history

13. Sir John Harington to Sir Hugh Portman, Oct. 9, 1601, in Thomas Park, ed., *Nugae Antiquae* . . . (London, 1804), I, 317.
14. Alfred Harbage, *As They Liked It: An Essay on Shakespeare and Morality* (New York, 1947), p. 73.

of the age with their monumental failures. In the foreground of this *fin-de-siècle* picture of high ambition and catastrophic failure loomed the great figures who filled the public eye with their successes, achievements, defeats, disgraces, and falls from royal favor—Essex, Raleigh, Mountjoy, Cumberland, and other such glittering names. And behind them crowded many other, lesser men, men of the stature of Sir John Burgh and Anthony Bacon, whose aspiring lives and tragic deaths filled the background with somber tones. Then too, there were the repeated failures of the grand schemes. There were the attempted colonies in Newfoundland and Virginia and Guiana and Ireland. There were the expeditionary forces to the Netherlands and France, and the great fleets which struck the coasts of Spain and Spanish America, or combed the Atlantic year after year in futile search for the treasure fleet they never caught. Many of these grand enterprises were complete fiascos, and almost all were financial failures. All about them, Elizabethans saw pitiful failures—futile suits pursued for years, exhausting fortunes and corrupting youth; young future governors of England killing each other over a point or honor, or falling to a chance musket ball or a bout of dysentary; all the abortive plans and futile voyages that the poets did not write about.

The writers of this generation, who crystallized and expressed its moods, shared its melancholy fate. Most of the literary younger generation—Kyd, Peele, Greene, Nashe, Marlowe, Watson, Sidney, and Spenser—did not survive the reign. Robert Greene, who caught the changing moods of the 1580's and '90's better than any other writer of his time, died abandoned in a slum tenement. Kit Marlowe, the stentorian voice of the aspiring mind, was cut down in a tavern brawl. And most of their fellows in this generation of "university wits" found little success in their short lives. Miserable bohemianism or uneasy patronage were the best they could hope for.

This was the pattern of the aspiring mind of the generation of 1560, arching towards the zenith to end in the dust. Both these characteristics of the trajectory of younger-generation ambition had significant consequences for the intellectual history of that age. It has already been suggested that the soaring aspiration of this generation of the ruling class helped provide the impetus that launched one of the central notions of modern times, the idea of progress. The ending in dust and ashes, on the other hand, almost certainly contributed largely to the melancholy mood that was so characteristic of the following reign.

Again, a case history or two will help to clarify a comparatively unfamiliar fact of Elizabethan life. For the extent and nature of the failure of the younger Elizabethans has not received the attention it deserves. It will therefore be useful, first, to examine the military career of Sir John Burgh. Young Sir John went to war with the first wave of courtier-soldiers in 1585, and spent most of the following decade fighting on land and sea. For another kind of failure, we shall then look at the political career of Anthony Bacon, the philosopher's older brother, who was deeply involved in the political intrigues of the Earl of Essex during the 1590's. Each of these men, in his chosen field of activity, was an undoubted failure. As such, these two are distressingly typical of their generation of Elizabethans.

ii. A chivalric failure: Sir John Burgh

Sir John Burgh was one of the lesser lights of the glittering age of Elizabeth. But it is often the case that lesser men are more typical of their times than are the giants of the age. The latter are too often *sui generis*—men whose unique talents raise them to some extent above the trends of their own epoch. To illustrate the general tendencies of a period of history, it is therefore sometimes better to turn to men of the second or even the third rank, men whose very obscurity guarantees that they were typical men of their times. Such men conform so nicely to the standards of their contemporaries that they almost disappear into their own historical background. They are second-raters, distinguished neither by unique talents nor eccentric genius; but it is often these who tell us most about the life of their age.

The response of twenty-three-year-old John Burgh, younger son of a North County baron, to the coming of the Spanish War was in fact typical of the reaction of many young gentlemen of the generation of 1560. In the late summer of 1585 he was busy raising troops in Lincolnshire; on August 25 he sailed from Hull as captain of a company of 150 men.[15] Throughout England young cavaliers were clamoring for such commands, eager to be off for the wars to win eternal honor and glory. John Burgh, who could trace his own lineage back to Hubert de Burge, was fortunate also in his patrons, among whom were the Earl of Lincoln and Lord Thomas Burgh, his older brother. Lord Thomas also served in the Netherlands, as a colonel and later as governor of Brill; the younger brother undoubtedly profited from the patronage of the older, despite occasional rivalry between them for military honor.

John Burgh was one of the first to arrive at Bergen-op-Zoom, the town he was to help garrison; but it was the following spring before he found an opportunity to demonstrate his prowess.[16] Then, in April of 1586, he won mention in dispatches for a costly display of courage in a skirmish before the city of Grave. The melee was a "most valiant encounter" and "a great overthrow" for the enemy, and Captain Burgh was commended for having "served very bravely."[17] But the honor was dearly bought, for the young gentleman lost the middle finger of one hand to a random musket ball.

The following autumn Captain Burgh was again prominent at the taking of Doesburgh. In this battle he was granted command of the van—despite his older brother's demands that he be given that honor—and both the Burgh brothers won reputations as "gentlemen of great valor."[18] Not long thereafter, John Burgh was knighted for his services by the Earl of Leicester himself, one of a brilliant company of aspiring young gentlemen to be so honored, a group that included Henry Unton, Robert Sidney, and the Earl of Essex.[19] Further, Captain John Burgh was made military governor of the captured town of Doesburgh—yet another bright new feather in his plumed hat.

Doesburgh was, as it happened, a poor place, with "nothing to answer either the need or greediness of the soldier" within its crumbling old brick walls.[20] Nevertheless, it was a great advance-

15. *C. S. P., Dom., Eliz.,* CLXXXI, 33, 64.
16. *C. S. P., For., Eliz.,* XX, 50.
17. *Ibid.,* XX, 530, 533, 534-535, 558.
18. *Ibid.,* XXI (pt. ii), 151, 153.
19. *Ibid.,* XXI (pt. ii), 214.
20. *Ibid.,* XXI (pt. ii), 152.

ment for the younger son of a North County baron, and garrisoned by some of the brightest stars in the firmament of the rising young generation. For a few months during that winter of 1586-1587, Sir John Burgh commanded the companies of the younger Sidney, of Lord North, and of the Earl of Essex himself, already singled out as the most brilliant of his contemporaries.[21] The spring came, the season for campaigning; Sir John staged a splendid review of his troops and marched off for services elsewhere. Thus briefly, still in his middle twenties, Sir John Burgh had tasted the honor and the power that appertained to high rank. He undoubtedly considered this no more than the first step up the ladder of success: he hunted for fame and wealth in Elizabeth's wars for the rest of his life. But despite his best efforts, on land and sea, he never really climbed higher than the governorship of that poor brick-walled city in the Low Countries.

Sir John Burgh's career in the Netherlands was that of most of his fellow captains. He fought with savage, reckless courage, shed his blood for his Queen, and was rewarded with commendations and a knighthood—and with the briefest taste of honorable authority. But his troops died or deserted; he went into debt to pay and victual those that remained; and neither funds nor reinforcements were forthcoming.

At the apex of his career in the Netherlands, Captain Burgh commanded two companies of 150 men each, having purchased a second command—a company of cavalry—at great cost. But by the summer of 1588 his original company of foot was described as "so feeble we shall take shame and loss whenever we shall be seriously by the enemy attempted."[22] And when he finally debarked his horse company for England less than a year later, an eye-witness reported succinctly: "Burgh's . . . were 22 strong, of whom 10, or at most 12, fit for service."[23] Casualties and desertion had decimated his command.

At least as early as 1587, Captain Burgh's pay and victualing allowances were months behind, and he was himself many hundreds of pounds in debt.[24] At one point his pay and allowances were in arrears by the staggering sum of £1448 15s. 10d.[25] Nor

21. *Ibid.*, XXI (pt. iii), 142.
22. *Ibid.*, XXI (pt. iv), 490.
23. *Ibid.*, XXIII, 111.
24. *Ibid.*, XXI (pt. iii), 364.
25. *Ibid.*, XXII, 199.

was Burgh among the greatest sufferers. He was twice paid in full by special royal warrant, so highly were his services coming to be valued, or so influential were his friends at court.[26] Nevertheless, in 1589, he required further special funds before he could sail with his horse company, due to his "great debts" and to the company's "horses being pledged for hay and straw. . . ."[27]

Sir John Burgh did not remain long in England. In the fall of 1589, he secured a new command—no less than a colonelcy in Lord Willoughby's expeditionary force to France.[28] He commanded six companies, one quarter of the four-thousand-man force. In the fields of France, Burgh found still more opportunities to do valiant service for Queen and country. He was knighted a second time, for valor at the great Battle of Ivry, and that by one of Europe's most celebrated cavaliers, King Henry of Navarre.[29] When Peregrine Bertie, Lord Willoughby—an even more rapidly rising member of the generation of 1560—was summoned home, King Henry personally requested that Sir John be allowed to remain behind, in command of a special group of English auxiliaries.[30] Sir John Burgh was winning honor in plenty; and, at least to the casual eye, his future must have seemed bright. But once again misfortune came upon him, and again in a typical form.

The French intervention had proved too costly, and not successful enough, for the Queen's liking. Her commanders came home under a cloud: her Majesty was very irritated with Willoughby, and "much displeased with Sir John Burgh. . . ."[31] Elizabeth and Burghley always worried about the cost of their military expeditions—much to the disgust of their field commanders, who felt seriously handicapped by the parsimony of their civilian commanders. Not even the Earl of Essex could pry additional subsidies for his French service out of "a sovereign whose policy was not dictated by ideal considerations and ambitions, but rather adapted to the somewhat limited resources of her country."[32] Burgh's failure and subsequent disgrace, however, were probably

26. *Ibid.*, XXII, 358, 412.
27. *Ibid.*, XXIII, 59.   28. *A. P. C.*, XVIII, 113.
29. John Knox Laughton, *DNB*, s. v. Burgh, John.
30. *A. P. C.*, XVIII, 292.   31. *C. S. P., Dom., Eliz.*, CCXXX, 19.
32. R. B. Wernham, "Queen Elizabeth and the Siege of Rouen, 1591," *Trans. of the Royal Hist. Soc.*, 4th ser. XV (1932), 165, 169, 173.

not due to royal stinginess, but simply to the physical limitations of the time.[33] One authority even goes so far as to state flatly that "negative results . . . were alone to be looked for from large-scale military operations under sixteenth-century conditions. . . ."[34] Supplies and reinforcements could not be transported in time to be useful; disease and desertion decimated the hosts; strategically simple troop movements proved in practice to be wretchedly difficult and costly. For ambitious young commanders like Burgh, these were bitterly frustrating facts of military life. Sixteenth-century armies proved dull and fragile instruments in the hands of would-be Tamburlaines.

It is impossible to determine whether Sir John Burgh remained long out of favor after the French expedition of 1589. He may have been kept at court by the Queen for precisely the opposite reason, because she valued his company too much to risk his life, as was the case with even such great soldiers as Charles Blount, the future Lord Mountjoy. For one reason or another, Burgh saw no service for the next two years, during which time he was "by her Majesty's special commandment stayed here in England."[35] It is more than likely that the Queen desired the young knight's attendance at her court, since special payments were made to him for his "entertainment."[36]

In any event, Sir John had had enough of those unprofitable wars in the Low Countries and in France.[37] In 1592 he took to the sea, in command of a little fleet dispatched by no less a personage than Sir Walter Raleigh.[38] And on his first privateering voyage, he captured the kind of prize that made the blood beat fast in Elizabethan veins. It was the celebrated "Great Carrack," as the publicists dubbed it, the *Madre de Dios*, one of the richest Spanish treasure ships ever brought into an English port.[39] The sea fight with the *Madre de Dios* lasted all day and half the night,

---

33. *Ibid.*, XV, 177-179; J. E. Neale, "Elizabeth and the Netherlands, 1586-7," *EHR*, XLV (1930), 396.

34. Wernham, 176.

35. *A. P. C.*, XXI, 104.

36. *Ibid.*, XIX, 183; XXI, 104.

37. *Ibid.*, XX, 330.

38. Edward Edwards, *The Life of Sir Walter Raleigh . . . with His Letters* (London, 1868), I, 146-149.

39. *Ibid.*, I, 149; Richard Hakluyt, "A True Report of the Honorable Service at Sea Performed by Sir John Burrough Knight," *The Principal Navigations, Voyages, Traffiques & Discoveries of the English Nation* (Glasgow, 1903-1905), VII, 116-117.

and left the huge carrack strewn with corpses.[40] After such bitter fighting, the looting was uncontrolled—and, so Burgh claimed, uncontrollable. And hardly had the treasure ship put down its anchor in an English port when the vultures moved in to parcel out the spoils.

Thus the rich prize slipped like sand through the fingers of its captor. A government investigating committee at once took charge to see that all who had helped to finance the fleet had their share of the loot.[41] Inevitably, the lawyers and the great magnates walked off with most of the ship's immensely valuable cargo. The largest shares went to the Queen herself and, on a technicality, to the Earl of Cumberland, while Raleigh barely broke even.[42] The share of Sir John Burgh's ship, worked out on the basis of vessels actually participating in the capture, came to the dazzling figure of more than £20,000. But a quick refiguring, based on a legal agreement of consortship with other privateering vessels, left Burgh's ship with only £5,880.[43] The government commission hinted darkly at "great booties of Sir John Burgh"; and in fact it is unlikely that he allowed such a prize to pass unscathed through his hands.[44] But it is also unlikely that he profited as much as he might have, or as much as he felt he deserved, from his brilliant feat. They seldom did, these debt-ridden, passionately ambitious young soldiers of the Queen.

Three bits of documentary evidence bring the story of Sir John Burgh's military career to a close. The first of these is a pedigree of the Burgh family, compiled at the order of Lord Burghley.[45] This may well mean that real promotion was in store for this ambitious younger son of obscure Northern nobility. If so, it was a pity: for he was never to receive whatever preferment the Queen's chief minister intended for him.

For, in early March of 1594, Sir John Burgh sent a series of angry challenges to one John Gilbert, perhaps a West-Country

40. Edwards, II, 62; Hakluyt, VII, 114.

41. Sir John Burgh to Lord Burghley, Aug. 17, 1592, in Thomas Wright, ed., *Queen Elizabeth and Her Times* (London, 1838), II, 419; *C. S. P., Dom.,* CCXLIII, 14.

42. Henry Ellis, *Original Letters, Illustrative of English History* . . . (Third Series, London, 1846), IV, 102-108.

43. Ibid., 103-104, 106.　　　　　*45. Ibid.,* CCXLVI, 95.

44. C. S. P., Dom., Eliz., CCXLIII, 17.

associate of Raleigh.[46] A duel was obviously intended—apparently with an adversary for whom Burgh felt nothing but contempt. Sir John threatened to "beat him like a boy" and offered to "travel all night" to London to meet him, if Gilbert's schedule really precluded a later encounter. Burgh's letters were bitter and choleric; in a fit of rage, he "stabbed the bearer" of one of Gilbert's more evasive replies. A final letter from Gilbert arranged a meeting, required "that when they come out of town, he [Burgh] be well searched, and . . . chooses a single rapier as the weapon." Sir John Burgh, with almost a decade of hard fighting behind him, was obviously confident of winning this typical affair of honor.

But, as was so often the case with Elizabeth's aspiring young cavaliers, Sir John lost his last fight. The last piece of evidence we have of this young gentleman who was so avid for glory is the inscription on his tomb. Here is simply recorded his death, on March 7, 1594, at the hands of a "bold and crafty enemy whom Burgh despised."[47] He died as he had lived, sword in hand, defending his honor. His crammed and desperate life was over—at the age of thirty-two.

iii. A political failure: Anthony Bacon

Like Sir John Burgh, Anthony Bacon was one of those lesser Elizabethans who were so often more typical of their time and place than their more celebrated contemporaries. But where the passage of time has condemned Burgh to oblivion, history has preserved the memory of Anthony Bacon—though in a strangely distorted form. For Anthony Bacon had the misfortune to be born the brother of Francis; and the same process of historical interpretation which has raised Francis to the heights has warped the image of Anthony. To put it simply, Anthony has become for posterity little more than Francis' big brother. The highest compliment the biographer can pay him is to stress his fraternal affection for Francis. His loyalty, his generosity, his unselfish

46. *Ibid.*, CCXLVIII, 54.
47. Quoted in Laughton, *DNB*, s. v. "Burgh, John."

devotion to his younger brother's interests are commonly extolled.

The true picture, however, seems to be rather different from that painted by biographers and historians dazzled by the subsequent achievements of the younger brother. During the 1590's, when this undeniably close fraternal relationship was at its height, it was in fact Anthony who impressed contemporaries as the more prominent and successful brother. While Francis labored fruitlessly for preferment in the legal profession, Anthony became the "foreign secretary" of the Earl of Essex—an enviable position indeed. During this decade of surging political ambitions, "it was Anthony who grew in importance, and Francis who, if he did not decrease, at least retired."[48] In general, we must agree with one of the few scholars who has done Anthony justice: "The greater fame of the younger brother has hidden from us the more immediate importance of the elder."[49]

If anything, Anthony Bacon was the more ambitious of the two. For unlike his younger brother, Anthony inherited enough lands and revenues from their father "to become a gentleman of leisure if he so minded."[50] Francis, like many younger sons of the Elizabethan ruling class, was actually compelled to seek preferment if he wished even to maintain the status he had enjoyed —until his father's death—as a son of the Lord Keeper. Anthony, on the other hand, seems to have deliberately and freely abandoned a life of moderate affluence and local prestige in the home county for a political career among the ruling circles of England and the continent. This was the choice of the true aspiring mind: for such men, the father's patrimony was only the beginning, the first upward step of a successful career.

Certainly, too, the older Bacon brother had every right to expect that his ambitions would be realized. His father was Lord Keeper of the Great Seal, one of the builders of the Elizabethan polity, and an old personal friend of the Queen; his mother was Lord Burghley's sister-in-law. During his prolonged continental tour, he moved in the highest circles. He could write from France of a visit by the King of Navarre, "who, doing me the honor to

48. Charles Williams, *Bacon* (London, 1933), p. 44.
49. *Ibid.*
50. Bryan Bevan, *The Real Francis Bacon* (London, 1960), p. 46.

come to my lodging, accompanied with the Prince of Condé, the Vicomte of Turenne, and other nobility, declared how much he was bound to your Majesty. . . ."[51] A young man so singularly favored had every right to aspire to higher things.

Anthony Bacon was also a young man of real and recognized talent. Of course, considering Anthony's high family connections, the description of him given by Henry of Navarre's Secretary of State—as "a worthy gentleman, praised and esteemed by all honest men"—may perhaps be suspect.[52] This is also true of Francis Bacon's characterization of his brother as "a gentleman whose ability the world taketh knowledge of for matters of state, especially foreign."[53] But we need not suspect Lord Bacon's secretary, writing after the death of both brothers, of any prejudice when he wrote of the two that Anthony was "a gentleman equal to [Francis] in height of wit."[54] In general, it appears that Anthony, too, had the family brains, though he seems to have applied them exclusively to practical matters. Given half a chance, such talents might well have brought him to a place of great power in England.

Finally, Anthony Bacon could base his claim to some share of political power on many years of faithful and valuable service to Elizabeth's government. Throughout the 1580's he lived in Europe, serving as a vital cog in Walsingham's celebrated foreign intelligence operation.[55] The voluminous correspondence which survives indicates that he took his duties seriously, and that he was employed in important and often highly confidential affairs. Bacon also made important contacts abroad, through whom he received much valuable information of use to his government.[56] From time to time, too, he acted as paymaster to others of Walsingham's agents, or as an intermediary between them and London.[57] He was, in fact, one of his government's "most valued agents" abroad.[58] Nor did his good service go unrecognized. Walsingham declared himself "greatly beholden" to young Anthony

51. *C. S. P., For., 1584-1585*, XIX, 335.   52. *Ibid.*, XIX, Suppl. Addenda, 719.
53. "Apology" for Essex prosecution, quoted in Spedding, I, 107.
54. William Rawley, "The Life of the Honorable Author," in Francis Bacon, *The Works of . . .* ed. Spedding *et al.* (London, 1864), I, 38.
55. Bevan, p. 61.   57. Bevan, p. 62.
56. *C. S. P., Dom., 1581-1590*, CCXXIII, 66.   58. *Ibid.*

Bacon for his reports.[59] The Queen herself, speaking through the Earl of Leicester, announced her satisfaction that she had "so good a man as you to have and receive letters by."[60] To ambitious young courtiers, such expressions of royal approbation were meat and drink. Indeed, they had to be, for any more tangible rewards were few and far between. Bacon's services, typically, were apparently unpaid; and it is known that his private resources were badly strained by the years of expensive living abroad.[61] Nevertheless, Anthony Bacon had every reason to expect some suitable political reward for his twelve years' service.

And yet the political career of Anthony Bacon in the 1590's was a dreary tale of false starts, an early plateau, and final, catastrophic failure. There were many reasons for this, most of them far from unique, but one reason in particular stands out in stark simplicity. Bacon, like so many others of his generation, became involved in the fratricidal feud between Essex and the Cecils. First on one side, then on the other, he found that neither faction could give him the success he sought and felt he deserved.

First came cruel rejection by his own kinsmen, the mighty Cecils. It was to their all-powerful uncle that the Bacon brothers naturally looked first for advancement in their chosen careers. The aging Lord Burghley responded to their petitions with repeated assurances of his "intention to do them good."[62] And yet somehow no good ever came to Anthony Bacon through the vast influence of his uncle. In time, Anthony Bacon came to believe that their rejection of him was deliberate, that the Cecils, the all-powerful father and the crafty son, actually bore him a mortal enmity. It has more than once been suggested that jealousy and fear of anyone who might provide serious competition for ambitious young Sir Robert Cecil were at the root of this rejection of the Bacon brothers. In any case, Anthony came to hate the Cecils cordially. For his long years of service, he got in return only "such words as make fools fain; and yet, even in these, no

59. Sir Francis Walsingham to Anthony Bacon, n.d., quoted in *ibid.*, p. 63.
60. Oct. 7, 1583, quoted in Edwin Abbott, *Francis Bacon: An Account of His Life and Works* (London, 1885), p. 16 n. 2.
61. Bevan, p. 62; F. Allen to Anthony Bacon, Aug. 17, 1589, in Spedding, I, 110-111.
62. Aug. 29, 1593, quoted in Francis Steegmuller, *Sir Francis Bacon, The First Modern Mind* (New York, 1930), p. 46.

offer or hopeful assurance of real kindness, which I thought I might justly expect at the Lord Treasurer's hands. . . ."[63]

Cold-shouldered by his powerful relatives, Anthony Bacon sought out a new patron in the early 1590's—Essex, the Queen's greatest favorite among the younger generation. Bacon's work as Essex's foreign secretary, and the part this work played in the Earl's effort to build himself a reputation as a mature, well-informed statesman—these aspects of his career are well known. The contacts he had made on the Continent, and the insights he had gleaned during his years of residence there, were put at the disposal of the young Earl in his bid for political power. Our concern here, however, is with Anthony Bacon's own ambitions, and these did not prosper under the Earl's patronage.

Bacon did not hesitate to put pressure on his patron to do more for him and even to threaten to return to the Cecils if he were not better rewarded for his invaluable services.[64] Nevertheless, his rewards in Essex's service were few and scanty; once more, he had only hopes for the future to sustain him. Again, he apparently got no financial remuneration for his work, despite some impressive talk of a thousand pounds a year—a munificent compensation, had it ever been forthcoming.[65] He was assigned rooms at Essex House, true, but he paid for his own food and wine.[66] In return for all his arduous labor, he received no preferment through the influence of the impetuous Earl, who more than once made promises he could not keep. The career of Anthony Bacon was stalled: he had risen so far, but it seemed increasingly as the years passed that he would rise no farther.

Meanwhile, other factors further handicapped this increasingly frustrated aspiring mind. One of these was the recurring suspicion —fatal to greater men than himself—that Anthony Bacon was soft on Papists. His long stay abroad, largely in Catholic France, aroused the common suspicion of religious corruption; and even after his return to England, he was rumored to be associating

63. Quoted in Abbott, p. 34 n. 1.

64. Henry Wotton, *A Parallell betweene Robert Late Earle of Essex and George Late Duke of Buckingham* (London, 1641), p. 5.

65. Bevan, p. 86; Wotton, p. 6. Wotton's statement that Bacon actually received this remuneration is not generally accepted.

66. Bevan, p. 119.

too freely with disloyal Romanists, both laymen and priests.[67] In those days, when the Pope and the King of Spain seemed united in a sinister alliance against Protestant England, Catholicism was synonymous with subversion. Elizabeth herself marveled at Edward Somerset, who in his own person "reconciled what she believed impossible, a stiff papist to a good subject."[68] In most cases, connections with Catholicism could be fatal to a political career.

Another difficulty was the crushing load of debt which any young man soon accumulated at the court of Elizabeth. At Grey's Inn in the early 1590's, Anthony and Francis were already spending lavishly on "luxurious dinners" for themselves and appropriate guests.[69] They purchased a coach and horses, still a rare luxury in Elizabethan London, but useful for lending to fellow courtiers whose voices might count for something in the future.[70] Naturally, both were soon deeply in debt. The story of Anthony's desperate efforts to wriggle out of the financial impasse into which his high ambitions had driven him was typical of his times. He borrowed heavily from his family and from his friends and associates.[71] Puritanical Lady Bacon wrung her hands in helpless indignation over her sons' extravagance and their frequent applications to her for financial help: "I have been too ready for you both," she wrote Anthony, "till nothing is left."[72] It was the Elizabethan commonplace of the young courtier frittering away the prudent accumulation of decades in a few gilded years. Few handicaps were so difficult to overcome as the exhaustion of his operating capital.

But one final obstacle, of a sort not often enough considered by historians, seems to have proved absolutely insurmountable for Anthony Bacon. Like a surprising number of Elizabethans, he was frequently in bad health. From the "rheumatic disorders" of his early years to the gout that all but incapacitated him in

67. *Ibid.*, pp. 65-66; Walter Bourchier Devereux, *Lives and Letters of the Devereux, Earls of Essex* (London, 1853), I, 318.

68. David Lloyd, *State Worthies*, quoted in A. F. Pollard, *DNB*, s.v. Somerset, Edward, 4th Earl of Worcester.

69. Steegmuller, p. 14.   70. *Ibid.*, p. 13; Williams, p. 6.

71. See, for example, the negotiations over the sale of Anthony Bacon's estate of Barly to one Alderman Spencer, in Spedding, I, 246-250.

72. Lady Bacon to Anthony Bacon, April 17, 1593, in Spedding, I, 244.

middle age, physical suffering was almost a chronic fact of his working life.[73] Particularly in the 1590's, when he might have made his bid for political prominence, he was an invalid, "crippled with gout," and almost continuously under a doctor's care.[74] That he was able to perform the taxing services he undertook, first for his kinsmen and later for Essex, was in itself remarkable.[75] But under the circumstances, the social maneuvering at court, so necessary a part of any successful political career, was completely beyond his strength. Essex did what he could by communicating to the Queen Anthony's "excuse for not seeing her Majesty all this while, and [his] grief for the want of doing that duty."[76] The grief of the elder Bacon brother, his career blighted by chronic illness, was surely very real.

The taint of subversive religious connections, the exhaustion of his financial resources, and the paralyzing grip of physical illness—all these handicaps played their part in the failure of Anthony Bacon's career. All of these difficulties were common enough among his contemporaries; they were among the occupational hazards of high aspiration for the generation of 1560.

As the tense, frustrating decade of the 1590's drew to a close, so too did the political career—and the life—of Anthony Bacon. The ultimate collapse of his political fortunes followed a familiar pattern: when his patron fell, the ambitious courtier's own hopes of advancement were also doomed. During the Earl of Essex's year of disgrace, following the failure of his disastrous Irish expedition, Anthony Bacon and his brother "worked frantically to save Essex"—and incidentally to salvage Anthony's own fortunes.[77] In Essex's mad attempt to raise the city of London against his enemies at the court, his invalided secretary apparently had no hand. But Anthony was already deeply involved in his master's "treasonable" correspondence, especially that with the King of Scots; and this fact was known to his arch enemies, the Cecils.[78] Thus the final arrest and trial of Essex and his more active followers must have given the weary sick man many a sleepless night.

73. Bevan, pp. 62, 67, 69.   74. *Ibid.*, pp. 67, 69, 85, 118-119, 160.
75. *C. S. P., Dom., Addenda, 1580-1625*, XXXIII, 70.
76. The Earl of Essex to Anthony Bacon, 1593?, in Devereux, I, 289.
77. Bevan, p. 163.
78. Devereux, I, 318-319; Bevan, pp. 129-130; Williams, p. 100.

Though he escaped punishment for his share in the Earl's ambitious schemes, Anthony Bacon did not survive this final disastrous turn of Fortune's wheel. He was never brought into the dock; in fact, his name was hardly mentioned at the trial, though it must have been in the back of many minds. The reasons are problematical, but one was almost certainly his brother Francis' passionate disavowal of his own connection with Essex, and his appearance as one of the Earl's prosecutors. By reaffirming his loyalty to the establishment, Francis probably won some measure of pardon for his brother as well.[79] In the end, it did not much matter, for Anthony died himself that spring, in such obscurity that even the day of his death is unknown. One of the most prolific of Elizabethan letter-writers noted in late May of 1601 that "Anthony Bacon died not long since, but"—he added with the callous realism of those times—"so far in debt that I think his brother is little the better by him."[80] We can only presume that, within a few weeks of the execution of his patron, Anthony Bacon was finally overcome by the diseases that had all but incapacitated him in his middle years. We may surmise also that this mortal blow to his high aspirations made some psychological contribution to his final illness.

One wonders if, in those last dark days, he ever regretted his decision, more than twenty years before, to abandon the peaceful satisfactions of a country gentleman's life for the hectic and dangerous career of an ambitious courtier. Perhaps he wished he had taken his own advice, jotted down in a cynical piece of doggerel:

> Cog, lie, flatter and face,
> Four ways in Court to win your Grace.
> If you be thrall to none of these,
> Away, good Piers! home, John Cheese![81]

Anthony Bacon had undoubtedly done his share of lying and flattering; but he would surely have been better off if he had stayed at home with good Piers and John Cheese.

79. Williams, p. 100.
80. John Chamberlain to Dudley Carleton, May 27, 1601, in *The Letters of John Chamberlain*, ed. Norman Egbert McClure (Philadelphia, 1939), I, 123.
81. Quoted in Bevan, p. 80.

iv. The roots of Elizabethan failure

Many of the more obvious causes of the failure of this generation of Elizabethans in their quest for honor and power have been illustrated on the preceding pages. Debt, disease, desertion of troops, failure of a patron, subversive religious connections, jealousy of rivals, an unfavorable wind, the fortunes of war, the fortunes of politics—these and many other miseries beset these young courtiers on all sides. And any single one of these multifarious misfortunes could lead to the ultimate disaster—withdrawal of that royal favor which was the essential condition of success under the courtier system of government. Once again, however, it will prove useful to look beneath these common but superficial causes, to seek out some of the deeper roots of Elizabethan failure. Only by probing to this more fundamental level of causation will it be possible to understand why this generation in particular, for all its high ambitions, found only chronic and ignominious failure.

What had defeated the generation of 1560? Why had all their talent, training, and energetic, tireless ambition so often gone for nothing? Their first and most obvious enemy seems to have been the older generation. The second, and least obvious, was probably their own overactive imaginations. The third, and historically the most important, was the fact that the goals of their aspirations were out of date, and were fast becoming impossible in a changing world. Let us examine these basic reasons for Elizabethan failure, the causes beneath the causes which the Elizabethans themselves complained about.

Little more need be said about the struggle between the generations, or about the social, economic, and political trends which made much of that struggle inevitable. It remains perhaps to stress the fact that these younger aspiring minds were among the Queen's best servants during the last two decades of her reign, and that they were very poorly rewarded. They served her as justices of the peace and lords lieutenants in their counties, and as judges and members of Parliament and councilors in London. They served her as captains and generals, as spy-masters and diplomats in foreign lands. Lord Mountjoy saved Ireland for her;

the Earl of Cumberland dispatched or personally led a dozen fleets against her enemies; Sir Walter Raleigh labored mightily to add an American empire to her realm; Sir Robert Cecil succeeded his father as her Majesty's most faithful and efficient servant. Many other names could be added, some famous and some less so, all of whom did the Queen good service at home or in foreign parts. There were lawyers like hard-bitten Sir Edward Coke, who prosecuted many of her domestic enemies, or like Judge Julius Caesar, who awarded many a privateering prize or lion's share of the booty to the crown. In her Majesty's foreign service, there were such talented men as Thomas Edmondes, the rising diplomat who even won the respect of the Venetians, and such famous military men of the generation of 1560 as Sir Francis Vere, Black John Norris, and Peregrine Bertie, Lord Willoughby. Objectively considered, it was a brilliant cavalcade of talent and courage in the service of the Queen.

They were, of course, motivated more by personal ambition than by zeal for the service of Elizabeth. But this fact did not prevent their feeling genuinely ill-treated when their efforts were so inadequately rewarded. Their actual motivation was probably not too clear in their own minds; but they knew the rules of the game, the courtier system of government by means of which they, their elders, and the Queen ran the country. Not unnaturally, they resented the drying up of the flow of places, patents, and favors, of honor and power, which were their legitimate rewards for service. Repeatedly, they suffered personal losses in royal service which were never repaid, saw their pet schemes frustrated and their humble petitions again and again ignored. The normal relationship between younger and older generations inevitably became one of mutual distrust and enmity. The older generation became the first enemy of the ambitious leaders of the younger generation; and for twenty years the institutional cards were stacked against youth, until the death of the Queen cleared the board.

The second enemy of the typical aspiring mind was his own romantic imagination; for it was this highly developed imagination which made it possible for him to take seriously the insubstantial pageant that was the court of Elizabeth. The artificial, unreal atmosphere of the court, and of much of ruling-class life beside, simply did not prepare young courtiers for the harsh facts of life in the real world. In their youth, these men learned to fight with chivalric grace, and to scheme and maneuver for royal favor. But they did not learn the common-sense limits of aspiration. They did not learn realistic methods of achieving their high ambitions: they did not learn to control impatience and proceed with devious slowness, or to co-operate despite personal differences, or to accept setbacks with equanimity, nor even how to be cautious. These sensible, pragmatic rules, which their parents had learned in the brutally real world of the mid-Tudor revolutions, the young men found hard to swallow in the peaceful, prosperous England of Elizabeth.

In neither the military nor the political sphere were the young gentlemen properly prepared to confront the real world. Skill at the medieval sport of tilting and a willingness to meet any man rapier to rapier, for instance, were poor preparations for the wars they were actually called upon to fight. Such training did not help appreciably with the logistic, strategic, and tactical problems of capturing a strongly fortified city in Normandy, or of defeating a guerrilla army of wild Irish kerns. The romantic atmosphere of the court was an equally poor background for would-be politicians, who would in time be called upon to play the game of court intrigue for high stakes, and with real penalties for error. It was all very well to learn the labyrinthine ways of the courtier system by heart, and to accumulate a vast number of clients and an unsurpassed array of powerful patrons and allies. But no ambitious subject who, blinded by pampered egotism, could even for a moment so forget the rules as to turn a haughty back upon divine Majesty—as the Earl of Essex did—would long succeed in Elizabethan politics.

These were imaginations richly fed on too much hyperbolic praise. These were pampered youths, encouraged to live magnificently beyond their means, surrounded by troops of liveried retainers, of clients and sycophants. Such men obviously lived in an unreal world of their own which had too few points of contact with reality to allow of long success. Inevitably, it became clear in time that aspiration conceived in such terms would win neither wars nor high places—but by that time, it was too late for many to retrace their steps. The eventual fading of this insubstantial pageant left the disillusioned aspiring mind alone with his failure in a desolate world of hard realities. In large measure, he had been defeated by his own soaring imagination.

Most important of all, however, was the fundamental historical fact that the objectives of this generation were simply out of date, and increasingly so with each passing decade. Naturally, as these goals fell further behind the times, they became more and more difficult to achieve in the changing world. Many young men, to cite an obvious example, aspired to be paragons of chivalry, knights errant in the tradition of Lancelot, Roland, the Chevalier Bayard, and other heroes of a vanished age. They seriously indulged in such fantastic notions in the late sixteenth century, when chivalry had long since ceased to have any real social function, when even romantic revivals of chivalry were becoming matter for parody through most of Europe. Or they aspired to be the conquistadors of golden American empires, scouring the forests of Newfoundland or Virginia for precious metals, or sailing up the feverish Orinoco in search of El Dorado. And this they undertook half a century after the only Indian empires had been destroyed, and at a time when any such expeditions would bring them into conflict, not with naked savages, but with Spain herself, the greatest power in the civilized world.

In the realm of the intellect, a few of these young Elizabethans aspired to profound knowledge of the world, and sought to penetrate the secrets of the universe. But more often than not, their mentors and wise masters were astrologers and alchemists, necromancers and heretical philosophers: for every Thomas Harriot, there were two John Dees and Edward Kelleys. And all this dabbling in animistic claptrap, this esoteric pottering about with essences and qualities, was actually contemporaneous with the birth of empirical, quantitative science on the continent.

The generation of 1560 was just as old-fashioned in the goals they set for their political and financial ambitions as in their aspirations to be knights, conquistadors, and alchemists. Financially, the more enterprising courtiers seem to have aspired to become merchant princes on the cultured Italian model. In pursuit of these magnificent aims, they pinned all their hopes on royal monopolies which the Queen could revoke at a word, or dispatched argosies of privateers which periodically put them on the brink of ruin. But the large-scale economic individualism of Elizabeth's colorful pirates and monopolists was also rapidly going out of date. Obvious necessity was even then bringing about the development of more effective forms of capitalistic organization—most notably, of course, the joint-stock company, of which the East India Company became the outstanding example.

Politically, most of these ambitious young Elizabethans sought power in the old-fashioned forms enjoyed by the medieval or humanistic royal councillor. These were the men closest to the throne, the source of all political power in the courtier system of government; they earned their places by winning the favor of the reigning monarch, and they were responsible only to the crown. There was, of course, room for only a very limited number on the Privy Council and in the inner circle of favorites and advisers: thus, by the very nature of things, such ambitions were doomed to failure in the majority of cases. And in focusing their attention so exclusively on the Council and the court, these aspiring minds of the generation of 1560 ignored the great and growing potential power of the Parliament. In a country where economic and social change had for a century been multiplying the ruling class, the House of Commons was rapidly becoming the real assembly of the rulers of England—not the Council with its small group of great magnates dependent on the monarch. This fact would become only too clear within half a century. But in the 1590's, for every Francis Bacon who used the House of Commons in his early years as a ladder to power, there were many courtiers who still considered a seat as nothing more than a prestige symbol in the home county.

The main reason for this singular shortsightedness in so many fields of activity was essentially simple: times were changing too fast in England for any generation to keep up. And after drifting into a cultural backwater in the middle third of the century, during the troubled decades of the mid-Tudor revolutions, Englishmen had a lot of catching up to do. The generation of 1560 tried to absorb too much too fast. Not surprisingly, they missed a number of significant developments, in many areas of life, at home and abroad. Then, too, the younger generation followed their fathers' examples in many practical things—in choosing the goals of their political ambitions, for instance. It was the theory and practice of the older generation which encouraged these young men to seek seats on the Privy Council instead of prominence in the House of Commons. Finally, this pampered generation was allowed to squander its energies on too many "luxury goals," if we may so style aspiration for beauty, love, esoteric lore, and the like. In selecting these basically non-functional objectives, they naturally chose almost entirely on the basis of emotional or imaginative interest, or simply on snob appeal. Such choices seldom had any relevance to the life of the late sixteenth century. Often, in fact, such motives as romantic nostalgia, love of the exotic, or the prestige value of artificiality may well have dictated the deliberate choice of out-of-date and irrelevant goals, chosen precisely because they were medieval and impractical. For all these reasons, the goals of these young aspiring minds were too often rooted in the needs and values of past and passing societies, and as such were simply unattainable in Elizabethan England.

The Elizabethan younger generation, then, could not succeed. Frustrated at every turn by the power of the older generation, stumbling through a harsh world only half-seen through the eyes of their own romantic imaginations, pursuing goals that were decades or centuries out of date—they were beaten before they started. Judged by their own standards, as they judged each other and themselves, the high aspiring minds of the generation of 1560 were failures. Gaudy failures, perhaps, but failures nonetheless. And these men were bitterly aware of this failure to achieve their highest aspirations. This very consciousness of failure is important in itself; for it seems probable that this feeling of failure contributed significantly to the darkening mood of Jacobean melancholy in which the generation of 1560 lived out its later years.

v. The melancholy mood

The Reverend John Donne—no longer ambitious Jack Donne of Elizabeth's days—described the mood of Jacobean England as one of "extraordinary sadness, a predominant melancholy, a faintness of heart, a cheerlessness, a joylessness of spirit."[82] This melancholy mood came gradually over Elizabethan England. In the eighties it was a cloud no bigger than a man's hand, hardly noticeable in the background of those aspiring times. Then in the nineties the dark clouds of discontent billowed up, till they covered half the Elizabethan sky. The century turned, and the sun itself was blotted from the firmament of those stricken times. For two decades thereafter, gloom darkened the Jacobean landscape: it was a time of faintness of heart, a predominant melancholy. This pattern of developing melancholy has often been traced in literature; it was true also in life—especially in the lives of the aging generation of 1560.

Both the literary and the social phenomena have been the subject of considerable research and speculation. Evidence has been culled from both spheres and correlated to establish a number of general facts about the melancholy malady which seems to have afflicted later Elizabethan and Jacobean England. But there is a certain disjointedness about the various monographic contributions: they do not seem to form a coherent chronological picture. Frustrated ambition has been mentioned as a prime cause of Elizabethan melancholy, but so has the Copernican world-view, and travel to Italy, and poor dietary habits. What seems to be lacking is a central organizing principle which will include and structure as many of these elements as possible into a meaningful whole. The concept of generational development seems to a considerable extent to fill this need.

The literary voices of the generation of 1560 spoke for them in this, as in other things. The change in Elizabethan literary taste during the nineties has been pithily characterized by an outstanding authority as "a noticeable progress from romance to realism, from realism to satire, from satire to nausea. . . ."[83] Shakespeare's shifting attitude toward the melancholy malady—to which he himself apparently fell victim—has been taken as typical by more than one expert. To cite G. B. Harrison again:

82. Quoted in Lawrence Babb, *The Elizabethan Malady: A Study of Melancholia in English Literature from 1580 to 1642* (East Lansing, Mich., 1951), p. 185.
83. G. B. Harrison, "An Essay on Elizabethan Melancholy," appended to Nicholas Breton, *Melancholike Humours*, ed. Harrison (London, 1929), p. 56.

"In 1594, he mocked lightly; when he came to write *As You Like It* melancholy was still a joke, but the laughter was uneasy; two years later when he wrote *Hamlet* it was a reality; when he wrote *Timon* and *Lear* it was almost an obsession."[84] In the late 1590's the satirists flourished, chief among them Hall, Marston, and the young John Donne. These were poets who dipped their pens in gall and venom; they declared themselves to be disillusioned men and bitter haters of this corrupted world. "Society is utterly rotten," they snarled: "all is degenerate, all is corrupt. . . ."[85] And across the Elizabethan stage now stalked the melancholy men, railing and lamenting over life and the world— the despairing heroes of Marston, Webster, and Tourneur.[86]

Taller than all the rest of these tragic protagonists who swept the conquering heroes of Marlowe from the *fin-de-siècle* stage was the melancholy Hamlet, Prince of Denmark. Hamlet summed up the Marlovian self-image of his predecessors, the aspiring minds, in a half-dozen bombastic phrases:

What a piece of work is man! how noble in reason! how infinite in faculty! in form and moving how express and admirable! in action how like an angel! in apprehension how like a god!

But Hamlet could only turn sadly away from this image of perfection:

And yet, to me, what is this quintessence of dust? man delights not me. . . .[87]

It was the epitaph of a generation, the recognition that the quintessential nature of even the highest aspiring mind was dust and ashes.

Nor was the melancholy view of man a mere literary affectation. In the first place, many of the writers who filled their pages with satirical railing and tragical heroes were themselves melancholy men. Greene, Chapman, Marston, Ford, Donne, Shakespeare, and even Robert Burton, the author of the famous *Anatomy* of the subject, were all probably troubled with the disease

---

84. *Ibid.*, p. 73.   85. Cruttwell, pp. 19-20.
86. See Theodore Spencer, "The Elizabethan Malcontent," in *Joseph Quincy Adams Memorial Studies*, ed. James G. McManaway *et al.* (Washington, 1948), p. 533, for one such list of melancholy dramatic heroes.
87. *Hamlet*, II, ii, 316-322.

of melancholy.[88] More important, there is general agreement that the darkening tone of Elizabethan literature reflected a real change in the mood of Elizabethan society. "It was as if the assurance and confidence following the defeat of the Armada, the praise of England's greatness in early drama, and the self-conscious and magnificent vigor of Marlowe had been but the dreams of men awakening at last to the sober, even repulsive realities of life. . . ."[89] This description, though intended to characterize the age as a whole, surely applies more accurately to the generation of 1560. In the city of London, with its comparatively sophisticated and informed populace, the melancholy mood was much more widespread by 1600 than it had ever been before. Melancholy gentlemen, their wide-brimmed black hats pulled low over downcast eyes, were an increasingly common sight in the city. They were to be seen everywhere, strolling abstractedly in the far aisles of St. Pauls, slouching dejectedly over their dinners in fashionable London ordinaries, even sulking in the antechambers of the court. Donne and Shakespeare and their fellows produced their satirical rantings and their tragic heroes, not only because they themselves took an increasingly jaundiced view of life, but because this embittered outlook was increasingly common in the society in which they lived.

But what exactly was this melancholy malady which so afflicted the generation of 1560 in its last years? The term "melancholy" was commonly used to denote one of the basic personality types, the gloomy temperament resulting from the predominance of the melancholy humor, or black bile, in the human body. The primary Elizabethan concern, however, was with the *disease* of melancholy, a form of mental illness resembling the melancholy temperament, but far more intense.[90] This kind of melancholy was "a psychosis caused by a black bilious humor and characterized by morbid depression, continuous or recurrent."[91] The "primary symptom" of this psychological ailment was "gloominess," or, more precisely, a combination of "fear and sorrow without ap-

88. Harrison, "Elizabethan Melancholy," pp. 70-83; Babb, pp. 181-183.

89. Charles Monroe Coffin, *John Donne and the New Philosophy* (New York, 1937), p. 265.

90. For a detailed discussion of the melancholy temperament and the melancholy disease, see Babb.

91. Babb, p. 37.

parent cause."[92] The typical melancholic was spare and lean of frame, hollow-eyed, pale, silent, slow-moving.[93] He was a sullen, despondent individual as a rule, but was given to sudden outbursts of anger or frenzy that sometimes carried him across the line into madness.[94] Always he was suspicious and envious of his fellows, and sometimes he developed "a venemous hatred of mankind."[95] Men in the grip of the melancholy malady suffered such agonies of self-doubt and bitterness that they seriously contemplated suicide. Melancholy was thus a very serious form of mental illness, one which could end in madness or death. It was generally believed to be a disease of the later years, of the autumn of a man's life.[96] In fact, as we shall see, many of the leaders of the generation of 1560 fell victim to this disease in their late thirties and early forties—the "autumn" of human life by Elizabethan standards. It is the spread of this "psychosis," and above all, the causes of the epidemic, that primarily concern the student of Elizabethan ambition, and of the generation of 1560.

The history of the psychology of humors in England goes back at least as far as the first half of the sixteenth century. During this period, there was certainly some interest—perhaps a growing interest—in physiology and related psychological subjects.[97] But there is no evidence of any specific concern with the melancholy personality or the melancholy malady during these years. It was during the first two decades of Elizabeth's reign—while the generation of 1560 was growing up—that a particular interest in melancholy apparently took hold of the English aristocracy.[98] Some knowledge of the psychology of the melancholic was thus part of the intellectual milieu in which this aspiring generation was raised. But the information can have made little immediate impression on these young men, blinded to all else by the vision of their own glorious futures.

In the 1580's melancholy became something of a fashionable

92. Hardin Craig, Introduction to Timothy Bright, *A Treatise of Melancholie* (New York, 1940), p. v; Babb, p. 30.

93. Bright, p. 124.   94. *Ibid.*, p. vi.

95. Babb, pp. 71, 32.

96. Lily B. Campbell, *Shakespeare's Tragic Heroes, Slaves of Passion* (New York, 1961), p. 60.

97. Hardin Craig, *The Enchanted Glass: The Elizabethan Mind in Literature* (New York, 1936), p. 119; Cruttwell, p. 110 n. 1.

98. Babb, p. 74.

affectation.[99] During this period it was alluded to and represented in Elizabethan literature with increasing frequency.[100] Knowledge of this form of mental illness was also spread widely in the 1580's and '90's by "a perfect flood of psychological works in the vernacular."[101] These included translations from foreign sources, didactic poetry by men of the celebrity of Sir John Davies and Davies of Hereford, and at least two serious treatises, Timothy Bright's *Treatise of Melancholy* and Thomas Wright's *The Passions of the Mind*. Bright and Wright, in particular, appear to have had a real "concern with the unhealthy English state of mind."[102] Ironically, their main achievement was to spread familiarity with melancholy still more widely, and thus quite possibly to increase the incidence of the disease. It has been suggested that Bright's work, published in 1586, "not impossibly . . . affected the Elizabethan imagination much as popularized theories . . . of the subconscious have affected our generation."[103] As sophisticated, intellectual circles took Freudian psychology to their bosoms in the 1920's and '30's, so the well-educated Elizabethan upper classes were fascinated by the psychology of humors in the 1580's and '90's.[104] For "melancholic," we may almost read "neurotic": the former term had as many fuzzy popular meanings in Elizabethan times as the latter has in our own, and both were applied broadly to any emotionally disturbed individual whose symptoms included intense anguish of spirit.

But there was more to the spread of the melancholy mood than dissemination of knowledge: there was also the social and intellectual prestige which came to be associated with this particular ailment. During the 1580's melancholy became socially almost de rigueur as the disease of the continental traveler, and particularly of the Italianate Englishman. Intellectually, melancholy became known at the same time as the affliction of genius, the mental illness to which the man of extraordinary talent was particularly liable.

99. *Ibid.*, p. 75.
100. *Ibid.*, p. 73.
101. Craig, *Enchanted Glass*, p. 119.
102. William B. Mueller, *The Anatomy of Robert Burton's England* (Berkeley and Los Angeles, 1952), p. 13.
103. Mary Isabelle O'Sullivan, "Hamlet and Dr. Timothy Bright," *PMLA*, XLI (1926), 668.
104. Cf. L. C. Knights, *Drama and Society in the Age of Jonson* (Harmondsworth, England, 1962), p. 262.

The melancholy traveler became a recognized "social type" in England during the last two decades of the century.[105] It was apparently these melancholy travelers who imported the melancholy outlook—or affectation, as it often was—into England from the continent, and above all from Italy. Melancholy had become a common characteristic of Italian aristocrats and artists as early as the later fifteenth century, and had spread across the Alps to France and perhaps to Spain during the sixteenth century.[106] Traveling in these countries, then, many members of the Elizabethan younger generation acquired the mannerisms and some of the mood of the fashionable melancholic. Since these young grand tourists were usually gentlemen, melancholy itself came to have "aristocratic connotations" in England, and to spread among the social elite.[107]

As early as the 1580's, then, some few young governors of England might be seen gravely pacing the narrow lanes of London in Italianate suits of solemn black.[108] They affected the French sloppiness of dress, hose ungartered and floppy black hat without a band. They combined unequal parts of Italian gravity and Italian vices, and added perhaps a touch of Spanish pride. For all their pompous airs of virtue betrayed, they were often wretchedly out-at-elbows, having squandered their patrimonies on foreign travel and court living. Such was the melancholy traveler of the 1580's, seen as a social phenomenon.

And yet, unappetizing though he might appear on the surface, the melancholic considered himself a man of extraordinary talents: in his own eyes, at least, he was a misunderstood genius.[109] This conception of the melancholic as a man of outstanding talent came to the generation of 1560 from classical antiquity, by way of the celebrated humanists of Italy. Aristotle had pointed out that many of the great men of history, and particularly the men of genius—Ajax and Hercules, Socrates and Plato—had been of a melancholy temperament.[110] Marsilio Ficino, the famous Floren-

---

105. Babb, p. 74.

106. Z. S. Fink, "Jaques and the Malcontent Traveler," *Philol. Quart.*, XIV (1935), 241-242; Babb, p. 81 n. 40.

107. Babb, p. 74.

108. Fink, "Jaques and the Malcontent Traveler," 242-243, 238 n. 7.

109. Babb, pp. 58, 76, 180.

110. Aristotle, *Problems*, trans. W. S. Hett (Loeb Classical Library; Cambridge, Mass., 1937), Prob. XXX, 1.

tine humanist, had seized upon this remark of Aristotle's to justify and dignify his own "melancholy disposition."[111] In time, it came to be widely believed that many of the great minds and talents of early sixteenth-century Italy were melancholics. Aristotle's dictum that many talented men were melancholy was gradually transformed into the popular belief that all melancholics were *ipso facto* men of genius. It was this exalted view of the melancholy mood which English travelers picked up and carried home with them. Back in England, this flattering interpretation was reinforced with Christian sanctions by Timothy Bright in his *Treatise of Melancholy*. Bright saw the melancholic as a Christian hero, held like liquid gold by " 'that heavenly refiner . . . in this hot flame' to 'make hereafter a more glorious vessel for his service.' "[112]

The essence of the intellectual superiority of the melancholy mood, however, remained in the classical conception passed on by the Italian humanists. The melancholy genius, according to this way of thinking, walked a high and narrow way, far above the common herd. But precisely because of this lofty elevation of spirit, the melancholy man walked in continual danger of falling, of toppling into the abyss of frenzy or madness.[113] For arrogant, adventurous young men, this exalted conception of the *furor melancholicus*—further identified by humanistic neoplatonists with their master's idea of the *furor divinus,* the creative frenzy—made melancholy an extremely attractive mental condition. The suggestion that moral and religious excellence were also characteristics of the true melancholic must have filled the cup to overflowing for those of the younger generation who were inclined—or affected—that way.

To be melancholy in later Elizabethan times thus indicated to the world at large that one was an aristocrat, or at least a gentleman, and a man of great, if unrecognized, talents. It is not surprising, then, that there were increasing numbers of melancholics among the generation of 1560 in the later 1580's and the early nineties. And yet, the overpowering impression remains that it was not till close to the turn of the century that the

111. Erwin Panofsky, *Albrecht Durer* (Princeton, N. J., 1943), pp. 165-166.
112. Bright, p. 47, quoted in O'Sullivan, "Hamet and . . . Bright," 679.
113. Panofsky, p. 165.

melancholy mood really laid hold of the nation.[114] Much of the earlier, fashionable melancholy had surely been in part affectation; by 1600 the generation of 1560 was melancholy in good earnest. The sincere melancholic of the 1580's and earlier '90's had been eccentric, out of step with his aspiring times; about 1600, he suddenly found that his had become "the prevailing mood."[115] In this transformation, the failure of the aspiring mind played a major role.

The single most important cause of the melancholy mood that descended over England at the end of the reign of Elizabeth was quite probably the fundamental failure of Elizabethan ambition.[116] For this widespread sense of frustration and failure transformed an optimistically ambitious generation into a generation of malcontents; and the malcontent was the basic type of the melancholy man. The malcontent was described, apparently for the first time, in 1588: he was, essentially, an embittered man, hating his superiors because they were above him and his equals because they dared claim parity.[117] Francis Bacon explained the close causal connection between the aspiring mind and the malcontent in his essay "Of Ambition":

Ambition . . . maketh men active, earnest, full of alacrity, and stirring . . . if they find the way open for their rising, and still get forward . . . but if they be checked in their desires, they become secretly discontent, and look upon men and matters with an evil eye. . . .[118]

They became, in short, malcontents.

The close connection between the malcontent and the melancholy humor was even more clearly recognized by other Elizabethans. As one authority points out, "to the Elizabethan mind, the word 'malcontent' implied 'melancholy'—denoted . . . an ex-

114. Fink, "Jaques and the Malcontent Traveler," 248 n. 39; Theodore Spencer, "Donne and His Age," in *A Garland for John Donne*, ed. Spencer (Cambridge, Mass., 1931), p. 186 n. 1; Knights, p. 201.

115. Harrison, "Elizabethan Melancholy," p. 49.

116. Spencer, "Elizabethan Malcontent," pp. 531-532; Babb, p. 76.

117. William Rankins, *The English Ape*, quoted in Oscar James Campbell, *Shakespeare's Satire* (New York, 1943, p. 142). Rankins, writing in 1588, refers to the term as "the new found name."

118. Francis Bacon, "Of Ambition," Harl. MS. 5106, 1607-1612, in *A Harmony of the Essays*, ed. Edward Arber (London, 1871), p. 222; cf. Walter Raleigh, *The Cabinet-Council . . .*, ed. John Milton (London, 1858), p. 108.

treme form of it."[119] Robert Burton, whose *Anatomy* was the
definitive work on melancholy, deserves to be heard on this, even
though he wrote when most of the generation of 1560 were in their
graves. Burton listed ambition as one of the major causes of
melancholy as a mental illness.[120] He described with heartfelt
eloquence the melancholia that afflicted the ambitious: "with what
waking nights, painful hours, anxious thoughts, and bitterness
of mind . . . distracted and tired, they consume the interim of
their time." Final failure hurled these malcontents into the
maelstrom of the *furor melancholicus*: "If he chance to miss . . . he
is in hell . . . so dejected that he is ready to hang himself. . . ."
Ambition thus led to a malcontented outlook, and the malcontent
was by definition melancholy: "so long as his ambition lasts, he
can look for no other but anxiety and care, discontent and grief
. . . madness itself, or violent death in the end."

The melancholy man of late Elizabethan and Jacobean times
was thus most typically a malcontent, a man frustrated in his ambitions. The generation of 1560 took their failures seriously.
Raleigh bitterly lamented the endless delays of his Guiana voyage:
"This long stay hath made me a poor man, the year far spent, and
what shall become of us God knows. The body is wasted with
toil; the purse with charge; and all things worn." And later, he
wrote simply: "this wind breaks my heart."[121] The awful transformation of Charles Blount, Lord Mountjoy, when disgrace
overtook him in his last years, was far from unique: "his countenance was cheerful, and as amiable as ever I beheld of any man,"
wrote one who knew him well, "only some two years before his
death, about the time of the scandal . . . his face grew thin, his
ruddy color failed . . . and his countenance was sad and dejected."[122] Such repeated disappointments drove these men into
melancholy by way of discontent. Francis Bacon, whose career
under Elizabeth has been described as "one long disappointment,"

119. Elmer Edgar Stoll, "Shakespeare, Marston, and the Malcontent Type," *Mod. Philol.*, III (1906), 284.
120. Robert Burton, *The Anatomy of Melancholy* . . . (New York, 1924), pp. 184-186.
121. Sir Walter Raleigh to Sir Robert Cecil, Sept. ?, 1594?, and same to same, Dec. 26, 1594, in Edwards, II, 101, 103.
122. Fynes Moryson, *An Itinerary Containing His Ten Yeares Travel* . . . (Glasgow, 1907), II, 261.

wrote to a friend in the bitterness of his failure to attain a coveted office: "This is a course to quench all good spirits, and to corrupt every man's nature."[123] And he saw plainly the direction this corruption of his nature was tending. As he wrote to Essex after a similar outburst of bitterness: "I humbly pray your Lordship to pardon me for troubling you with my melancholy."[124]

The brilliant young Earl of Essex, whose downfall shook his generation, provided the perfect illustration of the curdling of unsuccessful ambition into malcontented melancholy. Contemporaries blamed the follies of his last dark months on his own malcontented humor, and on the evil counsel of the equally frustrated aspiring minds who surrounded him.[125] Certainly he exhibited many of the classic symptoms of the *furor melancholicus*. Sir John Harington described with a shudder the melancholy frenzy which came over the Earl in this final period of his aspiring life:

It resteth with me in opinion, that ambition thwarted in its career, doth speedily lead on to madness; herein I am strengthened by what I learn in my Lord of Essex, who shifteth from sorrow and repentence to rage and rebellion so suddenly, as well proveth him devoid of good reason or right mind. . . . His speeches becometh no man who hath *mens sana in corpore sano*.[126]

Harington concluded with a description that would have done for more courtiers than Essex in those last years of an expiring reign: "the haughty spirit knoweth not how to yield, and the man's soul seemeth tossed to and fro, like the waves of a troubled sea." The mind of this generation, like that of the doomed Earl, was tempest-tossed indeed as the century drew to a close.

The close connection between the malcontent humor of frustrated ambition and the melancholy mood was evident also in both the earlier forms of melancholy, the melancholy traveler and the unrecognized genius. The young man, like Anthony Bacon or Robert Sidney, who traveled widely abroad, did so partly as preparation for a successful career in the Queen's service. When his newly acquired linguistic skill and geopolitical knowl-

123. Francis Bacon to Fulke Greville, 1595?, in Spedding, I, 359.

124. Francis Bacon to the Earl of Essex, March 30, 1593, in *ibid.*, I, 291.

125. Spencer, "Elizabethan Malcontent," p. 531; G. B. Harrison, *The Life and Death of Robert Devereux Earl of Essex* (New York, 1937), p. 276.

126. John Harington, "Brief Notes and Remembrances," in Park, I, 179-180.

edge failed to assure him the expected preferment, the aspiring mind turned malcontent and melancholy. Thus "Bruto the traveler" gloomily promenaded at Westminster:

> And now he sighs. Oh thou corrupted age,
> Which slight regard'st men of sound carriage;
> Virtue, knowledge, fly to heaven again
> Deign not among those ungrateful sots remain.
> Well some tongues I know, some countries I have seen
> And yet these oily snails respectless been
> Of my good parts.[127]

The misunderstood genius, the superior individual driven into melancholy fits by the refusal of this unperceptive world to recognize his talents, was also, obviously, a malcontent.[128] This feeling of innate superiority was a fundamental part of the Marlovian mind. These would-be Tamburlaines and Caesars saw themselves as men of great parts, as the very Phoenixes of their age. When their brilliance went unrecognized, unemployed, and unrewarded, these "unwise witty Malcontents," as a critic unfeelingly labeled them, railed bitterly on the blindness of the times that could thus ignore such "men of worth" as they.[129]

Even such comparatively abstract causes of melancholy as the feeling that society was corrupted, or that the cosmos itself was decaying, were not unconnected with frustrated ambition. Modern scholarship has paid a good deal of attention to these two presumed causes of Elizabethan melancholy, and neither seems at first glance to have much to do with disappointed ambition. But there does seem to be a connection; nor would this be the first time that men's personal fortunes have colored their views of their society and their universe.

Elizabethan society certainly seemed threatened from many directions in the last years of the reign. There was the war with Spain and the possibility of a civil war between Puritan and Catholic extremists; there were depressions and crop failures and the plague; there was the uneasy feeling that their bustling new

127. Satire 2, "The Metamorphosis of Pigmalion's Image," in *The Poems of John Marston*, ed. Arnold Davenport (Liverpool, 1961), pp. 75-76.
128. Babb, p. 76.
129. John Davies of Hereford, "Microcosmos," in *The Complete Works of . . .*, ed. Alexander Grosart (Edinburgh, 1878), I, 72.

commercial society was morally inferior to the pious Middle Ages; there was the inevitable backswing of the pendulum, the "sudden revulsion of feeling" against "the sensuousness and expansiveness" of their own age.[130] But if Elizabethan society looked particularly bleak during the Queen's last years, it was in large measure because that society had not satisfied the expectations of a generation of aspiring minds. Particularly during the tense period of transition from one reign to another, ambition was screwed to a high pitch of expectancy, and disappointment was correspondingly bitter. This was the moment in time, from the fall of Essex to that of Raleigh, when the generation of 1560 began at last to see the end of its road—"every man expecting mountains and finding molehills."[131] Even those who, like Sir Robert Cecil, successfully crossed the threshold of the new reign, began to lament the past and brood on the future. Busy little Sir Robert wrote with more than nostalgia of "our blessed Queen's time":

I wish I waited now in her presence-chamber, with ease at my food and rest at my bed. I am pushed from the shores of comfort, and I know not where the winds and waves of a Court will bear me; I know it bringeth little comfort on earth; and he is, I reckon, no wise man that looketh this way to heaven.[132]

In their forties, with the great transition behind them, the probability of failure became more apparent to this aging generation than ever before. It was no wonder society seemed utterly corrupt to what was fast becoming a generation of melancholy malcontents. The society which in their youth had seemed to promise them everything had ended by betraying their highest aspirations.

Not only society, but the framework of the universe itself seemed uncertain and tottering in the last years of the sixteenth century; and confusion and apprehension on this score have also been cited as an important cause of the melancholy mood. Two basic metaphysical difficulties plagued thinking men—one exceedingly modern, the other ancient. The new, open, Copernican cosmology deprived man's world of its central place, and seemed to question man's own primacy in God's universe. The ancient doctrine of universal decay and mutability, on the other hand,

130. Spencer, "Donne and His Age," p. 185; cf. Knights, p. 261.
131. Clifford, p. 5.
132. Sir Robert Cecil to Sir John Harington, May 29, 1603, in Park, I, 345.

convinced many that theirs was the last age, the age of "the degeneration of man and the growing senility of the world," with Doomsday not far distant.[133] Again, we may presume that the metaphysical views of this generation, like their social views, were warped by the failure of their high aspirations. In their egotistical youth, the universe had been on their side: they had been England's chosen governors, the Phoenixes of their age, men of godlike power, destined for glory. By the turn of the century, the very nature of things seemed to be against them, and as melancholy malcontents they raged against an unjust, unfair universe. For Hamlet, not only was there something rotten in Denmark, but the times themselves were out of joint, the universe infected:

. . . indeed, it goes so heavily with my disposition that this goodly frame, the earth, seems to me a sterile promontory, this most excellent canopy, the air, look you, this brave o'erhanging firmament, this majestical roof fretted with golden fire, why, it appears no other thing to me than a foul and pestilent congregation of vapours.[134]

It would seem, then, that more than any other single factor, the failure of personal ambition lay at the root of the melancholy mood of late Elizabethan and Jacobean times. In addition, an integral part of this somber mood of an aging generation was the conservative revival of the early seventeenth century. This resurgence of conservatism in the generation of 1560, the Elizabethans who survived Elizabeth, has, furthermore, led to much confusion about that untenable abstraction, the Elizabethan spirit.

What seems to have happened was simple enough. As the melancholy view of the world became widespread, the generation of 1560 began at last to see the great truth of the lessons their fathers had taught. Like their predecessors half a century before, they began to realize that overweening ambition did in fact all too often lead to disaster. And so a generation of overreachers turned

133. Don Cameron Allen, "The Degeneration of Man and Renaissance Pessimism," *Stud. in Philol.*, XXXV (1938), 215.

134. *Hamlet*, II, ii, 9-16. It has been suggested that in Hamlet's complex character, "filial grief shades into the grief of disappointed ambition" (Stoll, p. 297; O'Sullivan, pp. 676, 677).

back to the conservative lessons of their youth, to the melancholy classical commonplaces their fathers had drilled into them.[135] That "great reservoir of gloomy commonplace," as one scholar has put it, "made it very easy for anyone . . . whose ambition had received a rebuff to find expression for his feelings. . . ."[136] The generation of 1560 began to realize at last that overreaching ambition could be a real social evil. Now they were willing to believe that such ambition might be in very truth an unnatural rebellion and a sin against God. Most agonizingly, now they knew in the depths of their embittered souls that high aspiration was indeed a futile passion in a delusive world. In the pride of their golden youth, these truths had been committed to memory—and promptly forgotten. Now psyches in search of words to express the misery of their failure dredged up the ancient truths.

Thus a final paradox of this aspiring generation seems to be resolved. The life and works of Sir Walter Raleigh, for instance, expressed some singularly contradictory views of ambition. His career was "a record of striving for . . . position and power," and even in his writings, "the courtier and politican intrude. . . ."[137] And yet, his monumental meditation on the human past, *The History of the World*, was "unceasing in its condemnation of personal ambition."[138] For one biographer, this "paradox between words and deeds" reveals a serious flaw in Raleigh's character, politely described as "lack of logic and consistency."[139] Strathmann, however, has taken the trouble to investigate the admittedly controversial chronology of these conflicting words and deeds. He agrees with Bishop Hall on the importance of the fact that "The Court had his youthful . . . times, the Tower his later age": the one meant the possibility of ultimate success, the other the certainty of failure.[140] Raleigh in his later years could thus reproduce with melancholy sincerity the orthodox view of ambition he had once learned as a set of irrelevant commonplaces. Ambi-

135. Spencer, "Elizabethan Malcontent," pp. 524-525; Spencer, "Donne and His Age," pp. 184-185; Coffin, p. 266.

136. Spencer, "Elizabethan Malcontent," p. 525.

137. Philip Edwards, *Sir Walter Raleigh* (London, New York, Toronto, 1953), p. 54; Ernest A. Strathmann, *Sir Walter Raleigh, A Study in Elizabethan Skepticism* (New York, 1951), p. 170.

138. Edwards, p. 54.

139. Ibid., p. 55.

140. Strathmann, pp. 170-171.

tion was a terrible social evil, he wrote in his *History*—"the disease of Kings, and of States, and of private men."[141] Ambition was a crime against God and against the natural order: "Such is human ambition, a monster that neither feareth God . . . neither hath it respect to nature. . . ." And for an older, wiser Raleigh, the futility of high aspiration and the fickleness of Fortune had become melancholy truisms. "Experience hath oft proved," he was compelled by his own unhappy experience to admit, "that Men in best Fortune, and such as esteem themselves most secure, even then fall soonest into disadventure . . . . for the Day knows not what the Night bringeth. . . ."[142]

Night was coming over all this generation, and with the darkness came disillusionment. "Youth had dreamed dreams beyond the capacity of age to fulfill," as one authority on this melancholy time sums it up: "its enthusiasm had accumulated experience that would require generations to assimilate. . . ."[143] There were the commercial, political, and religious beginnings made by the generation of 1560; its tremendous literary achievement; its intuitions of the idea of progress. But they had aspired too high: they could not possibly achieve all they had set out to do, "and as the Elizabethan was conscious of his vigor and ambition at the dawn, he was aware of his shortcomings at the close of the day. . . ."

Thus the Elizabethan younger generation, driven by a unique aspiration for honor and power, grew, strove, made their contributions, and passed away. There were great men and glittering names among them—Essex, Raleigh, Mountjoy, Francis Bacon, Sir Robert Cecil, Sir Philip Sidney. There were lesser men, too often doomed by circumstance rather than by lack of quality in themselves—men like Sir John Burgh and Anthony Bacon and Sir Philip's little brother Robert Sidney, like the mighty Cumberland and the dashing Sir Henry Unton and shrewd Thomas Edmondes. There were the men of genius who were so meagerly rewarded by their own generation—Shakespeare, Spenser, Kit Marlowe, and the university wits. Born in a uniquely favorable time, these young gentlemen and scholars were all the Phoenixes of

141. Walter Raleigh, *The History of the World* (London, 1614), Bk. V, chap. i, par. 6; Bk. III, chap. xiii, par. 7.
142. Raleigh, *Cabinet-Council*, pp. 146, 148.   143. Coffin, p. 265.

their age. In youth, they were enthusiastic soldiers; in their middle years, ruthless politicians; in old age, a generation of malcontents. Like the legendary Phoenix, they were unique; and like the Phoenix, they consumed themselves—in the flames of their own exalted ambitions, in the ardor of their high aspiring minds.

Appendix: leading courtiers and writers of the generation of 1560*

Sir Walter Raleigh, 1552-1618
Sir Edward Coke, 1552-1634
Gilbert Talbot, Earl of Shrewsbury, 1553-1616
Edward Somerset, Earl of Worcester, 1553-1628
Sir Philip Sidney, 1554-1586
Sir Fulke Greville, 1554-1628
Peregrine Bertie, Lord Willoughby, 1555-1601
Philip Howard, Earl of Arundel, 1557-1595
Sir Henry Unton, 1557-1595
Anthony Bacon, 1558-1601
George Clifford, Earl of Cumberland, 1558-1605
Dr. Julius Caesar, 1558-1636

Sir Francis Vere, 1560-1609
Sir Edward Hoby, 1560-1617
Francis Bacon, later Baron Verulam, Viscount St. Albans, 1561-1626
Lord Thomas Howard, 1561-1626
Sir John Burgh, 1562-1594
Charles Blount, Lord Mountjoy, 1563-1606
Sir Robert Cecil, later Earl of Salisbury, 1563-1612
Sir Robert Sidney, later Earl of Leicester, 1563-1626
Sir Thomas Edmondes, 1563-1630
Sir Thomas Sherley, 1564-1630
Henry Percy, Earl of Northumberland, 1564-1632
Sir Anthony Sherley, 1565-1635

Sir Ferdinando Gorges, 1566-1647
Robert Devereux, Earl of Essex, 1566-1601

Edmund Spenser, 1552-1599
Richard Hakluyt, 1552-1616

John Lyly, 1554-1586
Richard Hooker, 1554-1600

Thomas Watson, 1557-1592

Thomas Kyd, 1558-1595
George Peele, 1558-1597

Thomas Lodge, 1558-1625
George Chapman, 1559-1634
Robert Greene, 1560-1592

Robert Southwell, 1561-1595

Samuel Daniel, 1563-1619

Michael Drayton, 1563-1631

William Shakespeare, 1564-1616
Christopher Marlowe, 1564-1593

John Davies of Hereford, 1565-1618

Thomas Nashe, 1567-1601

* Based on information contained in the *Calendars of State Papers, Foreign* and *Domestic*, the *Cambridge Bibliography of English Literature*, and G. B. Harrison's *Elizabethan Journals*.

Bibliography of works cited

PRIMARY SOURCES

An Advertisement from a French Gentleman, touching the intention and meaning which those of the house of Guise have in their late levying of forces. N. p., 1585.

Andrewes, Lancelot. *Ninety-Six Sermons by the Right Honourable and Reverend Father in God, Lancelot Andrewes.* Oxford, 1899.

Ariosto, Ludovico. *Orlando Furioso.* Translated by W. S. Rose. London, 1823.

Aristotle. *The Magna Moralia.* Translated by Hugh Tredenick. The Loeb Classical Library. London, 1935.

———. *The Politics.* Translated by H. Rackham. The Loeb Classical Library. London, 1932.

———. *Problems.* Translated by W. S. Hett. The Loeb Classical Library. Cambridge, Mass., 1937.

Ascham, Roger. *The Scholemaster.* Edited by John E. B. Mayor. London, 1863.

Bacon, Francis. *The Moral and Historical Works of Lord Bacon.* Edited by Joseph Devey. London, 1909.

———. *Selected Writings.* Edited by Hugh D. Dick. New York, 1955.

———. *The Works of Francis Bacon.* Edited by James Spedding, Robert Leslie Ellis, and Douglas Denon Heath. London, 1864–.

Baldwin, William, *et al. The Mirror for Magistrates.* Edited by Lily B. Campbell. Cambridge, 1938.

———. *A Treatyce of Moral Philosophy containing the sayinges of the wise.* Revised edition. London, 1564.

Barclay, Richard. *A Discourse of the Felicitie of Man Or His Summum Bonum.* Revised edition. London, 1603.

Birch, Thomas, editor. *Memoirs of the Reign of Queen Elizabeth from the Year 1581 till Her Death.* London, 1754.

Bright, Timothy, *A Treatise of Melancholie.* Introduction by Hardin Craig. New York, 1940.

Burton, Robert. *The Anatomy of Melancholy: What It Is With All The Kinds, Causes, Symptoms, Prognostics, Several Cures Of It.* New York, 1924.

Calendar of Letters, Dispatches, and State Papers Relating to the Negociations between England and Spain. Preserved in the Archives at Simancas. . . . London, 1862–.

Calendar of State Papers and Manuscripts Relating to English Affairs, Existing in the Archives and Collections of Venice and . . . Northern Italy. London, 1864—.

Calendar of State Papers, Domestic Series, of the Reign of Edward VI, Mary, Elizabeth, 1547-1580. London, 1856.

Calendar of State Papers, Domestic Series, of the Reign of Elizabeth. London, 1867—.

Calendar of State Papers, Foreign Series, of the Reign of Elizabeth. London, 1863—.

Camden, William. *Annales, or The History of the most Renowned and Victorious Princess Elizabeth, Late Queen of England*. Translated by R. N. 3rd edition. London, 1635.

Carey, Robert, Earl of Monmouth. *Memoirs of the Life of Robert Cary, Baron of Leppington, and Earl of Monmouth*. London, 1759.

Castiglione, Baldassare. *The Book of the Courtier*. Translated by Thomas Hoby. Everyman Edition. London and New York, n.d.

Cavendish, George. *The Life and Death of Cardinal Wolsey*, in *Two Early Tudor Lives*. Edited by Richard S. Sylvester and Davis P. Harding. New Haven and London, 1962.

Caxton, William. *The Auncient Historie of the Destruction of Troy*. Preface by Thomas Fiston. London, 1596.

Cecil, Robert, Earl of Salisbury. *The State and Dignitie of a Secretarie of Estates Place, With the care and perill thereof*. London, 1642.

Chamberlain, John. *The Letters of John Chamberlain*. Edited by Norman Egbert McClure. Philadelphia, 1939.

Churchyard, Thomas. *A pleasant Discourse of Court and Wars: with a replication of them both*. London, 1596.

Cicero, M. Tullius. *De officiis*. Translated by Walter Miller. The Loeb Classical Library. New York, 1921.

Clifford, Anne. *The Diary of Lady Anne Clifford*. Edited by V. Sackville-West. New York, n.d.

Cogan, T. *The Well of Wisdome, Conteining Chiefe and Chosen sayinges which may leade all men to perfect and true wisdome*. London, 1577.

Coignet, Martin. *Politique Discourses Upon Truth and Lying*. London, 1586.

[Colet, Claude.] *The Famous, Pleasant, and variable Historie of Palladine of England*. London, 1588.

Collier, J. Payne, editor. *The Egerton Papers. Chiefly Illustrative of the Times of Elizabeth and James I*. London, 1840.

Collins, Arthur, editor. *Letters and Memorials of State in the Reigns of Queen Mary, Queen Elizabeth, and King James*. London, 1746.

Colynet, Antony. *The True History of the Civill Warres of France between the French King Henry the 4 and the Leaguers.* London, 1591.

Coningsby, Thomas. *Journal of the Siege of Rouen, 1591.* Edited by John Gough Nichols. Camden Society Publications, Vol. 39. London, 1847.

Conybeare, John. *Letters and Exercises of the Elizabethan Schoolmaster, John Conybeare.* Edited by F. C. Conybeare. London, 1905.

Daniel, Samuel. *The First Fowre Bookes of the civile wars between the two houses of Lancaster and Yorke.* London, 1595.

Dasent, John Roche, editor. *Acts of the Privy Council of England.* London, 1901.

Davies of Hereford, John. *The Complete Works of John Davies of Hereford.* Edited by Alexander Grosart. Edinburgh, 1878.

Donne, John. *The Complete Poetry and Selected Prose of John Donne.* Edited by Charles M. Coffin. New York, 1952.

Dudley, Robert, Earl of Leicester. *Correspondence of Robert Dudley, Earl of Leycester, during His Government of the Low Countries, in the Years 1585 and 1586.* Edited by John Bruce. London, 1844.

Edwards, Richard. *A Paradyse of daynty devises. Conteyning sundry pithy preceptes.* London, 1578.

Ellis, Henry, editor. *Original Letters, Illustrative of English History.* . . . First Series. London, 1825.

———. *Original Letters Illustrative of British History.* . . . Second Series. London, 1827.

———. *Original Letters Illustrative of English History.* . . . Third Series. London, 1846.

———. *Original Letters of Eminent Literary Men of the Sixteenth, Seventeenth, and Eighteenth Centuries.* Camden Society Publications, Vol. 23. London, 1843.

Elviden, Edmund. *The Closet of Counsels: Conteining the advise of diverse wise Phylosophers.* London, 1573.

Elyot, Thomas. *The Boke named the Governour.* Edited by Henry Herbert and Stephen Croft. London, 1883.

Erasmus, Desiderius. *Apophthegmes, that is to saie, prompte, quicke, wittie, and sentencious saiynges.* London, 1564.

———. *A booke called in Latyn Enchiridion militis christiani and in englyshe the manuell of the christian knyght.* [London, 1533.]

Felippe, Bartolome. *The Counseller: A Treatise of Counsels.* Translated by John Thorius. London, 1589.

Fenne, Thomas. *Fennes Fruites . . . wherein is decyphered . . . the reward of aspiring mindes.* London, 1590.

Fenton, Geoffrey, editor. *Golden Epistles, Contayning various discourses both Morall, Philosophical, and Divine.* London, 1575.

Ferrarius, Joannes. *A Work of Ioannis Ferrarius Montanus, touchynge the good orderynge of a common weale.* Translated by William Bavende. London, 1559.

Floyd, Thomas. *The Picture of a perfit Common wealth, describing as well the offices of Princes . . . as also the duties of subiects towards their Governours.* London, 1600.

A fruitfull Sermon upon the 3.4.5.6.7. & 8. verses of the 12. Chapter of the Epistle of St. Paule to the Romanes. London, 1586.

Fuller, Thomas. *The History of the Worthies of England.* Edited by John Nichols. London, 1811.

Furio Ceriol, Fadrique. *A verie briefe and profitable Treatise declaring . . . what maner of Counselers a Prince that will governe well ought to have.* Translated by Thomas Blundeville. London, 1570.

The Garden of Prudence . . . touching the vanities of the world. London, 1595.

Gardiner, Samuel. *Portraiture of the prodigle sonne.* London, 1599.

Gibson, Charles. *The Praise of a good Name . . . Wherin every one may see the Fame that followeth laudable actions. . . .* London, 1594.

Gifford, George. *Eight Sermons upon the first foure Chapters, and part of the fift, of Ecclesiastes.* London, 1589.

Gomara, Francisco Lopez de. *The Pleasant Historie of the Conquest of the West India, Now Called New Spayne, atchieved by the worthy Prince Hernando Cortes, Marques of the valley of Huaxacac.* Translated by T. Nicholas. London, 1578.

Goodman, Godfrey. *The Court of King James the First. . . .* Edited by John S. Brewer. London, 1839.

Grafton, Richard. *Abridgement of the Chronicles of Englande, newely corrected and augmented.* London, 1572.

———. *Grafton's Chronicle or History of England.* London, 1809.

Great Britain. Historical Manuscripts Commissions. *Calendar of the Manuscripts of the Most Hon. the Marquis of Salisbury, Preserved at Hatfield House, Herefordshire.* London, 1883.

Greene, Robert. *The Plays and Poems of Robert Greene.* Edited by J. Churton Collins. Oxford, 1905.

Guevara, Antonio de. *The Familiar Epistles of Sir Anthony of Guevara, Preacher, Chronicler, and Counsellor.* Translated by Edward Hellows. London, 1574.

———. *The Golden Booke of Marcus Aurelius, Emperour and eloquent Oratour.* London, 1586.

H. B. *Moriemini: A Verie Profitable Sermon Preached before Her Maiestie at the Court.* London, 1593.

Hakluyt, Richard. *The Principal Navigations, Voyages, Traffiques & Discoveries of the English Nation.* Glasgow, 1903-1905.

Harington, John. *The Letters and Epigrams of Sir John Harington.* Edited by Norman Egbert McClure. Philadelphia, 1930.

Harvey, Gabriel. *Gabriel Harvey's Marginalia.* Edited by G. C. Moore Smith. Stratford-upon-Avon, 1913.

———. *Letter-book of Gabriel Harvey, A. D. 1573-1580.* Edited by E. J. L. Scott. Camden Society Publications, new series, Vol. 33. Westminster, 1884.

Haydn, Hiram, editor. *The Portable Elizabethan Reader.* New York, 1955.

Henry III, King of France. *Directions from the King . . . concerning the Death of the Duke of Guise.* Translated by E. A. London, 1589.

Higgins, John, and Thomas Blenerhasset. *Parts added to the Mirror for Magistrates. . . .* Edited by Lily B. Campbell. Cambridge, 1946.

Holinshed, Raphael. *Holinshed's Chronicles of England, Scotland, and Ireland.* London, 1807-1808.

Hopper, Clarence, editor. *London Chronicle during the Reigns of Henry the Seventh and Henry the Eighth.* Camden Society Publications, Vol. 93. London, 1859.

Hutchinson, Lucy. *Memoirs of the Life of Colonel Hutchinson.* Revised edition. London, 1885.

[Innocent III.] *The Mirror of Mans Life. Plainly describing What weake moulde we are made of.* Translated by H. Kirton. London, 1577.

James VI, King of Scotland. *Correspondence of King James VI with Sir Robert Cecil. . . .* Edited by John Bruce. Westminster, 1861.

Keymys, Lawrence. *A Relation of the Second Voyage to Guiana.* London, 1596.

The Lamentable Tragedy of Locrine, the eldest sonne of King Brutus. Edited by R. B. McKerrow. London, 1908.

La Noue, Francois de. *The Politike and Militarie Discourses of the Lord de la Nowe.* Translated by E. A. London, 1587.

Le Roy, Louis. *Of the Interchangeable Course, or Variety of Things in the Whole World.* Translated by Robert Ashley. London, 1594.

[Lily, William.] *A Short Introduction of Grammar, Generally To Be Used.* Oxford, 1651.

Lloyd, David. *The Statesmen and Favorites of England Since the Reformation.* London, 1665.

Lloyd, Ludowick. *The Pilgrimage of Princes, penned out of sundry Greeke and Latine aucthours.* London, [1573].

Lodge, Edmund, editor. *Illustrations of British History, Biography, and Manners, in the Reigns of Henry VIII, Edward VI, Mary, Elizabeth, and James I.* London, 1791.

Machiavelli, Niccolo. *The Prince and the Discourses.* Edited by Max Lerner. New York, 1940.

Marlowe, Christopher. *The Jew of Malta and the Massacre at Paris.* Edited by H. S. Bennett. New York, 1931.

———. *Tamburlaine the Great in Two Parts.* Edited by U. M. Ellis-Fermor. New York, 1930.

Marston, John. *The Poems of John Marston.* Edited by Arnold Davenport. Liverpool, 1961.

Moffet, Thomas. *Nobilis or A View of the Life and Death of A Sidney.* . . . Translated and edited by Virgil B. Heltzel and Hoyt H. Hudson. San Marino, Calif., 1940.

Moryson, Fynes. *An Itinerary Containing His Ten Yeares Travel.* . . . Glasgow, 1907.

Mulcaster, Richard. *The Educational Writings of Richard Mulcaster (1532-1611).* Edited by James Oliphant. Glasgow, 1903.

Murdin, W., editor. *A Collection of State Papers Relating to Affairs in the Reign of Queen Elizabeth from the Year 1571 to 1596.* London, 1759.

Nares, Edward. *Memoirs of the Life and Administration of the Right Honorable William Cecil, Lord Burghley.* London, 1829-1831.

Nashe, Thomas. *The Works of Thomas Nashe.* Edited by Robert B. McKerrow. Revised by F. P. Wilson. Oxford, 1958.

Naunton, Robert. *Fragmenta Regalia.* Edited by Edward Arber. London, 1870.

Nichols, John Gough, editor. *The Chronicle of Queen Jane, and of Two Years of Queen Mary, and Especially of the Rebellion of Sir Thomas Wyatt.* London, 1850.

———, editor. *The Progresses and Public Processions of Queen Elizabeth.* London, 1823.

Palmer, A. Smythe, editor. *The Ideal of a Gentleman.* London and New York, n. d.

Park, Thomas, editor. *Nugae Antiquae: Being a Miscellaneous Collection of Original Papers . . . written during the Reigns of Henry VIII, Edward VI, Queen Mary, Elizabeth, and King James.* London, 1804.

Peele, George. *The Works of George Peele.* Edited by A. H. Bullen. London, 1888.

Phiston, William, translator. *The Welspring of wittie Conceites: Containing a . . . varietie of pithy Sentences, vertuous sayings, and right Morall Instructions.* London, 1584.

Pricket, Robert. *Honors Fame In Triumph Riding (1604)* [and] *A A True Coppie of a Discourse written by a Gentleman, employed*

in the late Voyage of Spaine and Portingale . . . 1589. Edited by
Alexander B. Grosart. Manchester, 1881.

Rainolds, John. *A Sermon Upon Part of the Eighteenth Psalm Preached
to the publik assembly of Scholars in the Universitie of Oxford
. . . 1586.* Oxford, 1586.

Raleigh, Walter. *The Cabinet-Council: Containing the Chief Arts
of Empire, and Mysteries of State. . . .* Edited by John Milton.
London, 1858.

———. *The Discoverie of the large rich and bewtiful Empire of Guiana.*
Edited by V. T. Harlow. London, 1928.

———. *The History of the World.* London, 1614.

———. *The Poems of Sir Walter Raleigh.* Edited by Agnes M. C.
Latham. Cambridge, Mass., 1951.

———. *The Works of Sir Walter Raleigh.* Edited by Thomas Birch.
London, 1751.

S. I. *Bromleion. A Discourse of the most substantial points of Divinity,
Handled by divers Common places.* London, 1595.

Sansovino, Francisco. *The Quintessence of Wit, being a current comfort of conceites, Maximes, and poleticke devices.* Translated by
Captain Hitchcock. London, 1590.

Shakespeare, William. *The Complete Works of Shakespeare.* Edited
by Hardin Craig. Chicago, 1951.

Sidney, Philip. *The Complete Works of Sir Philip Sidney.* Edited by
Albert Feuillerat. Cambridge, 1922-1926.

———. *The Correspondence of Sir Philip Sidney and Hubert Languet.*
Edited and translated by Steuart A. Pears. London, 1845.

Slingsby, Henry. *The Diary of Sir Henry Slingsby of Scriven, Bart.*
Edited by Daniel Parson. London, 1836.

Smith, Henry. *The Sermons of Master Henry Smith, gathered into
one volume.* Edited by Thomas Man. London, 1611.

Somers, John. *A Collection of Scarce and Valuable Tracts.* London,
1748.

Spedding, James. *The Letters and Life of Francis Bacon Including
All His Occasional Works.* London, 1890.

Spenser, Edmund. *The Poetical Works of Edmund Spenser.* Edited by
Ernest de Selincourt. Oxford, 1909-1910.

Storer, Thomas. *The Life and Death of Thomas Wolsey, Cardinall . . . .*
Oxford, 1826.

Stow, John. *The annales of England, from the first inhabitation until
1592.* [London,] 1592.

———. *A Summarie of the Chronicles of England.* London, 1598.

Stubbes, Phillip. *Phillip Stubbes's Anatomy of the Abuses in England
in Shakespeare's Youth, A. D. 1583.* Edited by Frederick J. Furnivall. London, 1877.

Thomas à Kempis. *The Imitation or Following of Christ, and the contemning of worldly vanities.* Translated by Edward Hake. London, 1567.

Traherne, John Montgomery, editor. *Stradling Correspondence: A Series of Letters Written in the Reign of Elizabeth.* London, 1840.

Unton, Henry. *Correspondence of Sir Henry Unton, Knt. Ambassador from Queen Elizabeth to Henry IV, King of France, in the Years MDXCI. and MDXCII.* Edited by Joseph Stevenson. London, 1847.

Vaughan, William. *The Golden grove, moralized in three Bookes.* London, 1600.

W. S. *The True Chronicle Historie of the whole life and death of Thomas Lord Cromwell.* London, 1602.

Walsingham, Francis. *Manual of Prudential Maxims for Statesmen and Courtiers,* in *Instructions for Youth, Gentlemen and Noblemen.* London, 1722.

Warnke, Earl, and Ludwig Proescholdt, editors. *Pseudo-Shakespearean Plays.* Halle, 1883.

Wilbraham, Roger. *The Journal of Sir Roger Wilbraham, Solicitor-General in Ireland and Master of Requests, For the Years 1593-1616.* Camden Society Publications, 3rd series, Vol. 4. London, 1902.

Wood, Anthony à. *Athenae Oxoniensis.* 2nd edition. London, 1721.

Wotton, Henry. *A Parallell betweene Robert late Earle of Essex, and George late Duke of Buckingham.* London, 1641.

Wright, Thomas, editor. *Queen Elizabeth and Her Times: A Series of Original Letters. . . .* London, 1838.

Zarate, Augustin de. *The Strange and Delectable Historie of the Discovery and Conquest of the Provinces of Peru. . . .* Translated by T. Nicholas. London, 1581.

SECONDARY SOURCES

Abbott, Edwin A. *Francis Bacon: An Account of His Life and Works.* London, 1885.

Allen, Don Cameron. "The Degeneration of Man and Renaissance Pessimism," *Stud. in Philol.,* XXXV (1938), 202-227.

Anders, H. "The Elizabethan ABC with the Catechism," *The Library,* 4th series, XVI, No. 1 (1935), 32-48.

Anderson, F. H. *The Philosophy of Francis Bacon.* Chicago, 1948.

Anthony, Irvin. *Raleigh and His World.* New York and London, 1934.

Appel, Louis David. "The Concept of Fame in Tudor and Stuart Literature," *Summaries of Doctoral Dissertations Submitted to the Graduate School of Northwestern University,* XVII (1949), 9-13.

Ascoli, Georges. *La Grande-Bretagne devant l'opinion française depuis la Guerre des Cent Ans jusqu'à la fin du XVIᵉ siècle*. Paris, 1927.

Babb, Lawrence. *The Elizabethan Malady: A Study of Melancholia in English Literature from 1580 to 1642*. East Lansing, Mich., 1951.

Barber, C. L. *The Idea of Honor in the English Drama, 1591-1700*. Goteborg, 1957.

Baroja, Pio. "Tres generaciones," *Obras*, Vol. LV. Madrid, 1926.

Bates, E. S. *Touring in 1600: A Study in the Development of Travel as a Means of Education*. Boston and New York, 1912.

Bateson, F. W. *The Cambridge Bibliography of English Literature*. New York, 1941.

Battenhouse, Roy W. *Marlowe's Tamburlaine: A Study in Renaissance Moral Philosophy*. Nashville, Tenn., 1941.

Berryman, Audrey. "Themes and Techniques in Mid-Tudor Lyric Poetry," *Summaries of Doctoral Dissertations Submitted to the Graduate School of Northwestern University*, XVII (1949) 35.

Bevan, Bryan. *The Real Francis Bacon*. London, 1960.

Bindoff, S. T. *Tudor England*. Penguin Books edition. Harmondsworth, England, 1950.

Boas, Frederick S. *Sir Philip Sidney, Representative Elizabethan*. London, 1955.

Bourne, H. R. Fox. *Sir Philip Sidney, Type of English Chivalry in the Elizabethan Age*. New York and London, 1891.

Bradbrook, M. C. *Themes & Conventions of Elizabethan Tragedy*. Cambridge, 1960.

Bradburn, Norman M., and David E. Berlew. "Need for Achievement and English Industrial Growth," *Economic Development and Cultural Change*, X (1961), 8-20.

Bryson, Frederick Robertson. *The Point of Honor in Sixteenth Century Italy: An Aspect of the Life of the Gentleman*. Chicago, 1935.

Bury, J. B. *The Idea of Progress*. London, 1924.

Bush, Douglas. *Themes and Variations in English Poetry of the Renaissance*. Claremont, Calif., 1957.

Cam, Helen M. "The Decline and Fall of English Feudalism," *History*, XXV (1940), 216-233.

Camden, Carroll. *The Elizabethan Woman*. Houston, New York, and London, 1952.

Campbell, Lily B. *Shakespeare's Tragic Heroes, Slaves of Passion*. New York, 1961.

Campbell, Oscar James. *Shakespeare's Satire*. New York, 1943.

Cavaignac, Eugène. "La Succession des générations en histoire," *Inter-*

national Congress of Historical Sciences, VIII Meeting. Zurich, 1938.

Cayley, Arthur. The Life of Sir Walter Raleigh. 2nd edition. London, 1806.

Cecil, Algernon. A Life of Robert Cecil, First Earl of Salisbury. London, 1915.

Charlton, Kenneth. "Holbein's 'Ambassadors' and Sixteenth-Century Education," JHI, XXI (1960), 99-109.

Cheyney, Edward P. A History of England from the Defeat of the Armada to the Death of Elizabeth. New York, 1948.

Chidsey, Donald Barr. Sir Walter Raleigh, That Damned Upstart. New York, 1931.

Clark, Eleanor Grace. Raleigh and Marlowe: A Study in Elizabethan Fustian. New York, 1941.

C[ockayn], G. E. The Complete Peerage. London, 1926.

Coffin, Charles Monroe. John Donne and the New Philosophy. New York, 1937.

Comte, Auguste. Cours de philosophie positive. Paris, 1830-1842.

Craig, Hardin. The Enchanted Glass: The Elizabethan Mind in Literature. New York, 1936.

Crane, Ronald S. The Vogue of Medieval Chivalric Romance during the English Renaissance. Menasha, Wisconsin, 1919.

Crowther, J. G. Francis Bacon, The First Statesman of Science. London, 1960.

Cruttwell, Patrick. The Shakespearean Moment and Its Place in the Poetry of the 17th Century. New York, 1960.

Daniells, Roy. "English Baroque and Deliberate Obscurity," The Journal of Aesthetics and Art Criticism, V (1946), 115-121.

Davis, Maxine. The Lost Generation: A Portrait of American Youth Today. New York, 1936.

Dennis, G. Ravenscroft. The Cecil Family. Boston and New York, 1914.

Devereux, Walter Bouchier. Lives and Letters of the Devereux, Earls of Essex . . . 1540-1646. London, 1853.

Dewar, Mary. Sir Thomas Smith, A Tudor Intellectual in Office. London, 1964.

Dewey, Rebecca Arnell. "The Idea of Progress in Elizabethan Literature," Abstracts of Dissertations [Stanford University] . . . 1946-47, pp. 31-36. Stanford, Calif., 1947.

Dickens, A. G. Thomas Cromwell and the English Reformation. London, 1959.

Dietz, Frederick C. English Public Finance, 1558-1641. New York and London, 1932.

Dilthey, Wilhelm. Das Erlebnis und die Dichtung. Leipzig, 1906.

———. *Gesammelte Schriften.* Leipzig and Berlin, 1924.

Dromel, Justin. *La Loi des revolutions.* Paris, 1862.

Dublin, L. I., A. J. Lotke, and M. Spiegelman. *Length of Life.* Revised edition. New York, 1949.

Edwards, Edward. *The Life of Sir Walter Raleigh . . . Together with His Letters. . . .* London, 1868.

Edwards, Philip. *Sir Walter Raleigh.* London, New York, Toronto, 1953.

Einstein, Lewis. *The Italian Renaissance in England.* New York, 1913.

———. *Tudor Ideals.* New York, 1921.

Ellis, Havelock. *A Study of British Genius.* London, 1904.

Ellis-Fermor, U. M. *Christopher Marlowe.* London, 1927.

Elton, G. R. *The Tudor Revolution in Government.* Cambridge, 1953.

Esdaile, Arundell. *A List of English Tales and Prose Romances Printed before 1740.* London, 1912.

Esler, Anthony. "Influence of Social and Cultural Developments and of Traditional Geography on Elizabethan Concepts of the Nature of the American Indian." Unpublished Master's thesis, Duke University, 1958.

Evans, F. M. C. *The Principal Secretary of State: A Survey of the Office from 1558 to 1680.* Manchester, London, New York, 1923.

Falls, Cyril. *Mountjoy: Elizabethan General.* London, 1955.

Farrington, Benjamin. *Francis Bacon, Philosopher of Industrial Science.* New York, 1949.

Ferguson, Arthur B. *The Indian Summer of English Chivalry.* Durham, N. C., 1960.

Fink, Z. S. "Jaques and the Malcontent Traveler," *Philol. Quart.,* XIV (1935), 237-252.

Fisher, F. J. "The Development of London as a Center of Conspicuous Consumption in the Sixteenth and Seventeenth Centuries," *Trans. of the Roy. Hist. Soc.,* 4th series, XXX, 37-50.

Friedrich, Carl J. *The Age of the Baroque 1610-1660.* Harper Torchbooks edition. New York, 1952.

Fuller, Thomas. *The Church History of Britain.* Edited by J. S. Brewer. Oxford, 1845.

Gosse, Edmund. *Raleigh.* London, 1886.

Handover, P. M. *The Second Cecil: The Rise to Power, 1563-1604, of Sir Robert Cecil, Later First Earl of Salisbury.* London, 1959.

Harbage, Alfred. *As They Liked It: An Essay on Shakespeare and Morality.* New York, 1947.

Harrison, G. B. *The Elizabethan Journals: Being a Record of Those Things Most Talked of during the Years 1591-1603.* London, 1928-1933.

———. "An Essay on Elizabethan Melancholy." Appended to Nicholas Breton, *Melancholike Humors.* Edited by Harrison. London, 1929.

———. *The Life and Death of Robert Devereux, Earl of Essex.* New York, 1937.

Heffner, Ray. "The Earl of Essex in Elizabethan Literature," *Johns Hopkins University Dissertation Collection,* Vol. I, No. 2. Baltimore, 1934.

———. "Essex, the Ideal Courtier," *ELH,* I (1934), 7-36.

Heltzel, Virgil B. "Young Francis Bacon's Tutor," *MLN,* LXIII (1948), 483-485.

Henry, L. W. "The Earl of Essex as Strategist and Military Organizer, 1596-7," *EHR,* LXVIII (1953), 363-393.

Herr, Alan Fager. *The Elizabethan Sermon: A Survey and a Bibliography.* Philadelphia, 1940.

Hume, Martin A. S. *Sir Walter Raleigh: The British Dominion of the West.* London, 1897.

Hurstfield, Joel. "Robert Cecil, Earl of Salisbury: Minister of Elizabeth and James I," *History Today,* VII (1957), 279-289.

Ingram, John H. *Christopher Marlowe and His Associates.* London, 1904.

James, D. G. *The Dream of Learning: An Essay on "The Advancement of Learning," "Hamlet," and "King Lear."* Oxford, 1951.

Jantz, Harold Stein. "Herder, Goethe, and Friedrich Schlegel on the Problem of the Generations," *Germanic Review,* VIII (1933), 219-238.

Jasinski, René. *Histoire de la littérature française.* Paris, 1947.

Joel, Karl. "Der sakläre Rhythmus der Geschichte," *Jahrbuch für Soziologie,* Vol. I (1925).

Kelso, Ruth. *The Doctrine of the English Gentleman in the Sixteenth Century.* University of Illinois Studies in Language and Literature, Vol. XIV. Urbana, Illinois, 1929.

Knights, L. C. *Drama and Society in the Age of Jonson.* Penguin Books edition. Harmondsworth, England, 1962.

Kocher, Paul H. "Francis Bacon and His Father," *HLQ,* XXI (1958), 133-158.

Kummer, Friedrich. *Deutsche Literaturgeschichte des neunzehnten Jahrhunderts, dargestellt nach Generationen.* Dresden, 1909.

Laín Entralgo, Pedro. *Las generaciones en la historia.* Madrid, 1945.

Langston, Beach. "Essex and the Art of Dying," *HLQ,* XIII (1950), 109-129.

Latham, Agnes M. C. "Sir Walter Raleigh's Gold Mine: New Light on the Last Guiana Voyage," in Geoffrey Tillotson, editor, *Es-*

says and Studies, 1951 . . . Collected for the English Association. London, 1951.

Laughton, John Knox. "Sir John Burgh," DNB.

Lee, Sidney. "The Call of the West and Elizabethan England—The Example of Spain," Elizabethan and Other Essays. Edited by F. S. Boas. Oxford, 1929.

———. "Sir George Abbot," DNB.

———. "Sir Maurice Abbot," DNB.

———. "Sir Nicholas Bacon," DNB.

Lewis, C. S. English Literature in the Sixteenth Century, Excluding Drama. Oxford, 1954.

Lindabury, Richard V. A Study of Patriotism in the Elizabethan Drama, Princeton University Studies in English, No. 5. Princeton, N. J., 1931.

Lindsay, Philip. The Queenmaker: A Portrait of John Dudley, Viscount Lisle, Earl of Warwick, and Duke of Northumberland, 1502-1553. London, 1951.

Lorenz, Alfred. Abendländische Musikgeschichte im Rhythmus der Generationen: Eine Anregung. Berlin, 1928.

Lorenz, Ottokar. Die Geschichtswissenschaft in Hauptrichtungen und Aufgaben. Berlin, 1886-1891.

Lovejoy, Arthur C. The Great Chain of Being: A Study of the History of an Idea. Cambridge, Mass., 1936.

Lowenthal, Leo. Literature and the Image of Man: Sociological Studies of the European Drama and Novel, 1600-1900. Boston, 1957.

Lowers, James K. Mirrors for Rebels: A Study of Polemical Literature Relating to the Northern Rebellion of 1569. University of California Publications in English Studies, No. 6. Berkeley and Los Angeles, 1953.

[Macaulay, Thomas Babington.] "Review of Basil Montagu, editor, Works of Francis Bacon," Edinburgh Review, LXV (1837), 1-104.

MacCaffrey, Wallace T. "Place and Patronage in Elizabethan Politics," in S. T. Bindoff, J. Hurstfield, and C. H. Williams, editors, Elizabethan Government and Society. London, 1961.

McCarthy, Margaret. Generation in Revolt. London and Toronto, 1953.

McClelland, David C. The Achieving Society. New York, 1961.

McClelland, David C., John W. Atkinson, Russell A. Clark, Edgar L. Lowell. The Achievement Motive. New York, 1953.

McShane, Edith. Tudor Opinions of the Chivalric Romance. Washington, D. C., 1950.

Malkiewicz, A. J. A. "An Eye-witness Account of the Coup d'Etat of October, 1549," EHR, LXX (1955), 600-609.

Mallet, Charles Edward. A History of the University of Oxford. New York, 1924.

Mannheim, Karl. "Das Problem der Generationen," *Kölner Viertel-jahrshefte für Soziologie,* VII (1928), 157-185, 309-329.

Marias Aguilera, Julian. *El método historico de las géneraciones.* Madrid, 1949.

Mayes, Charles F. "The Sale of Peerages in Early Stuart England," *Journ. Mod. Hist.,* XXIX (1957), 21-37.

Mentré, François. *Les Générations sociales.* Paris, 1920.

Mohl, Ruth. *The Three Estates in Medieval and Renaissance Litera-ture.* New York, 1933.

Mueller, William R. *The Anatomy of Robert Burton's England.* Berkeley and Los Angeles, 1952.

Murray, James A. H., *et al. The Oxford English Dictionary.* London, 1933.

Neale, J. E. "Elizabeth and the Netherlands, 1586-7," *EHR,* XLV (1930), 373-96.

———. *The Elizabethan Political Scene.* London, 1948.

———. *Queen Elizabeth I: A Biography.* Anchor Books edition. New York, 1957.

Nef, John U. *Industry and Government in France and England, 1540-1640.* Ithaca, N. Y., 1957.

Notestein, Wallace. "The English Woman, 1580 to 1650," in *Studies in Social History: A Tribute to G. M. Trevelyan,* edited by J. H. Plumb. London, New York, Toronto, 1955.

Oakeshott, Walter. *The Queen and the Poet.* London, 1960.

Ortega y Gasset, José. *El tema de nuestro tiempo.* Madrid, 1923.

———. "En torno de Galileo," *Obras completas,* Vol. V. Madrid, 1946-1947.

O'Sullivan, Mary Isabelle. "Hamlet and Dr. Timothy Bright," *PMLA,* XLI (1926), 667-679.

Panofsky, Erwin. *Albrecht Dürer.* Princeton, N. J., 1943.

Petersen, Julius. *Die literarischen Generationen.* Berlin, 1930.

Peyre, Henri. *Les Générations littéraires.* Paris, 1948.

Pinder, Wilhelm. *Das Problem der Generation in der Kunstgeschichte Europas.* 2nd edition. Berlin, 1928.

Pollard, A. F. *The Evolution of Parliament.* 2nd edition. London, New York, Toronto, 1934.

———. *The History of England from the Accession of Edward VI to the Death of Elizabeth (1547-1603).* London, 1910.

———. *Wolsey.* London, 1953.

Powell, Chilton Latham. *English Domestic Relations, 1547-1653.* New York, 1917.

Praz, Mario. "The Politic Brain: Machiavelli and the Elizabethans," *The Flaming Heart.* New York, 1958.

Prothero, Rowland Edmund, Baron Ernle. *The Light Reading of Our Ancestors.* London, n. d.

Quinn, David B. *Raleigh and the British Empire.* London, 1947.

Read, Conyers. *Mr. Secretary Cecil and Queen Elizabeth.* New York, 1955.

———. *Mr. Secretary Walsingham and the Policy of Queen Elizabeth.* Cambridge, Mass., 1925.

Renouard, Yves. "La Notion de génération en histoire," *Révue historique,* CCIX (1953), 1-23.

Ribner, Irving. "The Idea of History in Marlowe's *Tamburlaine,*" *ELH,* XX (1953), 251-266.

Riedl, John O. *A Catalogue of Renaissance Philosophers (1350-1650).* Milwaukee, Wisconsin, 1940.

Rowse, A. L. *The England of Elizabeth.* New York, 1961.

———. *Sir Walter Raleigh: His Family and Private Life.* New York, 1962.

Ryman, Elizabeth Rosemary. "The Scientific Attitude of Francis Bacon," *Abstracts of Dissertations . . . in the University of Cambridge . . . 1952-1953,* pp. 111-112.

Salzman, L. F. *England in Tudor Times: An Account of Its Social Life and Industries.* London, 1926.

Schumann, Detlv W. "Cultural Age-Groups in German Thought," *PMLA,* LI (1936), 1180-1207.

Seneschal, Christian. *Les Grands courants de la littérature française contemporaine.* Malfère, France, 1934.

Spedding, James. *The Letters and the Life of Francis Bacon, Including All His Occasional Works.* London, 1890.

Spencer, Theodore. "Donne and His Age," in *A Garland for John Donne,* edited by Spencer. Cambridge, Mass., 1931.

———. "The Elizabethan Malcontent," in *Joseph Quincy Adams Memorial Studies,* edited by James G. McManaway *et al.* Washington, D. C., 1948.

Stahlin, Karl. *Sir Francis Walsingham und seine Zeit.* Heidleberg, 1908.

Stebbing, William. *Sir Walter Raleigh, A Biography.* Oxford, 1891.

Steegmuller, Francis. *Sir Francis Bacon, the First Modern Mind.* Garden City, N. Y., 1930.

Stoll, Elmer Edgar. "Shakespeare, Marston, and the Malcontent Type," *Mod. Philol.,* III (1906), 281-303.

Stone, Lawrence. "The Inflation of Honours, 1558-1641," *Past and Present,* No. 14 (1958), 45-70.

Strathmann, Ernest A. *Sir Walter Raleigh: A Study in Elizabethan Skepticism.* New York, 1951.

Thibaudet, Albert. *Histoire de la littérature française de 1789 à nos jours.* Paris, 1936.

Thomas, Henry. *Spanish and Portuguese Romances of Chivalry.* Cambridge, 1920.

Thompson, Edward. *Sir Walter Raleigh, Last of the Elizabethans.* New Haven, Conn., 1936.

Tillyard, E. M. W. *The Elizabethan World Picture.* Modern Library Paperback edition. New York, 1958.

Toledano, Ralph de. *Lament for a Generation.* New York, 1960.

Traill, H. D., editor. *Social England.* New York and London, 1895.

Troeltsch, Ernst. *Protestantism and Progress.* New York, 1912.

Tucker Brooke, C. F. *The Reputation of Christopher Marlowe.* New Haven, Conn., 1922.

———. "Sir Walter Raleigh as Poet and Philosopher," *ELH,* V (1938), 93-112.

Turgenev, Ivan. *Fathers and Sons.* Translated by Barbara Makonowitzky. Bantam Books edition. New York, 1959.

Tuveson, Ernest Lee. *Millennium and Utopia: A Study in the Background of the Idea of Progress.* Berkeley and Los Angeles, 1949.

Tytler, Patrick Fraser. *England under the Reigns of Edward VI and Mary . . . Illustrated in a Series of Original Letters Never Before Printed.* London, 1839.

———. *Life of Sir Walter Raleigh.* Edinburgh, 1833.

Valois, Georges. *D'un siècle à l'autre: Chronique d'un génération (1885-1920).* Paris, 1921.

Venezky, Alice S. *Pageantry on the Shakespearean Stage.* New York, 1951.

Waggoner, G. R. "An Elizabethan Attitude toward Peace and War," *Philol. Quart.,* XXXIII (1954), 20-33.

———. "The School of Honor: Warfare and the Elizabethan Gentleman," *Summaries of Doctoral Dissertations* [University of Wisconsin] *for 1947-1949,* X, 624-626.

Waldman, Milton. *Sir Walter Raleigh.* New York, 1928.

Wallace, Malcolm William. *The Life of Sir Philip Sidney.* Cambridge, 1915.

Watson, Foster. *The English Grammar Schools to 1660: Their Curriculum and Practice.* Cambridge, 1908.

Wechssler, Eduard. *Die Generation als Jugendreihe und ihr Kampf um die Denkform.* Leipzig, 1930.

Wernham, R. B. "Queen Elizabeth and the Siege of Rouen, 1591," *Trans. of the Roy. Hist. Soc.,* 4th series, XV (1932), 163-179.

Williams, Charles. *Bacon.* London, 1933.

Williamson, G. C. *George, Third Earl of Cumberland (1558-1605), His Life and His Voyages.* Cambridge, 1920.

Williamson, George. "Mutability, Decay, and Seventeenth-Century Melancholy," *ELH*, II (1935), 121-150.

Wilson, Mona. *Sir Philip Sidney*. London, 1950.

Wingfield-Stratford, Esme. *The Making of a Gentleman*. London, 1938.

Yates, Frances A. "Elizabethan Chivalry: The Romance of the Accession Day Tilts," *Journ. of the Warburg and Courtauld Institutes*, XX (1957), 4-25.

Zilsel, Edgar. "The Genesis of the Concept of Scientific Progress," *JHI*, VI (1945), 325-349.

———. "The Sociological Roots of Science," *Amer. Journ. of Sociol.*, XLVII (1942), 544-566.

Index

Abbot, George, Archbishop of Canterbury, 74
Abbot, Maurice, 74
Alexander the Great, 30, 119
Amadis of Gaul, 109-110, 122
Ambition, x, xviii-xxiv, 3-9, 11, 16-18, 20-29, 47-50, 71-72, 79-86, 135-136, 143-145, 155, 170-172, 181-185, 215; Marlovian Aspiration, xxii, 51, 66, 78-86, 146-153, 163-164, 169-171, 188-189, 196-198, 238
Analogy, importance of, 39, 85, 149-150
Andrewes, Lancelot, 33, 151
Apsley, Sir Allen, sons of, 203
Aquinas, St. Thomas, 122
Ariosto, Lodovico, 110, 122, 178
Aristocracy, xix-xx, 3, 51, 60-61, 66, 106, 137-138, 154, 201, 232-233
Aristotle, 28, 30, 33-34, 40, 63, 67, 69, 75, 122, 186, 233-234
Armada, defeat of, xviii, 79, 96, 203-204, 230
Ascham, Roger, 60, 62, 77
Aske, Sir Robert, 12
Augustine, St., 46, 49
Augustus, 119
Authorities, respect for, 68-69, 77-78, 119, 121-123
Avarice, 31-32

Babington Plot, xviii
Bacon, Lady Ann, 130, 133, 219
Bacon, Anthony, 53, 63, 75, 206, 208, 214-221; and the Cecils, 130, 217-218, 220, debts of, 219, 221; and Elizabeth, 217, 220; and Essex, 130, 215, 217-218, 220-221; foreign service of, 216-217, 237; and Francis Bacon, 130, 214-216, 219-221; influential connections of, 69, 75, 215-216; poor health, 58, 219-220
Bacon, Francis, xvii, 50, 53-54, 63-64, 75, 115, 141, 156-157, 206, 215, 235; and the advancement of learning, 170, 182-192; ambitious nature, 181-185; and Anthony Bacon, 54, 214-216, 219-221; early career, 131-132, 142, 182, 205, 226; education of, 63-64; and Essex, 130-133; family of, 53-54, 69-70, 75; and the idea of progress, 197, 199-200;

and Robert Cecil, 130-133; *Essays*, xvii, 182; *Great Instauration*, 182, 186-187; *New Atlantis*, 182, 186, 190-191
Bacon, Sir Nicholas, 54, 67, 69-70, 181, 215
Baldwin, William, 26, 40, 157; *Mirror for Magistrates*, 26, 43-44
Baroque spirit, 163-164
Battenhouse, Roy W., 148
Bayard, Chevalier, 225
Berlew, David E., xxiii
Bernard, St., 31
Bertie, Peregrine, Lord Willoughby, 91, 211, 223
Blount, Charles, Lord Mountjoy, xiv, 64, 70, 100-101, 120-121, 152-153, 206; and Elizabeth, 74-75, 138-139, 212, 222; and Essex, 97, 140
Blount, Sir Christopher, 56-57
Bodley, Sir Thomas, 132
Boleyn, Anne, 12, 22
Bradbrook, M. C., 147
Bradburn, Norman N., xxiii
Bright, Timothy, 232, 234
Brothers, competition between, 53-55
Burgh, Sir John, 108, 206, 208-214; and capture of "Great Carrack," 212-213; and Cumberland, 213; debts of, 204, 210-211; and Elizabeth, 211-212; in France, 211-212; involved in duel, 213-214; in the Netherlands, 209-211; and Raleigh, 212; understrength companies of, 210
Burgh, Lord Thomas, 209
Burton, Robert, 229-230, 237
Bury, J. B., 195

Cadiz expedition, 96, 132-134
Caesar, Julius, 30, 119, 223
Calvin, John, 122
Cambridge University, 24, 63, 77, 126, 187
Camden, William, 18, 21, 173; *Britannia*, xvii
Carew, Sir Nicholas, 12
Carey, Robert, 94, 138
Castiglione, Baldassare, *Book of the Courtier*, 106-107, 122